AF653889

Language and Mind

Hyderabad Studies in Philosophy, no. 5

Language and Mind

Volume 2

The Classical Indian Perspective

Edited by

K.S. Prasad

Decent Books
New Delhi

Cataloging in Publication Data — DK
[Courtesy: D.K. Agencies (P) Ltd. <docinfo@dkagencies.com>]
**National Seminar on Language and Mind (2004 :
Hyderabad, India)**
Language and mind / edited by R.C. Pradhan.
2 vols. 23 cm. — (Hyderabad studies in philosophy ;
nos. 4-5)
Papers presented at the National Seminar on
Language and Mind, held at Hyderabad in 2004.
Includes bibliographical references.
Includes index.
Contents: **v. 1**. Western perspective / edited by R.C.
Pradhan; **v. 2**. The classical Indian perspective / edited by
K.S. Prasad.
ISBN 8186921354 (set)

1. Language and languages — Philosophy — Congresses.
2. Philosophy of mind — Congresses. I. Pradhan, R. C. (Ramesh
Chandra), 1950- II. Prasad, K.S. (Konda Siddeswara), 1953– III.
Title. IV. Series: Hyderabad studies in philosophy ; nos. 4-5.

DDC 401 22

ISBN 81-86921-35-4 (set)
ISBN 81-86921-45-1 (vol. 2)
First published in India in 2008
© Department of Philosophy, University of Hyderabad.

All rights reserved. No part of this publication may be reproduced or transmitted, except brief quotations, in any form or by any means, electronic or mechanical, including photocopying, recording, or any information storage or retrieval system, without prior written permission of the copyright holder, indicated above, and the publishers.
Published and printed by:
Decent Books
D-36/A-1, Mohan Garden, Najafgarh Road
New Delhi - 110 059
Ph. (011) 2535 3435

Distributed by:
D.K. Printworld (P) Ltd.
Regd. office : *'Sri Kunj,'* F-52, Bali Nagar
New Delhi - 110 015
Phones : (011) 2545 3975, 2546 6019; *Fax* : (011) 2546 5926
E-mail : dkprintworld@vsnl.net *Web* : www.dkprint.com

Contents

Acknowledgement

The present volume contains some of the papers presented in a National Seminar on "Language and Mind in Classical Indian Tradition" held between 03-05 March 2005. The seminar was organized under the UGC Special Assistance Programme of the Department of Philosophy, University of Hyderabad, Hyderabad.

The present volume entitled *Language and Mind, Volume 2: The Classical Indian Perspective* is the fifth under the series **Hyderabad Studies in Philosophy**. We are grateful to the University Grants Commission for providing the necessary grant for the publication of this volume under the Special Assistance Programme (SAP). We are thankful to the authors for their consent to include their papers in this volume.

We take this opportunity to place on record our gratitude to our Vice-Chancellor and the Chairman of the SAP Advisory committee, Dr Seyed E. Hasnain for providing all necessary help in undertaking this publication. We are highly indebted to Prof. Amitabha Dasgupta, Coordinator of the SAP for his keen interest and assistance in the publication of this volume and for extending all help in organizing the seminar. With a profound sense of gratitude we acknowledge the assistance and encouragement of all our colleagues in the Department of Philosophy in making this publication possible.

We are thankful to Rajendra Agarwal of Decent Books, New Delhi for undertaking this publication.

Hyderabad

January 2008 ***K.S. Prasad***

Key to Transliteration

VOWELS

अ *a*	आ *ā*	इ *i*	ई *ī*	उ *u*	ऊ *ū*	ऋ *ṛ*	ॠ *ṝ*[1]
(Roman)	(palm)	(it)	(police)	(put)	(rule)	(rig)	
ऌ *ḷ*	ॡ *ḹ*[1]	ए *e*	ऐ *ai*	ओ *o*	औ *au*		
(able)		(there)	(aisle)	(no)	(loud)		

CONSONANTS

Guttural	क *ka*	ख *kha*[2]	ग *ga*	घ *gha*[2]	ङ *ṅa*
	(skate)	(blockhead)	(gate)	(ghost)	(sing)
Palatal	च *ca*	छ *cha*[2]	ज *ja*	झ *jha*[2]	ञ *ña*
	(chunk)	(catch him)	(john)	(hedgehog)	(bunch)
Cerebral	ट *ṭa*	ठ *ṭha*[2]	ड *ḍa*	ढ *ḍha*[2]	ण *ṇa*
	(start)	(anthill)	(dart)	(godhead)	(under)
Dental	त *ta*	थ *tha*[2]	द *da*	ध *dha*[2]	न *na*
	(path)	(thunder)	(that)	(this)	(numb)
Labial	प *pa*	फ *pha*[2]	ब *ba*	भ *bha*[2]	म *ma*
	(spin)	(philosophy)	(bin)	(abhor)	(much)
Semi-	य *ya*	र *ra*	ल *la*[3]	व *va*[4]	
vowels	(young)	(drama)	(luck)	(vile)	
Sibilants	श *śa*[5]	ष *ṣa*[5]	स *sa*	ह *ha*	
	(shove)	(bushel)	(so)	(hum)	

अं (ं) *ṁ anusvāra* is a nasal off-glide that immediately follows the pronunciation of a vowel as in *saṁskṛti.*

अः *visarga* = *ḥ* consists in abrupt release of breath after a vowel as in *prātaḥ*.

ऽ *Avagraha* shows non-pronunciation, that is, deletion of "a" after "e" or "o" as in *ime 'vasthitāḥ*. In Vedic Sanskrit, it can also show word division.

1 Longer form of the preceding vowel.

2 Aspirated forms of the preceding consonants. The compound words given as examples should be pronounced without a syllabic break at the underlined places. "tha" and "pha" should not be pronounced as fricatives.

3 retroflexed and written as "L *la*" in certain phonetic contexts.

4 Pronounced like "w," without aspiration.

5 "śa" is palatal; "ṣa" cerebral or retroflex.

Introduction

IT has all through been assumed in the Western philosophical and linguistic traditions that there is a close connection existing between language and mind. The strongest and probably the clearest version of this connection is found in Descartes. According to Descartes, what distinguishes humans from animals is that the former possess a thinking faculty. It is a faculty which expresses itself through human action and linguistic behaviour. Language is thus conceived as intrinsically related to mind giving rise to the idea that it is a mental organ. This idea of language being a mental organ gets its overwhelming support from the recent studies in philosophy of mind, Chomskian linguistics and cognitive science.

In the classical Indian philosophical tradition the connection between language and mind in general was never denied. However Indian philosophers of language do not perceive the relationship between language and mind in the same way as Western philosophers do. It is well known that the Indian notion of mind (*manas*) is essentially different from the Western perspective of mind. In the Indian context mind is used as an instrument, so to say an internal organ (*antaḥkaraṇa*) for knowledge acquisition. The concept of mind, thus in Indian tradition, being an instrument or sense-organ is assumed to be devoid of consciousness. Consciousness has a separate locus and is associated with soul (*ātman*). Basically we are not entering into these theoretical details pertaining to Indian notion of mind in this volume. Our thrust is to discuss **the role of mind** (in whatever form) in language comprehension. Keeping this objective in view, we are using a broad-based notion of mind which includes consciousness also. The word mind is used here more as a cover term to include internal states of existence such as different mental states, thought and thought processes.

In the Indian philosophical tradition, the problem regarding the interface between language and mind arises due to certain specific needs. Indian philosophers of language raise the question: How does a hearer derive knowledge from a speaker's utterances? In the process of solving this issue, they developed some of the most important insights into language and cognition, language-generated awareness, the distinction between knowledge and understanding, etc. These issues may not always explicitly address the interaction between language and mind. But in many of their formulations the concept of the mental is assumed as the background of linguistic activity. By and large the main objective of the present volume is to explore the details of the point of contact between language and mind as conceived by the classical Indian philosophers. In fact, all schools of Indian philosophy considered language at some stage or other and each one had to ponder over questions concerning the relation of the word to reality and the validity of verbal testimony (*śabda*) as a source of valid knowledge (*pramāṇa*). However their metaphysical bias determined their answers to these questions.

Philosophical analysis of language in India emerged as a discernible field of intellectual activity since time immemorial. With certainty we can trace the beginning of speculation on language back to the Vedas, the Brāhmaṇas and the Upaniṣads. In *Ṛgveda* several hymns are devoted to *vāk* (the power of speech) and the same trend continued in the Brāhmaṇas and the Upaniṣads.

Broadly, in the classical Indian philosophical tradition, we come across three distinct views regarding the relation between language and Reality. The realists, notably the Naiyāyikas are of the view that language is competent to describe everything that is there. Whatever exists is potentially capable of being known and whatever is known is capable of being expressed; is their view. In contrast, there is a dominating view which says that language is not equipped to express the nature of Reality. It is a view held by the Mādhyamika school of Buddhists and the Advaita Vedāntins. In contrast the view that 'language is the Reality' is held by the Grammarians. Thus the relation between language and Reality can be addressed from these three different perspectives namely adequacy, inadequacy and identity. The volume begins with the inadequacy thesis proposed by the Mādhyamika school of Buddhism and the Vedāntins which suggests that language fails to express certain experiences. This is followed by papers dealing with the identity thesis held by the Grammarians which suggests that language is the Reality. When the Grammarian describes the Reality as *śabdabrahman* he neither means any articulate word form which is regarded as an evolution of the transcendental principle nor sound which is viewed as the medium for manifestation of the transcendental principle on the empirical plane. *Śabdabrahman* for Grammarians is the Supreme Reality which is subtle and transcends all that comes within the purview of human experience. This *śabdabrahman* is regarded as the material cause of the phenomenal world and is found to persist in every manifestation inasmuch as every object in the universe is determined by a verbal form. The volume ends with the adequacy thesis supported by the Naiyāyikas which suggests that whatever exists is potentially capable of being known (*jñeyatva*) and whatever is known is capable of being expressed in language (*abhidheyatva*).

How language is connected to things or objects of the world is a question which has been the major preoccupation of both the Indian and Western philosophical traditions. Purushottama Bilimoria in his paper "Bimal Matilal's Navya-Realism, Buddhist 'Lingo-Phobia' and Mental Things" takes Bimal Matilal's work to be central to the issue concerning the relationship between language and the world. Matilal while developing his approach brought many of the issues and view-points which were pertinent to the basic theme. It was indeed a comprehensive approach to the subject. Essentially, Matilal adopts the Nyāya-Vaiśeṣika approach which assumes a realist perspective of the relationship between language and the world. Through this perspective he seeks to construct a realist metaphysics being supported by a theory of language appropriate to it. It is due to adopting the realist approach, that Matilal finds that the Buddhist critique of language is unacceptable and characterizes the stand taken by Buddhism as lingophobia.

Bilimoria gives an analytic account of how Matilal develops a realist theory of language within the Nyāya and Navya-Nyāya framework of logic and epistemology. In the context of Nyāya, the issue of language mainly arises while dealing with *jñāna* or cognition. Cognition is always cognition of something, i.e. directed towards an object and is always expressed through some verbal form. There is an influential view in Indian epistemology which says that cognition necessarily consists of a sensory core required for the construction of particulars. Such a perspective denies any causal connection between the internal sensory experience and the external object of awareness. This sensory core remains ineffable. Matilal, as Bilimoria argues, seeks to show that this view is not unconnected to the view of language that it holds. Diṅnāga and many other Indian philosophers including Candrakīrti arrive at this view of cognition due to their supposition that private language is possible. But Matilal refutes this view by using the argument especially of Quine and Wittgenstein that language is a social behaviour. Wittgenstein's private language argument shows that the idea of language being private is unintelligible and thus to hold that private sensory experience can be expressed through language is equally unintelligible and logically incoherent. This is the reason why Buddhist critique of language, as Matilal claims, turns into a lingophobia that reduces mental things as mere mythical. The Nyāya view, on the other hand claims that any cognitive experience must be expressible in language. Gaṅgeśa rules out the presence of the ineffable sensory core to be the essence of cognition on the ground that it is merely physical and is thus non-cognitive. Matilal interprets this, according to Bilimoria, to be a version of metaphysical realism which argues for an inseparable connection between language and cognition. As Bilimoria puts it, it is a "linguistically compromised doctrine of knowing."

Language, according to Buddhists in general, is considered as *vikalpa,* so to say a mental construct devised to assist in day-to-day life and it is not capable of depicting or revealing the nature of Reality. The realistic standpoint that "knowability is co-extensive with expressibility" is not acceptable to Buddhism. The ultimate Reality, the Absolute, according to Buddhism is knowable and yet inexpressible. The Absolute, according to Ācārya Nāgārjuna, an exponent of Mādhyamika Śāstra, is transcendent to both thought and speech. C.D. Sebastian in his paper "Language and Mind: A Mādhyamika

Perspective" is of the view that Mādhyamika has language which does not have syntax but semantics and he terms it as the language of silence. In the Mādhyamika school of Buddhism we find a clear-cut distinction between the realms of things-in-themselves and commonsense-experiences which are termed as *sva-lakṣaṇa*s and *sāmānya lakṣaṇa*s respectively. The former is the sphere of *paramārtha satya,* i.e. transcendental reality while the latter is the sphere of *saṁvṛtti satya,* i.e. empirical reality. Whatever comes within the realm of empirical experience is characterized as mentally constructed, imagined and linguistically expressible. On the other hand, the transcendental experience is untouched by mental construction, imagination and is beyond the realm of language which is termed as *śūnyatā* in Mahāyāna Buddhism. *Śūnyatā* on the logico-linguistic level, as Sebastian argues, then means accepting the failure of predicate language as a viable mode of discourse. The Mādhyamika standpoint in this sense, as he concludes, does not have a first-order language.

The study of language necessarily leads to the study of what it means. But the word-meaning, in classical Indian philosophical tradition, was never confined to the verifiable meaning only. Its scope was extended to include metaphysical expressions. Metaphysical statements are meaningful because they are verifiable in a different sense. R.C. Pradhan in his paper "Language and Mind in the Upaniṣads" has suggested that the language of metaphysics is always different from the language of ordinary objects. He introduces a distinction between natural language and metaphysical language. Natural language, while it is suitable for describing the phenomenal world, is grossly handicapped to express the transcendental reality. Metaphysical language though fails to have cognitive meaning as found in natural language is not devoid of meaning altogether. The uniqueness of metaphysical language, according to Pradhan, lies in its introduction of non-natural meaning which takes us back to the Reality. The metaphysical statements such as, *tat tvam asi, ayam ātma brahman, prajñānam brahman, aham brahmāsmi* have the deeper import of conveying the essential identity of *Brahman* and *jīva* as pointers. However, Pradhan rightly points out that Ultimate Reality cannot be known except by one's own direct realization (*aparokṣānubhūti*). While emphasizing the revelatory character of Reality, Pradhan brings in the philosophy of Wittgenstein and Heidegger to substantiate his point.

G. Mishra in his paper "Limits of Mind and Universe of Language" has a twofold objective. The first is to show the relation between language and mind in Indian philosophy in general and the other is to explain the thesis proposed in Advaita Vedānta that there is a need to transcend both language and mind to attain a higher level of Reality identified as *Brahman.* Attaining such a state is usually described as a state of emancipation — an emancipation from empirical bondage. Language and mind do not have ultimate validity since they belong to the empirical world which is not real from the ultimate standpoint. Mishra while explaining the nature of mind examines major philosophical theories in the Indian context and takes pains to prove that it is not an internal sense-organ as understood in certain philosophical schools such as Nyāya. Advaita Vedānta while emphasizing the nature of Reality in terms of Pure Consciousness emphatically pronounces the illusory nature of mind and language. Taking a clue from the Upaniṣads, Mishra argues a case for Advaita Vedānta. *Śruti vākya*s which are the only means of the knowledge of *Brahman,* according to Advaita Vedānta turns out to be illusory on the onset of *Brahman* realization. To the question: how can an illusory *śruti vākya* be a means for the Real, the Advaitins argue that just as an illusory snake which can create a real fear in the cognizer, so also the *śruti vākyas* though illusory in nature, can help in realizing the *Brahman*. Mishra elucidates this point succinctly with an empirical illustration. Mishra argues that just as words that are no longer useful after conveying their sense in an ordinary discourse, similarly the *śruti vākyas* also cease to be authoritative on the onset of the knowledge of *Brahman*.

From the Advaita standpoint of language and mind the next issue that arises is regarding the relationship between language and consciousness. To be conscious means to be conscious of the world around us, the environment where we live and the life that we share with other people. Consciousness is inclusive of all our cognitive and mental states such as understanding, desire, feeling, etc. The defining feature of these states is that they are always directional, i.e. directed towards the world. Keeping this feature in mind, Brentano in the Western tradition defines consciousness in terms of intentionality. However, this approach to consciousness does not define what consciousness is, i.e. what consciousness is *per se* and how to identify it. We find such a task difficult. In fact, to define what consciousness is in linguistic terms can often be found to be inadequate if not futile. It is in this context that Meera Chakravorty's paper "Language and Consciousness: The Advaita Perspective" assumes its significance. For Advaita, consciousness is the ultimate basis of all that exists. Everyone is conscious of his own existence and never thinks he is not. In fact, it is impossible to entertain any doubt with regard to the existence of consciousness for doubt itself is an expression of consciousness. It is a self-evident reality. Further, it is that without which even the subject-object relationship becomes an impossibility; it is that which really exists as compared to that which has got phenomenal, temporary and relational existence. From this very consciousness of the self, Advaitins arrive at the existence of an infinite, eternal Universal consciousness which is free from predication. However, in the phenomenal world this non-relational, non-predicative nature of consciousness, as Chakravorty argues, changes its character because it is viewed differently. It is due to our inclination towards the objective standpoint that consciousness is defined in terms of observable attributes. In the phenomenal world, consciousness is thus always viewed as conscious of something which can be articulated in language. Chakravorty argues that there is a strong tendency to see the objective world and the mind as mutually incompatible since the one resists any fixed interpretation by the other and vice versa. If we take unsublatability (*abādhitaviṣayatva*) as the criterion for Reality then the dream experience is contradicted by the waking experience and the waking experience is contradicted by transcendental experience of pure consciousness which cannot be expressed in language. Failure to express is not something unique to transcendental experience alone. It is a fact that we have all felt certain things at certain privileged moments in our day-to-day lives, that words fail to describe. "The challenges presented by consciousness," according to Chakravorty, "impede our ability to develop a coherent linguistic expression of consciousness directed to certain experiences mentioned above." She suggests that instead of drawing a definite linguistic correlate of consciousness it would be appropriate to have a detailed survey of linguistic expressions which have been invented and used in different fields such as quantum physics, mythology, esoteric teachings, biology, philosophy, mysticism, poetry, etc. for understanding and describing the different aspects of consciousness. This may provide valuable clues that can explain the linguistic relation with consciousness.

We are all exposed to a variety of experiences and surely all are not of the same value. The cognitive content of one experience may at times come into conflict with the other and claim for greater reality which in turn may be contradicted by the other. Philosophy must rationally discriminate between one experience and the other and assign a proper place to each. In the light of such rational grounds the Advaitins classify all our experiences. In grading these experiences they followed the principle of unsublatability (*abādhita*). Momentary experiences such as dreams are sublated by the waking experience which in turn is sublated by a transcendental experience which is neither contradicted nor contradictable. Thus according to Advaita the principle of unsublatability which forms the criterion to validate an experience, states that an experience which is unsublatable at all times (*trikāla-abādhita*) is real. It rules out a situation where an experience which is at one time and is not at another time cannot be real. However, in all our phenomenal experiential episodes there is a transition of thought from sensation to determination, so to say from *nirivikalpaka* to *savikalpaka*. To determine a sensation is to predicate it in terms of substantive-adjective relation (*viśeṣya-viśeṣaṇa sambandha*) and is termed as *savikalpaka jñāna*, while *nirvikalpaka* is the knowledge of a thing as not related to anything, not even to itself. It is the knowledge of the identity of a thing as excluding all relations. Identity propositions such as 'This is that man' and the like according to Advaita are non-predicative and non-relational in nature. Vinay Kumar in his paper "Advaitic Language of Sublation" interrogates the role of language in all these experiences. Using the analogy of a postman who faithfully delivers the goods without tampering the contents, he argues that at least in the case of *tuccha vākyas* language acts like a not-so-trustworthy postman as there is no cognitive content in *tuccha vākyas*. Through an analysis of language Vinay Kumar concludes that what remains finally is the pure undifferentiated consciousness which does not need any postal articles to be delivered by the postman.

Indian philosophers belonging to different schools of thought in general emphasize the role of language in the context of cognition. Bhartṛhari argues for the inseparability of cognitive faculty from verbal faculty. According to him, verbalizability is immanent in our cognitive faculty. To cognize is to verbalize and in the same way to verbalize is to cognize. This may be characterized as an inextricability thesis which is possible due to the deeper relationship between language and thought. The relation between language and thought is so intimate that we cannot conceive of the possibility of one without the other. It is a well-known fact that we cannot isolate thinking from language for there are no meta-linguistic modes of thought. All thinking is invariably carried out in language. Language is not just a vehicle of thought but it constitutes a vital part of thought. Tandra Patnaik in her paper "Thought and Language: The Bhartṛharian Perspective" tries to explore Bhartṛhari's views on this issue. She approaches the problem from two important dimensions — (i) thought and language as components of linguistic communication, and (ii) thought and language as conceptual entities and their relative priority. According to her, Bhartṛhari prefers to prioritize language over thought. For Bhartṛhari the Supreme Reality is the *śabdabrahman* which is subtle and transcends all that comes within the purview of human experience. The words we speak are momentary and are simply the manifestations of the *śabdabrahman.* Committed to non-dualism, Bhartṛhari never maintained an absolute distinction of thought and language. Just as the empirical world cannot be established apart from and independent of consciousness, similarly consciousness in the sense of awareness cannot be established apart from and independent of language. Tandra Patnaik makes it abundantly clear that for Bhartṛhari consciousness means linguistic consciousness and there cannot be any pre-linguistic bare awareness. Thus, there is nothing without thought and there is no thought without language.

In the history of philosophy of language the place of Bhartṛhari is quite significant. For the first time he undertook an in-depth study of the *śabdabrahman,* the Word-Absolute, and demonstrated its logical implications. Maharana in his paper "Bhartṛhari on Word and Consciousness : The Advaita Perspective" seeks to explore the central philosophy of Bhartṛhari from his work *Vākyapadīya*. Further he tries to identify the relationship that can be drawn among Bhartṛhari and the Advaitins like Śaṅkara and Maṇḍana Miśra on the nature of word and consciousness. For Bhartṛhari the Supreme Reality is the *śabdabrahman* which is subtle and transcends all that comes within the domain of human experience. The whole world is an expression of the *śabdabrahman* which is of the nature of consciousness. Thus the Grammarian is as much an advocate of non-dualism as Śaṅkara is. However, Maharana points out that there are certain important points of difference between them. For Grammarians *śabdabrahman* in its essence is identical with *kālaśakti* which is its eternal and innate power. In fact, the two may be regarded as aspects of the same Reality. As transcendent it is beyond time and it is above all predications in thought and language, and as immanent it is in time and it is the subject and predicate of all judgements.

This *kālaśakti* has no independent being apart from *śabdabrahman* and is eternally real unlike the *māyā* of Śaṅkara. The powers of the *Brahman* according to Śaṅkara are illusory while for Bhartṛhari the *kālaśakti* of *śabdabrahman* is real and eternally present in the relation of identity.

Classical Indian thinkers, from the beginning, considered mind as something distinct from the Self. They regarded mind as an instrument of knowledge for the self. This idea that mind is an instrument directed by the Self and itself directing the other sense-organs is wonderfully illustrated with the help of a chariot in the *Kaṭhopaniṣad*. In Indian Grammatical tradition we come across two aspects of mind — the physiological component termed as *buddhi* and the transcendental component namely *citta*. Srimannarayana Murthy in his paper "Language and Mind in Grammatical Tradition" identifies the physiological component of mind with the empirical mind so to say the Brain which is responsible for all cognitions, while the transcendental mind is the one which controls the empirical mind. The communication of the mental disposition of the speaker to the listener is the purpose of language. In the science of language, according to Srimannarayana Murthy, the intention of the speaker should match with the physical effort in acoustics to bring out a correspondence with the empirical mind, which controls the articulatory processes, with the transcendental mind, which governs the psychological processes of the speaker and the listener. In order to account for continuity and consistency between the operations of the empirical mind and transcendental mind, the Grammarians maintained the eternality of the word, its sense and the relation between them. Bhartṛhari, according to Srimannarayana Murthy, gave a new dimension to relate mind and language by propounding *bauddhapadārthavāda* as the basis for understanding *sphoṭa,* the meaning bearer, and *pratibhā,* the meaning of a sentence, and *vivarthavāda* to substantiate the transitory nature of the mental world.

Vyākaraṇa (grammar) which is regarded as one of the Vedāṅgas is considered to be the gateway for other disciplines. Vyākaraṇa is taken to mean the process of analyzing language. The distinctive feature of Vyākaraṇa is such that unlike the ordinary language wherein the use of the word such as *ghaṭa* refers to its meaning, in Vyākaraṇa the use of the word refers to the word itself. The basic purpose of Vyākaraṇa is to distinguish correct word forms from incorrect ones. The nature of the word thus occupies an important place in the philosophy of language. Nirmalya Narayan Chakraborty in his paper "On the Nature of the Word and our Knowledge of it" has discussed the classical Indian Grammarian theory on the nature of the word. The study of grammar, according to him, leads to the knowledge of the word which in turn amounts to knowing the meaning of the word. The knowledge of the meaning of the word leads to the knowledge of the Upaniṣads which in turn leads to the knowledge of the *Brahman* which is regarded as a state of emancipation. Patañjali, according to Chakraborty, rejected any attempt to describe the nature of the words in terms of substance, quality, action and universal. To set aside these wrong notions Patañjali, according to Chakraborty, explained the word in terms of *dhvani,* the manifestation of which produces the knowledge of it.

There is another view in classical Indian tradition which argues for the autonomy and irreducible character of linguistic utterances as a separate source of knowledge. The same has been recognized as verbal testimony in the Western philosophical tradition. The most exhaustive account of this knowledge is found in Nyāya, which gives rise to the thesis called *śābdabodha*. The Nyāya considers language-generated knowledge as a separate type of *pramā*, as its causal inheritance can neither be understood in terms of perception or inference or comparison. In my paper "The Centrality of Mind in Cognitive Process: The Nyāya Perspective," I have discussed in detail the notion of cognition in Nyāya philosophy and the centrality of mind in the cognitive process. The purpose of *śābdabodha* thesis of Nyāya is to show how there is a close connection between linguistically-generated knowledge and mind.

In these papers there has been an attempt to discuss a number of issues philosophers are concerned with from time to time in the area of philosophy of language and mind. One important aspect of language is that the articulate linguistic forms of language and thought are intrinsically incapable of expressing the full knowledge of the Reality on the empirical plane. However, these forms of language though fail to express the Reality in full and present only a vague picture of it, still help as a pointer to the Reality. It is this function of language which saves it from being utter nonsense and helps the probing spirit in its effort to realize the Ultimate Reality. In fact, the articulate linguistic form of language shadows the Reality and is meaningful because of it.

1

Bimal Matilal's Navya-Realism, Buddhist 'Lingo-Phobia' and Mental Things

*Purushottama Bilimoria**

Abstract

THE vexed issue of the precise connection between words and things (or objects) has been a major preoccupation over the centuries summoning the resources of metaphysics, philosophy of language, linguistics, ontology and increasingly semiological analysis. Philosophy in India produced a number of different and often conflicting solutions, only to be rivalled by an equally bewildering variety witnessed in the ancient and modern West. I want to bring to the foreground the late Bimal K. Matilal's development of Nyāya-Vaiśeṣika realist approach to the aporia, and interject the analysis with dissident voices, especially of Mīmāṁsakas and Buddhists. Significantly, it will be the living ghosts of Putnam and Dummett that I will invoke to haunt Matilal's variation on metaphysical realism (after Davidson). Matilal veered closer to a realist metaphysic, which is inflected in his own formulation of a theory of language appropriate to this ontology, this despite his idealized attraction to phenomenalist-constructivism

* Professor, School of International and Political Studies, Faculty of Arts, Geelong Campus, Deakin University, Australia.

(especially Buddhist); his flirtations with Bhartṛharian holism (even Saussurean semiology) and lately with Derridean deconstruction (after G.C. Spivak) in his epiloquia. But my critique focuses on his famous earlier analysis of *jñāna* or cognition and his defence of a particular linguistic-ontology within a narrowly circumscribed naturalized epistemology (after Navya-Nyāya).

The Problem

The vexed issue of the precise connection between words and things (or objects) has been a major preoccupation over the centuries, summoning the resources of metaphysics, philosophy of language, linguistics, ontology and increasingly semiological analysis, to solve this problem. Indian philosophy produced a number of different and often conflicting solutions, only to be rivalled by the even more bewildering variety of approaches and theories witnessed in the West, traditional and modern, relying largely on various *models* of the 'word' (natural, ideal, scriptural, semiotic, etc.). In this paper I want to suggest that there is an even more intricate relationship between the model of the *word* or language and the background view of the *world*. In other words, it is not at all as simple as sitting down one fine morning and asking, "Well, ol' boy, what is the connection between the *word and the world*?" as though it is a question simpliciter about some given or givens in our environment. Many theories proceed on the basis of this assumed dualism, if not a complete asymmetry between language and the world that it is supposed to describe, represent, or whatever its function is taken to be in relation to each other; for instance, the strict 'atomistic' and propositional theories of language assumed a transparent distinction between words and the world, such that a correct use of language would successfully represent or picture the structure of the world. Language is the 'grammar of the world.' As Rorty has shown, there has been an obsession with the linguistic end of the analysis. The world is elusively the backdrop to which language has to be reconnected, at least in our understanding and intellectual charting; for common sense tells us that there is a connection, otherwise we would fail to communicate with each other, relate newspaper blotches to events elsewhere, carry on our daily social commerce, fetch the glass of water when asked for one, and take formal promises made by our partners or friends or *gurus* impeccably seriously. But to ponder whether in some logical or philosophical sense language could precede the world, give us the world, and might even be the condition for the possibility of the world is too often considered to be an evocation of sheer sophistry, or merely of mythological significance. Although there are those that did ponder along these lines: Plato with his theory of *Eidos*, the Mīmāṁsakas with their doctrine of *apauruṣeyatva*, Bhartṛhari who collapsed the ontology of the world with a higher speech form (*śabdabrahman*), and Wittgenstein in his more mystical aphorisms about language (continuing a Kantian insight into the apriocity of our categories of understanding). But I think there are even more radical critiques and divergent views of language and the world than these few idealistic tendencies might suggest. I want to bring to the foreground the late Bimal K. Matilal's development of Nyāya-Vaiśeṣika realist approach to the aporia, and occasionally interject the analysis with the dissident Buddhist voice, especially of Candrakīrti. More significantly, it will be the living ghosts of Putnam and Dummett (or Putmett for short) that I will invoke as it were to haunt Matilal's variation on metaphysical realism. The paper is dedicatory as it is programmatic, but I do hope that before long scholars of Indian philosophy will begin seriously to review Matilal's work, as some of us have been doing with the Bhattacharyyas, Mohanty, Potter, and Daya Krishna among others.

The late Matilal wrote a number of works in which he attempted to get a handle on the problem we have raised. Steeped deeply in classical (Indian) scholastic philosophy, and inspired by analytical currents in Western philosophy, he skilfully analysed and debated several of the major Indian systems (Nyāya, Buddhism, Grammarian, and Mīmāṁsā). But his own view was not always clear. It would not be unfair to say that he veered closer to a realist ontology or metaphysical realism as he christens it after Davidson (evident, e.g. in his masterful work on *Perception*), and this may have informed or impacted on his formulation of a theory of language appropriate to this ontology. In fact, I want to argue this to be the case, despite his enormous attraction to phenomenalist-constructivist theories (especially Buddhist ones), and his flirtations with Bhartṛharian holism, even Saussurean semiology and lately Derridean deconstructionism as he completed his essay on *The Word and The World*. I am intrigued by all this and so I wish to trace this line of thinking in Matilal's work, which I believe awaits a fuller response from the Buddhist dialectical CRITIQUE OF LANGUAGE, which Matilal chastises as 'lingophobia'. Again, it is for this reason that I choose to contrast Matilal on this problematic, as it would seem that at least one insight of Candrakīrti's poses a serious challenge to Matilal's ontologico-linguistics, viz. 'there is no real connection between the reflected image and the face,' or for that matter Diṅnāga's supposed utterance: 'Language issues from imaginative construction and vice versa.'

I will begin with some clues from Matilal's published works, and from a succinct paper entitled "Some Issucs of Nyāya Realism (SINR)" which I think is not yet published. Now the very first sentence of the first chapter in his *Navya-Nyāya Doctrine of Negation* (*NNDN*) begins thus:

> In the West logic has been primarily concerned with propositions or sentences. Navya-Nyāya, like other Indian systems of logic, deals rather with what it calls *jñāna*, by which it means something close to "particular instances of cognition." An instance of cognition, it is true, can be shown to be ultimately related to some verbal form, namely, to a statement or sentence. In the case of determinate or qualificative cognition (*savikalpa* or *viśiṣṭa jñāna*), with which Navya-Nyāya is chiefly concerned, the relationship is very close. But *jñāna* itself is not a form of language. . . .
>
> — NNDN, p. 7

Here then is a disavowal; *jñāna* essentially has nothing to do with sentences or verbal forms; certain of its qualificative forms might involve verbal delimiters, but its primary connection is with the world of objects, directly and inexorably. So *jñāna*s "are always cognitions *of* or *about* . . ., and what is denoted by the expression that fills the blank here is to be taken as the object or objects of such cognitions." Cognition always refers, beyond itself, to some object. As such the object is neither compromised nor ascribed a new property (such as *jñātata a' la* the Bhaṭṭas). The world is as it is and our cognitions simply bring its varied furniture into our sharp conscious focus, no more and no less. There are two other features about *jñāna* that we are urged to note.

The object of cognition, at least by the time of Navya-Nyāya, has nothing to do with some supposed residue of sensory core, the primitive unrepresentable or unstructurable given "on par with sense-data, percepts, or uninterrupted sensations" (SINR, p. 3). Some theories assume or posit this sensory core either to give legitimate support to an objective characterization of particulars in experience, or simply to force an argument towards an utter subjective, conceptual or indeed imaginative construction of a particular, conceding that there is no way of establishing any causal connection between this internal core of experience and what *appears* as the external object of awareness. Matilal attributes the latter motivation to Diṅnāga and makes the curious following observation (I shall quote this long passage since it is very intriguing): "These self-characterized objects," he writes, "which are similar to sense-data or percepts and which some philosophers in the modern West have described in language by such verbless complex 'Red here now' are unanimously regarded by Diṅnāga and other Indian philosophers [count Candrakīrti in here] as virtually and actually ineffable. This obviously depended upon a view of language. Use of language depends upon shared properties, which are results of the synthesizing aspect of mental construction. For language is a social affair (as Quine had once said). The private sensory core, which are unique particulars, cannot therefore be expressed in language. This is also reminiscent of the argument against the notion of a private language *a'la* Wittgenstein in modern times."

But what does Matilal intend by suggesting that "[T]his obviously depended upon a view of language"? What is the referent of 'This' here: the claim that there is an ineffable core of sensory private experience? Or its attempted description? I think he intends the former, but if so why is this metaphysical thesis about the unavailability of language made dependent upon a prevailing view of language? Isn't this a claim that stands on its own right, on par with other similar logical and epistemological claims? So I detect a slight bias here. And of course the remark about language being a social affair (how would Quine, a sterile man of no social graces, know?), which Wittgenstein presumably also underscored in his denial of private language (for very different reasons though) is, I am afraid to say, not much developed here or elsewhere in Matilal's work.

Nevertheless, we get a second clue a few lines down when we turn to the Nyāya view proper. Nyāya apparently disputed the relevance of this residual sensory core, as this is neither error, nor *jñāna* nor even a foundation for knowledge. Again I quote,

> Later on in the same realist tradition, even its cognitive role was called into question. For there was a prevalent theory of language (ascribed to Bhartṛhari) which maintained that language and thought (any cognitive experiences) are inextricably intertwined such that language anchors thought and vice versa. Being influenced by this theory [I really do wonder about this claim anyway], the Nyāya realist claimed that any cognitive experience must be expressible in language. The ineffable sensory core, if there is any, should be little more than the physiological surface irritation, and hence non-cognitive. Besides, by its very nature, it would not be even introspectable or amenable to inner perception. Introspectable states have a judgemental structure.
>
> — SINR, pp. 4-5

And so we are back to cognitions once again, although a more detailed concern with attributed predicate property, its prior knowledge, copula relations with universals (of cowhood, e.g. in the judgement '*x* is a cow') follows which need not detain us presently. What Matilal wants to stress is that Nyāya categorically denies the role, in any significant epistemological analysis, of the core sensory data: it is found to be almost superfluous, as structured thoughts or judgements are not (therefore) interpretations or organizations of these raw data, for we have no conscious verbal access to such data. (loc cit.).

What is being said? It seems to me the following: the raw sensory core might well be there, we do not know as we have no linguistic access to it; it is perhaps only a "surface physiological irritation" or physiogenic motions like our feelings and other sensations (indeed e-motions and like e-mail messages not terribly cognitive or intellectual in worth either). Language only comes into play or into the foreground when judgements are being formed or about to be formed: this is the structured perception; and language should be banished from having concerns with the pre-linguistic, uninterpreted and unstructured or pre-structured data. We should pause to note that while the Nyāya theory of cognition admits an indeterminate phase, namely, *nirvikalpa* prior to the arising of the determinate judgement, which is *savikalpa*, the pre-linguistic, pre-structured inchoate state which Matilal is denying is not to be identified with *nirvikalpa* phase. For the *nirvikalpa jñāna* already is on its way to be being structured, or one might say that it registers the logical pre-condition for the determinate *jñāna*. The difference is in degree rather than in kind (as Matilal once put it to me).

On this strong point of the rejection of the ineffable base, which Matilal attributes to Gaṅgeśa, he adverts to Donald Davidson's explosion of the myth of the core and inexplicable given which otherwise leads to a kind of conceptual relativism. So, he avers, "I find a support to Davidson's conclusion in Gaṅgeśa's clever move to direct our attention to the logical prerequisite of a propositional knowledge or judgement and omit our talk of the unstructured data or the pure pre-linguistic content of our perceptual experience." At core, what Matilal actually wants to endorse is a version of metaphysical or external realism that comes through as an implication of Davidson's doctrine and which he believes is upheld by the Nyāya-Vaiśeṣika philosophers, who were apparently in a head-on collision course with the 'idealists' and 'relativists' in India (pp. 1 & 8): It is significant, he notes, "that their mistrust in the availability of the pure, structureless data as well as their outright rejection of any form of representation, of intentional content or propositional entities intervening between us and the world seems not only compatible with but also conducive to their brand of realism (if we can omit some minor details)." This is a telling endorsement even as it underscores a motivation on Matilal's part. We must, at all cost, reject the so-called idealist and relativist versions of the theory which rely precisely on language's interventionist role and pander to paradigms of representation or of intentionality, and so on. Before I say anything more on the preferred paradigm or context-independent schema, let me refer to a thought experiment which might frame the distinction between schema and context alluded to in this realist critique. This comes from Hilary Putnam and it is highly instructive as it has been provocative (though I will modify it a bit). Imagine there are two identical *lokas* or twin earths; the respective inhabitants of both *lokas* behave in exactly identical ways towards a certain liquid substance which each side consumes when thirsty and use it in their cooking, and so on. Moreover, both the *loka*-dwellers call it 'water' in their respective (natural) languages. On earth *A* their scientists tell them that it is H_2O. Now is there any way in which we can say that on earth *B* their own scientists will also tell them that what they call and use as 'water' is actually H_2O? Putnam says emphatically 'No', for we have no access other than through what we are told from within the schema of each earth-community what the substance is: even if earth *B* scientists decide to call the liquid H_2O, and their propositional knowledge attests to this objective characterization, there is no gainsaying that it is exactly what is intended by use of the term H_2O in earth *A* and vice versa. In other words, both make judgements that look, on the face of it, to be identical, but there is no way in which we can say that each side shares the knowledge and therefore the linguistic contents involved in exactly identical terms. It so happens that their conventions or common sense discourses coincide, but this gives no warrant to suppose that they are perceiving and are therefore speaking about the same reality qua reality. Of course, Putnam uses this imaginary example to bolster his own theory of internal or what he now calls common sense realism which stops external or metaphysical realism on its tracks.

Now I am coming to my main argument: the central point to be made is not that, or not simply that, on the one hand there are no ineffable unstructured percepts and on the other hand that language anchors thought (or that all our cognitions are shot through with language), but to acknowledge that language anchors or might just well spread over and encompass the unstructured qua pre-structured content of our experience as well. I think Mark Siderits has made this plea more forcefully in his book on *Indian Philosophy of Language.* To put it more cynically: Why privilege language's anchor only in respect of cognitive or structured experiences, and deny its trekking all the way down to the sensory core, or onto other kinds of sensations? This latter denial, when forced, leads ultimately to the denial of the pre-structured core as well, which is an ontological claim and not therefore the business of epistemological or linguistic analysis — a fault too readily committed by the Naiyāyikas, despite cautionary reminders from the Buddhist quarters.

Returning to the question of the preferred paradigm, I want to suggest a reason for why I think the realists in India opted for this rather more simple-minded characterization of the role of language in relation to our awareness of things. Here I turn to the Nyāya theory of Perception, which again Matilal has best articulated for us. Details aside, we know that the theory moved from Gautama's cruder version of sense-organ contact with the object (*indriyārtha sannikarṣa*) to Gaṅgeśa's more elegant view of the directness of the presentation of the object to awareness (neither any sort of contact nor first-person ascertainment is deemed necessary). The mind directly "touches" the object. A Lockean type of representationalism, Berkeleyean idealism, Humean sense-data empiricism, Brentanoian 'intentional content' phenomenologism, are all set aside, and it would have no bar either with any kind of phenomenalism, constructivism or constructionalism. An *F*-attribute is all that one has in the initial grasping (i.e. in the *nirvikalpa* phase), which is absolutely unmediated and gets promptly completed when the *F*-attribute (which may be a simple universal or an unanalysable property) as the qualifier is conjoined with the qualificandum, *x*, the nebulous haze that floats into the awareness, whence immediately arises the cognition, $G = Fx$ (The relation that causally connects *F* and *x*, as *aRb*, is also said to be real and tacit in the awareness). Such a theory of perception indeed is also most conducive to the doctrine of realism being harnessed, albeit direct or metaphysical realism. Now for those more committed to the economy of this doctrine, nothing should be allowed or supposed to stand in the way of the directness of the perceptual grasp, the 'touching' of reality — language, i.e. words and concepts included. In other words, the *F*-attribute neither presupposes a cognition of the thing of which it is a cognition (which is the preserve of the vaguely floating *x* or 'this. . . .'); nor does the *x* presuppose a core sensory data to which it ascribes the attributes or features, for all such presuppositions would either lead to a paradox or be prolix and therefore are unwarranted.

To be sure the *F*-attributes are *linguistic* in a sense or linguistically-imbued, for otherwise it would make no sense to speak of universals, such as cowness, colour-sensations such as red patches, or other properties such as — blobs of coldness, or — very hotting, and so on, as featuring in the awareness. Qualifiers are property-instantiations in predicate form and as such they function in one of characterization. This must perforce involve them in quasi-linguistic behaviour, as it were. This admission, which Naiyāyikas have no difficulty in making, is probably what Matilal counts as the modified adoption of the Bhartṛharian thesis, according to which it is sensations that penetrate the linguistic level (not that the linguistic tropes penetrate the sensory level, as the Buddhists might have it). But the primacy of the process, we should note, is never given to the linguistic, it is given rather to the cognitive (recall Matilal's opening sentence earlier), and only secondarily to the linguistic. Hence the allusions to the Bhartṛharian influence is a bit of a red-herring or a misnomer, for the Naiyāyikas are no metaphysical *bhāṣāvādin*s (proper namesakes occur without the calling of the mother of necessity). Still, the assertion about all thought or judgement being expressible in words is needed in the Nyāya view so as to "avoid the reduction of the public concepts finally to the inexpressible phenomenal criteria. They are identified in terms of causal relations between agents and the world (there being nothing in between on this view)." But how much of the linguistic criteria has the Nyāya allowed to penetrate the cognitive process? This question is pertinent, for what is grasped or perceived is not a bit of language but an object qua object which is descriptively marked as possessing such and such a feature. Big deal, as the Americans might say.

Let me summarize the analysis and argument thus far. The Nyāya position is, as Matilal has it, that sensations have no core unstructured component: all cognitions worth their Howrah-salt arise structured; linguistic elements attach themselves like yokes, not ploughs, to the farming oxen, and their causal connection with the things of which they are cognitions is indubitably direct. This approach guarantees the conclusions of metaphysical realism. Or perhaps metaphysical (i.e. external) realism dictates just such a linguistically-compromised doctrine of knowing. Matilal says as much, thus, "All these, the Naiyāyikas asserted, were needed to remain true to their view of metaphysical realism." But whether they are *necessary* is of course another, and indeed the moot question; but this remains to be shown; though I believe Sibajiban Bhattacharyya with Stephen Phillips in their work on Gaṅgeśa have been making good progress on this very issue.

As to language *per se* or *śabda*, which as a whole is another *pramāṇa* since we obtain knowledge from using linguistic utterance, it too must operate in more or less the same way and conform to the same criteria or conditions of external, causal connectivity, otherwise the knowledge it delivers us will be much compromised or contaminated (not least by its own excesses). Worse still, if especially the Tower of Babel or babblers is admitted into the fray, we'd risk conceptual relativism; but most of all, if we are to remain committed to true blue (i.e. anticipating Davidson and Dummett) metaphysical realism, then we must find a way of talking about language that sustains this doctrine optimally. How can we achieve that? Well, there is one simple route: viz. use the model of sensory perception as the paradigm for linguistic knowledge, with all the devices, criterial requirements and descriptive categories opened up for us in the theory of propositional knowledge discussed thus far. Seek to ground this doctrine of word and knowledge in the "direct grasp" modality that Gaṅgeśa has insisted upon for sensory perception; do not allow concepts (*vikalpa*) thrown up randomly or unconsciously by the mind, through kārmic traces, or love's desires, or private reflective tropes, or other discursive items outside of the shared public language, etc. to interfere with and mediate the otherwise immaculate continuum between the word and the world. — This is not unlike the Kantian strictures on the categories of understanding which were to be strictly rational, i.e. universal, in form and were not to be mixed up with relative projections, artefacts of imagination, human intentionalities and so on. — Language, despite the temptations coming from the likes of Candrakīrti and more recently echoed in the post-Sausurean semiological movement led by Rolland Barthes in France and Derrida more famously in North America, is not to be regarded as a self-contained system of signs which makes reference only to internally bifurcated or constructed signifieds, or that it is only by a wild stretch of our imagination that any real-term reference or what Frege called Bedeuṭung is achieved: otherwise it is all *Sinn*.

If the latter were the case, we would not be able to distinguish between true and false sentences: the *F*-attributes must and do necessarily feature in the object of which it is a verbally-derived cognition for linguistic judgements that are true. That is how we know from words.

It is then little wonder that Arindam Chakravorty, following in the same tradition, would question whether it was even possible for someone to understand a patently false sentence, such as "Odourless green cheese utters Martian music," for one would be hard-pressed to make a logically coherent connection of *Fx* to *G*. This predilection for a realist thesis of language and the epistemic moves under-girding it is further borne out in K.C. Bhattacharyya's wonderful description of how *śabda* functions in the context of a *karaṇa:* the word, he says, reaches out to the thing, it *touches* the thing. (Professor Mohanty and I have commented in some detail on K.C. Bhattacharyya's immensely helpful insight, but again here I wish to point to the unargued but presupposed bias towards a realist schema which informs this insight.) Direct realism can only produce or issue in a theory of the direct relation between words and the world. Bhartṛhari may well have believed that world is *linguistically* given to us; but the Naiyāyikas for their part, including their modern day defenders it would be true to say, believe that not the world as a whole but only the public space and one-half-of-the-cognitive act (that too the predicate side) is linguistically riven. All else is thankfully free from the ravages and relativistic tendencies of a more general course of linguistics.

Why not, however, go all the way and take seriously the Buddhist dialectical argument that even this partial linguisticality, as conceded in the Nyāya cognitive theory, is an imaginative construction, that indeed language is a figment of our desires, intentionalities, which cover up the absence of real causal connections. In other words, we are far from having convincingly established necessary causality in respect of the *x* and *F*-attributes which float into and feature respectively in our awareness (as *prākārata* and *viśeṣaṇa*), or, alternatively, consider that as a shared public or collective discourse, language is not devoid of its own relativities, constructions, self-referentialities, community or tradition-transmitted intentionalities and so on, that get in the way of authentic grasping of the world, which can only be 'wordless.'

References

Acronyms for Matilal's work discussed:

NNDN – *Navya-Nyāya Doctrine of Negation* (Harvard Oriental Series), 1976.

ELG = *Epistemology Logic and Grammar* (Motilal Banarsidas, Delhi).

SINR = Some Issues of Nyāya Realism.

WW = *The Word and the World* (Oxford University Press, Delhi).

2

Language and Mind
A Mādhyamika Perspective

*C.D. Sebastian**

If the dictum 'a creature cannot have a thought unless it has language' of *linguistic interpretationism*[1] is taken seriously, the Mādhyamika[2] perspective of language might nearly be impossible, for the Mādhyamika does not have a language of his own to put forward. But a truth-seeking examination of the Mādhyamika will enable one to acknowledge that Nāgārjuna has a language. However, his language does not

---

* Assistant Professor of Philosophy, Department of Humanities & Social Sciences, Indian Institute of Technology, Bombay, Mumbai — 400 076, India.

1. Donald Davidson et al. held the view that the ascription of thought is inseparable from the interpretation of language. See for more details William Child, *Causality, Interpretation and the Mind*, Oxford, Clarendon Press, 1996, pp. 7-47.

2. The name of the school of Nāgārjuna is Mādhyamika, meaning "follower of the *madhyamā pratipad*, the Middle way or Path." There is little doubt that the term is taken from the first sermon of Buddha, where the Middle Path is preached. But the old meaning was transformed, and for Nāgārjuna it was the middle path between asserting the real existence of *dharmas* and denying them in the sense of negating a possible real.

have syntax,[3] but the semantics[4] is very clear in the soul-searching study of the Mādhyamika. Since there is no syntax in his language, unlike the language of mathematical logic,[5] there is room for misinterpretation of the semantics of the Mādhyamika language. We are aware of the fact that many have tried to interpret his language down through the ages, and in turn, they even misinterpreted it in their own biased approach.[6] His language was the language of silence, as it was in the case of Buddha.

---

3. By syntax I mean 'how we say things' (I am indebted to John N. Crossley for this understanding, Cf. John N. Crossley, "Mathematical Logic? A Survey," in *Programme and Abstracts: First Indian Conference on Logic and Its Relationship with Other Disciplines*, Mumbai, Indian Institute of Technology, Bombay, 8-13 January 2005, p. 33).
4. By semantics I mean 'what we mean' (Cf. John N. Crossley, "Mathematical Logic? A Survey," in *Programme and Abstracts: First Indian Conference on Logic and Its Relationship with Other Disciplines*, Mumbai, Indian Institute of Technology, Bombay, 8-13 January 2005, p. 33).
5. See for details, John N. Crossley, Chris Brickhill et al., *What is Mathematical Logic*, New York, Dover Publications, 1990.
6. The Philosophy of *śūnyatā* by Nāgārjuna, the greatest Mādhyamika (*c.* CE 150), has come down to us more through misunderstanding and misinterpretation than through an accurate appraisal and appreciation of its fundamental contention. That is why A.K. Chatterjee wrote three decades ago about the philosophy of *śūnyatā*: "It is a philosophy which is much feared and abused but little understood, a philosophy *more sinned against than sinning*" (A.K. Chatterjee, "The Mādhyamika and the Philosophy of Language" in *Our Heritage: Bulletin of the Department of Post-graduate Research*, XIX (1), 1971, Calcutta, Sanskrit College, p. 21). The history of the influence of the great Indian thinker named Nāgārjuna is even today far from over. Karl Jaspers listed Nāgārjuna among the 'great philosophers' (Karl Jaspers, *Die grossen Philosophen*, vol. 1, Munich, 1959, pp. 934-56) half a century ago and his influence in West remains an open question.

In this paper I will concentrate on the markedly Buddhist version of language with which I am more familiar. Modern philosophers of language have put forward a principle of expressibility, according to which it is held that for anything that a speaker desires to put across, there is an expression or demonstration present in the speaker's language which can express it.[7] B.K. Matilal of happy memory testifies it as, "Succinctly, this principle means: what can be meant can be said."[8] However, in this paper I am not endorsing this position, as it is impossible to regard this consideration in Mādhyamika perspective. In the first and second parts, I will deal strictly with the Mādhyamika perspective, and in the third part a sort of analysis of the same is made in the way I look at it. The fourth part is the summing up of what I have been saying so far.

I

To understand the Mādhyamika perspective of language, it is essential to appraise the silence of Buddha (on metaphysical issues). Silence as an attitude is open to a variety of interpretations: one can be silent due to a lack of interest in theoretical speculations (pragmatism) or due to an impossibility to take a stand (agnosticism and suspension of judgement) or due to a tacit expression of disagreement (negation or annihilation). However, for the Mahāyānists, the Mādhyamika in particular, Buddha's silence cannot be understood by any of these three interpretations. Buddha was not an agnostic, for he taught the four noble truths through which human beings can avoid the doubt and despair that

7. J. Searle, *Speech Acts*, Cambridge, Cambridge University Press, 1969, pp. 19-21.

8. Bimal Krishna Matilal, *The Word and the World*, New Delhi, Oxford University Press, 2001, p. 144.

emanate from agnosticism. His position was not nihilism because he propounded a way for *nirvāṇa* described by him in positive terms as bliss and peace. Above all, his rejection of speculative metaphysics indicates that he was aware of the indescribable nature of the Absolute Reality. The silence of Buddha is an indication, rather a proposition, that reason cannot describe transcendent reality. Buddha never answered certain questions of metaphysical bearings, because of the insufficiency of human language to express the highest truth, and silence was the best expression of reality.[9]

Buddha was the forerunner of the Mādhyamika dialectic. However, the philosophical position underlying the silence of Buddha did not get crystallized into a philosophy until the time of Nāgārjuna. Buddha tries to resolve the conflict of views, by raising the human mind beyond the empirical level of phenomena or *saṁvṛtti* to a higher level of reality, where neither existence nor non-existence can be asserted, rather where categories of thought and language do not apply. The unanswered questions are unanswerable because they are about the Unconditioned (*asaṁskṛta*), and it cannot be characterized by the phenomenal verbal-linguistic constructions. Phenomenal verbal constructions are linguistically ill-formed when it concerns the Ultimate or the Unconditioned, as it is virtually impossible to give a picture of it. Such constructions "use personal referring terms, which according to Buddhist thinking have no real referent; hence any answer given directly to them (i.e. to those questions) would necessarily confirm the misleading presupposition that such terms do refer to some real and permanent individual"[10]

9. Abraham Valez de Cea, "The Silence of the Buddha and the Questions about the *Tathāgata* after Death," in *The Indian International Journal of Buddhist Studies*, X (5), 2004, pp. 119-41.

10. Steven Collins, *Selfless Persons*, Cambridge, Cambridge University Press, 1982, p. 133.

as well. Thus, the silence of Buddha "can only be interpreted as meaning the consciousness of the indescribable nature of the Unconditioned Reality."[11]

Nāgārjuna is a *prāsaṅgika*,[12] as he does not have any tenet of his own, and he does not care to frame a theory or a language of his own.[13] The sole aim of Nāgārjuna is to free the human mind of the net of concepts (*vikalpa-jāla*) and verbal elaboration (*prapañca*).[14] That is why Nāgārjuna ends his *magnum opus* with *sarvadṛṣṭiprahāṇāya*:

> *sarvadṛṣṭiprahāṇāya yaḥ saddharmam adeśayat;*
> *anukampāmupādāya tam namasyāmi gautamam.*[15]

---

11. T.R.V. Murti, *The Central Philosophy of Buddhism*, New Delhi, Harper Collins Publishers, 1998, p. 48.

12. The *prāsaṅgika* is one who resorts to *reductio ad absurdum* arguments. This is the Mādyamika dialectic. This dialectic is a series of *reductio ad absurdum* arguments (*prasaṅgāpādanam*). *Prasaṅga* is not to be understood as an apagogic proof in which we prove an assertion indirectly by disproving the opposite. *Prasaṅga* is disproof simply, without any intention of proving a thesis. After Nāgārjuna and his immediate disciple āryadeva, the Mādhyamika School had a splitting up into two schools, namely, the Prāsaṅgika and the Svātantrika, represented by Buddhapālita and Bhāvaviveka respectively. Later on Candrakīrti (seventh century) becomes the champion of the Prāsaṅgika School.

13. Nāgārjuna says, *nāsti ca mama pratijñā*, "I have no proposition," or anything to put forward, for when all things are appeased (*atyantopaśānta*) and by nature isolated (*prakṛtivivikta*), how can there be a proposition? For details see Nāgārjuna's *Vigrahavyāvartanī* 29 and its commentary.

14. C.D. Sebastian, "Emptiness Appraised: A Critical Study of Nāgārjuna's Philosophy by David Burton," in *Indian International Journal of Buddhist Studies*, X (4), 2003, pp. 225-29.

15. The *Mādhyamika Kārikā* 27: 30.

Prapañca or *vikalpa* is used in the Mādhyamika system for verbal and linguistic constructions of mind. It is the "verbal proliferation" which does not have any worth in the above-said system. Such verbalization or description by language is a sort of distortion of what is real (*paramārtha satya*), rather perceived or experienced. Such verbal, linguistic and theoretical constructions (even termed as *dṛṣṭi* in Mādhyamika) contaminate the pristine purity of the real, for the real is *nirvikalpa* and *niṣprapañca* (or indeterminate). With his rejection of all views, of all constructive metaphysics, Nāgārjuna has advocated *śūnyatā sarva dṛṣṭinām*:

> *śūnyatā sarvadṛṣṭinām proktā niḥsaraṇam jinaiḥ;*
> *yeṣām tu śūnyatā dṛṣṭistānasādhyān babhāṣire.*[16]

Further, Nāgārjuna asserts that the heart of Buddha's teaching is the disposal of *prapañca.*[17] *Prapañca* is deceptive and illusory, and by saying this Buddha meant *śūnyatā.*[18] The attitude in philosophy consists in being beyond any views and theories, and remaining critical of all rational speculations and verbal constructions of language. It demonstrates the falsity of every philosophical language without claiming to be another. It practises the "silence" of Buddha, which the Mādhyamika upheld, in just observing the nature of things without uttering a single word, as it is said by Candrakīrti, *paramārtho hi āryāṇām tuṣṇīṁbhāvaḥ* (freedom is silence).[19]

16. The *Mādhyamika Kārikā* 13: 8.

17. *sarvopalambhopaśamaḥ prapañcopaśamaḥ sivaḥ* ।
na kvacit kasyacit kaścid dharmo buddhena deśitaḥ ॥
— *The Mādhyamika Kārikā* 25: 24

18. *tan mṛṣā moṣadharma yad yadi kim tatra muṣyate* ।
etat tūktam bhagavatā śūnyatā-paridīpakam ॥
— *The Mādhyamika Kārikā* 13: 2

19. A.K. Chatterjee, "The Mādhyamika and the Philosophy of Language," in *Our Heritage: Bulletin of the Department of Post-graduate Research,* XIX (1), 1971, Calcutta, Sanskrit College, p. 29.

I must add one more thing here. As it has been just stated above, the Mādhyamika does not have any position of his own in order to be able to refute the position of others. Further, he does not have a position of his own to be able to have a means to establish his rejection of others' standpoints. However, he criticizes others' position. Thus, the predicament and crucial trouble with the Mādhyamika is that he cannot say anything, and the moment he says something, he will contradict himself for he himself has stated *śūnyatā sarva dṛṣṭinām*[20] and hence his own position is *śūnya* if the same parameter is applied. We will be in a position to salvage this situation as we proceed further in the following pages.

II

Unlike the early Vedic literature and its conception of the word (*vāk*), Nikāya Buddhism never accepted the divine nature of words, because words have no intrinsic worth or a metaphysical grounding in a supreme power. They are only valuable in an instrumental way in order to accomplish something.[21] Words and any conceptions that they may form are not absolute.[22] Language is imperfect like everything else, for it has got its place within the cycle of causation and impermanence, and it cannot be expected to express any absolute truth. Although no absolute truth can be expressed in language, the *dhamma/dharma* (teachings) of Buddha is embodied in language in the Buddhist texts. Unlike the ordinary language, the unique supreme word of Buddha,

---

20. The *Mādhyamika Kārikā* 13: 8.

21 Harold Coward, *Sacred Word and Sacred Text: Scripture in World Religions*, Maryknoll, Orbis Books, 1988, p. 139.

22. *Majjhima Nikāya* 3: 234 (*The Middle Length Sayings*, vol. III, I.B. Horner (tr.), London, Luzac and Company Ltd., 1967).

buddha-vacana,[23] is not in a state of bondage, and the interpreter can comprehend its meaning. [24] Here it is useful to bring in the two significant notions of Mahāyāna Buddhism in this regard: *nītārtha* and *neyārtha*. The doctrine of these two truths enables the Mahāyāna philosophy in general and the Mādhyamika in particular, to synthesize and evaluate the scriptural texts and the doctrines. Texts are divided on the basis of *paramārtha satya* and *saṁvṛtti satya*, into *nītārtha* and *neyārtha* respectively. Thus *nītārtha* is the teaching of direct or ultimate import, whereas *neyārtha* is the teaching of the indirect or circumstantial import, having phenomenal validity only. The Advaita Vedānta makes a similar distinction of the *śruti* texts into *parā* and *aparā*. The language as such has got its appeal and value in the *neyārtha* level, but its meaning could be of *nītārtha* level. For this reason only, the learned Buddhist scholar E. Lamotte explained it as "the meaning is single and invariable, while the letter is multiple and infinitely variable."[25]

Further, Nāgārjuna denies that words acquire meaning by referring to something outside or external to language system of phenomenal level (*saṁvṛtti*). For words in a language are *saṁvṛtti* distinctions which have meaning only in their contextual relation to each other, and are not pinpointing to any ontological status. He brings to light that all distinctions we make, such as subject and object, the seer and the seen,

---

23. C.D. Sebastian, *Metaphysics and Mysticism in Mahāyāna Buddhism*, Delhi, Sri Satguru Publications, 2005, pp. 254-56.

24. George D. Bond, "The Gradual Path as a Hermeneutical Approach to *Dhamma*," in Donald S. Lopez, Jr. (ed.), *Buddhist Hermeneutics, Studies in East Asian Buddhism*, 6, Honolulu, University of Hawaii Press, 1988, p. 33.

25. Etienne Lamotte, *Histoire du Buddhisme Indien, des Origines a l' Ere Śaka*, Bibliotheque du Mussen, Bd. 43, Louvain, Universite de Louvain Institut Orientaliste, 1967, p. 13.

cause and effect,[26] or even motion and rest[27] are interdependent, and they are relative to each other. All such (interdependent) distinctions obtain their meaning only in contextual relation to each other, and they are *śūnya* or meaningless of any ontological standing.[28] It is significant that Nāgārjuna devotes a whole chapter (chapter 24) in his *Mādhyamika Kārikā* for explaining *śūnyatā*. He explicates that *śūnyatā* is not nihilism, but relativity, interdependence and conditionedness. It is not an outright denial of the world of becoming and the meaningfulness of life, but an exposition of *saṁvṛtti* as a course of conditioned becoming. Nāgārjuna says, "for him who is in concord with *śūnyatā*, everything stands in conformity/harmony; and for him who is not in concord with *śūnyatā*, nothing stands in conformity/harmony."[29]

It is important to be aware of the intellectual *locale* of Nāgārjuna. In his critiques, Nāgārjuna was critiquing the fundamental metaphysical concepts shared in common by the entire Indian tradition. They came in contradictory pairs: permanence and change, substance and quality, forms and relations, presence and absence, identity and difference, cause and effect, *pramāṇa* and *prameya*, etc. These concepts are logically incoherent, thus they are *śūnya* for him. So are, fundamentally, all concepts. Hence, Nāgārjuna's advice is to

---

26. The *Mādhyamika Kārikā*'s first chapter entitled *Pratyaya-parīkṣā* deals with causation.

27. The *Mādhyamika Kārikā*'s second chapter entitled *Gatāgata-parīkṣā* deals with motion and rest.

28. This very position is upheld by Fredrick J. Streng in his *Emptiness: A Study in Religious Meaning*, New York, Abingdon Press, 1967.

29. *sarvam ca yujyate tasya śūnyatā yasya yujyate* ।
sarvam na yujyate tasya śūnyam yasya yujyate ॥
— *The Mādhyamika Kārikā* 24: 14.

get rid of them all — *śūnyatā sarva-dṛṣṭinām.*[30] One has to go beyond all the plurality and categories (*sarva-prapañcātīta*). The inapplicability of the ways of concepts and language is *aprapañca*. Nāgārjuna had a piece of advice like this:

> Those who describe Buddha, who is transcendent to thought and word, and is not subject to birth and death in terms of conceptual categories, are all victims of *prapañca* (the verbalizing mind) and are unable to see *tathāgata* in his real nature.[31]

III

Our language is a coloured or translucent window, not a transparent one; it will always colour and shape the thing/ reality as one wishes to depict it. If one attempts to describe the reality, one cannot do it without describing it in a language,[32] thus we will be forced to acknowledge the plurality of language games. Let us remember that no language is exempt from context-sensitivity[33] and personal colouring of one's own perception. When one tries to speak of the Ultimate Reality, if at all there is one, then that presentation will be biased or one-sided, or even partial, as it is only the perception of the person concerned. Wittgenstein's counsel was in this line that "what is excluded by the law of causality cannot be

---

30. There is a beautiful exposition of this *śunyatā* concept by J.N. Mohanty. For details see J. N. Mohanty, *Explorations in Philosophy*, vol. I, New Delhi, Oxford University Press, 2001, p. 174.

31. *prapañcayanti ye buddham prapañcātītam-avyayam* ।
te prapañcahatāḥ sarve na paśyanti tathāgatam ॥
— *The Mādhyamika Kārikā* 22:15.

32. H. Putnam, *Renewing Philosophy*, Cambridge, Harvard University Press, 1992, p. 123.

33. H. Putnam, "Reply to Jean-Pierre Cometi," *Revieu Internazionale de Philosophie* 55, 2001, pp. 460-61.

described"[34] and also "whereof one cannot speak of, thereof one must be silent,"[35] he had no interest in portraying the indescribable. That is why, I take the liberty to say, the golden silence was powerful not only in Buddhist tradition, but in the entire Indian philosophy.

We try to express the unfamiliar in terms of the familiar. Language always seeks to express the spiritual by the analogy of the physical,[36] which is of *saṁvṛtti* (phenomenal) level for the Mādhyamika. Hence, the moment we speak of the *paramārtha,* we are phenomenalizing it, and it is not proper in the strictest philosophical sense for the Mādhyamika. Even if one is going to use language as only a symbol, it is inadequate. The symbol is always a material object, or the mental image of such an object; and the *paramārtha* is always non-sensuous. We cannot speak of the *paramārtha* adequately either positively, negatively, both ways or neither way.[37] It transcends both our concepts and the meaning of our words. Whatever our intellect conceives of the *paramārtha* falls short of representing it, so what it actually is could be better represented in our golden silence.

---

34. Ludwig Wittgenstein, *Tractatuṣ Logico-Philosophicus* 6.362, London, Routledge & Kegan Paul Ltd., 1983, p. 179.

35. Ludwig Wittgenstein, *Tractutus Logico-Philosophicus* 7, p. 189.

36. J. Venattumattom, "Truth as Reflected in the Sacred Scriptures," *Jñānatīrtha: Journal of Sacred Scriptures,* V (1), 2005, p. 93.

37. My reference here is to the *catuṣkoṭi-tarka.* Four and only four views are possible: two are primary and the other two are secondary. Nāgārjuna has clearly systematized these four and formulated them into *catuṣkoṭi* and, *Prajñā-pāramitā* is *catuṣkoṭi-vinirmukta.* Nāgārjuna tries to express the inexpressible through this. Nāgārjuna gives the four views in the 27th chapter entitled *Dṛṣṭi-parīkṣā* of the *Mādhyamika Kārikā.* We have these views in the *Mādhyamika Kārikā* 27:2. āryadeva in his *Catuḥ Śatakam,* 14: 21 also mentions the same.

It might be asked if the phenomenal (*saṁvṛtti*) has no value at all, and it should be rejected then how is it possible to speak of the Ultimate (*paramārtha*). How is the knowledge of the *paramārtha* possible? Further, if we were rooted in *paramārtha*, there should not be any need for *saṁvṛtti*, and we would not even care to make the distinction between the two. To this we have the answer. Nāgārjuna does not rule out our phenomenal existence of *vyavahāra*. We are in this *vyavahāra* and we need to overcome the tenets of *vyavahāra* to reach the *paramārtha*. *Paramārtha* is the end or goal that we seek out to attain by rooting ourselves in the *vyavahāra* or *saṁvṛtti*.[38] It is possible to realize the *paramārtha* only by the acceptance of our phenomenal existence. So we are advised not to ignore the *saṁvṛtti*, as it is there, but the keynote is that *saṁvṛtti* is imperfect and limited. It will never be able to portray the real. However, the real is identical with phenomenal,[39] though the ultimate or absolute is the only real. This difference between the two is only subjective, and not real.

Discursive thought, logic, and reason cannot reach the real or the knowledge of it. This is the keynote of all *prajñāpāramitā* teachings. Buddha always couples knowing (*jñāna*) with seeing (*paśya*),[40] for without seeing, knowing has no depths, and the reality will not be comprehended fully without seeing. We

---

38. *vyavahāramanāśrityā paramārtho na deśyate* ।
— *The Mādhyamika Kārikā* 24: 10 (a).

39. *na saṁsārasya nirvāṇāt kiñcidasti viśeṣaṇam* ।
na nirvāṇasya saṁsārāt kiñcidasti viśeṣaṇam ॥
nirvāṇasya ca yā koṭīḥ koṭīḥ saṁsāraṇasya ca ।
na tayorantaram kiñcit susūkṣmamapi vidyate ॥
— *The Mādhyamika Kārikā* 25: 19-20.

40. D.T. Suzuki, "The Basics of Buddhist Philosophy," in Richard Woods (ed.), *Understanding Mysticism*, New York, Image Books, 1980, p. 126.

find the first item in the *aṣṭāṅga-mārga* as *samyagdṛṣṭi*. Nāgārjuna also uses the word 'seeing' (*paśya*) for the realization.[41] This 'seeing' is the 'insight' or the experiencing of things in their state of such-ness or that-ness (*tathatā*). This seeing or insight is *bodhi*. It is the "seeing by means of *prajñā*-eye which is a special kind of intuition enabling us to penetrate right into the bedrock of Reality itself."[42] Let us remember that Indian philosophy in general is "an attempt to transcend the empirical and to lead us to something beyond."[43] The non-empirical is a kind of seeing, as we have mentioned just above. That is why the insistence on philosophy in India as *darśana*.

The insight is the immediate experience of the unsurpassable Reality, and this Reality is ineffable (or indescribable) and "can only be characterized in paradoxical or, at least seemingly, contradictory ways."[44] Even such characterization would be imperfect. Our language is the product of a world of numbers and individuals, which could only be applicable to this world (*loka*). Yes, it is true that the Mādhyamika presented his philosophy in a language which is again paradoxical. "The Mādhyamika philosophy can be taken to challenge language itself as a useful source of thought, which makes it appear paradoxical, since it is itself expressed in language."[45] However, our experience and insight extend

---

41. *yaḥ pratītya-samutpādam paśyanidam sa paśyati* I
duḥkham samudayam caiva nirodham mārgam eva ca II
— *The Mādhyamika Kārikā* 24: 40.

42. D.T. Suzuki, "The Basics of Buddhist Philosophy," p. 128.

43. A.K. Chatterjee, "Reasoning in Indian Philosophy," in *ānvīkṣikī: Research Bulletin of Centre of Advanced Study in Philosophy*, III (2), 1970, Varanasi, Banaras Hindu University, p. 45.

44. Charles Hartshorne, "Mysticism and Rationalistic Metaphysics," in Richard Woods (ed.), *Understanding Mysticism*, p. 415.

45. Oliver Leaman, *Eastern Philosophy: Key Readings*, London, Routledge, 2004, p. 211.

beyond this world, which is called *lokottara* (or transcendental world). That is why Vasubandhu calls it as *jñānam lokottaram ca tat*.[46] This experience is ineffable or in the Mahāyāna terminology it is *nirvikalpa* and *niṣprapañca*. It is *anirvacanīya* or indescribable. This Reality experienced is just termed as *śūnyatā* in Mahāyāna Buddhism.[47] This *śūnyatā* or *tathatā* defies all characterization and denotation. No words can express what it is. Thus, this insight and experience is mysticism.

For natural languages, the roles of grammar and semantics are harder to split apart; there may be no principled way of making this separation in general.[48] But for the language of the Mādhyamika it is different. One is convinced that the language of the Mādhyamika is such. Further, the critique of Mādhyamika was only directed against the *dṛṣṭis*, the language and the way the views were presented. One finds a similar kind of attitude in R.C. Pradhan's statement in his recent book on Wittgenstein, and it goes, ". . . the idea of having to draw the limits of thought is superseded by the idea of drawing the limits of language. This facilitates the idea of a philosophical critique of language. The critique is no more a critique of thought, but a critique of language."[49] Thus, there is "the limits of language."[50] Hence, one can give good reason for the position of Nāgārjuna in his consideration that all views and speculative systems are uncritical and dogmatic approaches

46. Vasubandhu's *Vijñapti-Mātratā-Siddhi*: *Triṁśikā* 29.

47. For details of this experience see John Hick, Mystical Experience as Cognition," in Richard Woods (ed.), *Understanding Mysticism*, p. 433.

48. Wilfrid Hodges, "Compositional Semantics for a Language of Imperfect Information," *Logic Journal of IGPL* 5 (1997), pp. 539-63.

49. R.C. Pradhan, *The Great Mirror: An Essay on Wittgenstein's Tractatus*, New Delhi, Kalki Prakash, 2002, p. 149.

50. Ludwig Wittgenstein, *Philosophical Investigations*, 119, G.E.M. Anscombe (tr.), Oxford, Basil Blackwell, 1963.

(*dṛṣṭis*) only, for what is ultimately real is *beyond concepts and language*. Nāgārjuna rejects speculative (dogmatic) metaphysics, not because there is no real that is transcendent, but because of its defective procedure in communicating in a language game. Nāgārjuna writes about the Real (*tattva*) as transcendent to thought, non-relative, non-determinate, quiescent, non-discursive and non-dual.[51]

Let us have a look at the critics of the Mādhyamika. Many have appropriated the Mādhyamika, but few have seen him whole. The Mādhyamika has been criticized by many an Indian thinker from inside and outside Buddhism. Among them are the Advaitins, whose own position bears a remarkable resemblance with the Mādhyamika. Śaṅkara dismisses the Mādhyamika Buddhism as 'not worth refuting' in his *Tarkapāda*, making reference to it in a line or two. His motives are unclear. A critical student of Indian philosophy might not be inclined to agree with some of the Advaitins' claim that Śaṅkara did not find any merit in the *śūnyavāda*. One is prepared to give weight to the assertion of the learned scholar Professor A.K. Chatterjee in this regard that Śaṅkara was "apprehensive of his own position being misconstrued as a variation on the theme of *śūnyatā*"[52] for the two philosophies are close to each other in their main contentions, and "Śaṅkara anticipated the charge of his preaching a kind of veiled *śūnyavāda*, and tried to ward off it by not spelling out a definitive stand *vis-a-vis śūnyavāda.*"[53] The sole comment Śaṅkara gives is a duplication

---

51. *apara-pratyayam śāntam prapañcairaprapañcitam* ।
    nirvikalpam anānārtham etat tattvasya lakṣaṇam ॥
    — *The Mādhyamika Kārikā* 18: 9.

52. A.K. Chatterjee, *Facets of Buddhist Thought*, Calcutta, Sanskrit College Research Publication, 1973, p. 21.

53. A.K. Chatterjee, *Facets of Buddhist Thought*, p. 21.

of Nyāya criticism on the Mādhyamika that a universal reproof of all *pramāṇas* is self-silencing. Thus, when one undertakes the journey to comprehend the language of Nāgārjuna, the greatest Mādhyamika, the advice of Nāgārjuna himself will come handy: "*Śūnyatā* should be handled with skill; it does great harm if wrongly understood, like a snake caught by the wrong end."[54]

IV

The Mādhyamika does not say anything about reality. He was an ardent opponent of canons, and to claim that he had a specific canon of his own will be self-contradictory. Otherwise it would be only another metaphysical construction; its oblique references to reality (*aparā pratyaya,* etc.) are all negative. To say that nothing can be said is not really to say anything, but only a *façon de parler,* a pretence so to speak.

The kind of language which we employ for the description of things is that which possesses a subject-predicate model. Without referring to the nature of predicates, Nāgārjuna points out that not only predicate creates problems for us but the very mould of predicate language is prone to engender certain problems for us,[55] because any predicate *qua* predicate is intended to bring out common, shareable or similar characteristics of things. According to Nāgārjuna, the things in the world are uniquely particular (*svalakṣaṇa*) and such that no two of them are similar or identical. On the logico-linguistic level, *śūnyatā* would amount to accepting the utter

---

54. *vinasyati durdṛṣṭā śūnyatā mandamedhasam* ।
sarpo yathā dugṛhito vidyā vā duṣprasādhitā ॥
— *The Mādhyamika Kārikā* 24: 11.

55. M.P. Marathe, "Nāgārjuna and Candrakīrti on Śūnyatā," *Indian Philosophical Quarterly,* VII (4), 1980, p. 533.

incompetence of predicate language, where every predicate implies a common property, descriptively used to usher in the nature of a uniquely particular thing.

The Mādhyamika never points out an incommunicability of our knowledge in any language whatever; rather he points out its incommunicability through the language we normally have.[56] Syntax and semantics are linguistic phenomena which come into play only when there is a language. Mādhyamika does not have a first-order language, or it would be vitiated by the same fallacies that it seeks to refute. But this refutation is itself expressed and communicated, and thus utilizes linguistic equipment so there have to be a syntax and a semantics for his use of language. Sentences have to be 'well-formed' (syntax) and have to say something (semantics) even if only about its own incompetence. Language creates pictures of reality and these pictures hold us in thralldom or bondage. So we utilize language to break out of it.

When critics characterize Mādhyamika as skepticism, positivism, negativism, nihilism or whatever, it is possible that Mādhyamika has used faulty methods and indulged in sophistry. But presumably the critics are not themselves imparting anything of their own to their critique of the Mādhyamika. They are rather engaged in pure disinterested analysis of the Mādhyamika position in a completely detached and dispassionate manner. This is precisely what the Mādhyamika is striving to do. He is not an 'other' to metaphysics, but metaphysics become self-aware. We can refute the Mādhyamika only by being Mādhyamika, and not from outside. The critics are all in this respect 'crypto-Mādhyamikas.' Let us bear in mind that after all the vicissitudes

56. A.M. Padhye, *The Framework of Nāgārjuna's Philosophy*, Delhi, Sri Satguru Publications, 1988, p. 82.

of misreading, misinterpretation and the misconception of the Mādhyamika, his philosophy of *śūnyatā* nevertheless survives, for "his arguments have a lasting philosophic value"[57] and that is the real worth of the Mādhyamika.

57. Bimal Krishna Matilal, *Perception: An Essay on Classical Indian Theories of Knowledge*, Oxford, Clarendon Press, 1986, p. 49.

3

Language and Mind in the Upaniṣads

*R.C. Pradhan**

In this paper I will discuss the nature of language and mind in the Upaniṣads which constitute one of the sources of the philosophy of Vedānta. The Upaniṣads are concerned with the nature of *ātman* in general, but they also discuss the nature of the human mind and language in their investigation into the nature of *ātman*. The concepts of language and mind have arisen in the course of the understanding of the psychological and moral behaviour of man. The Upaniṣads develop a well-grounded moral psychology and also the psychology of spiritual consciousness.[1] It is in this context that the concepts of language and mind come into prominence, language and mind being the instruments through which consciousness manifests itself. For the Upaniṣadic thinkers, mind and language are the organs through which the *ātman*, which is of the nature of consciousness, is embodied in the world.

---

* Professor, Department of Philosophy, University of Hyderabad, Hyderabad — 500 046, India.

1. See R.D. Ranade, *A Constructive Survey of the Upaniṣadic Philosophy* (Bharatiya Vidya Bhawan, Bombay, 1968), pp. vii-xxi.

Ātman, Consciousness and Human Beings

The central concept of the Upaniṣadic philosophy[2] is *ātman* or the Self which is the primal principle of reality. *Ātman* is the ultimate reality on which the reality of man and the universe is founded. *Ātman* is of the nature of consciousness, that is, it is the self-effulgent being known otherwise as *Brahman.*[3] From this consciousness which is primal and ultimate arise the different forms of consciousness manifest in human beings and other subhuman creatures of the world. Thus the Upaniṣads tend to propound a monistic theory of consciousness while admitting the diversity of the forms of consciousness embodied in the finite material bodies in the universe. The metaphysics of the diverse forms of consciousness is underpinned by the idea of oneness of the ultimate reality, the *ātman* or *Brahman.*

According to the Upaniṣads, the *ātman* is by its nature conscious, is immortal and eternal and infinite.[4] There can be no spatial and temporal limitations of it as it is not located in space and time. It is subtler than the subtle and finer than the fine.[5] It is such that it is never to be understood in terms of the limited binary categories like big and small, near and distant, gross and subtle, etc. That is to say, the *ātman* is a transcendental reality that cannot be placed in the midst of the finite and limited entities of the universe. Thus the Upaniṣads establish the foundations of a transcendent metaphysics of the *ātman* or the *Brahman* in the history of Indian philosophy.

2. Ibid., See also S. Radhakrishnan, *The Principal Upaniṣads* (George Allen and Unwin, London), Introduction (tr. into Hindi, Delhi, 1971).
3. *Kaṭhopaniṣad,* I.ii.20-25.
4. Ibid., I.iii.15.
5. Ibid., I.ii.20.

The most important aspect of the metaphysics of the *ātman* is that it identifies *ātman* with consciousness as consciousness is taken to be the original form of *ātman* which is in itself not embodied, but appears to be so because of its association with the human body. Human beings are the embodiments of this supreme consciousness and thus appear to limit it to the finite bodies. However, the *ātman* is not identical with the human being, though human beings bear this consciousness in their essential nature. The Upaniṣad dictum: *tat tvam asi*[6] (Thou art That) reveals the essential identity of the *jīva* (the individual human being) and the *ātman*, though outwardly they are different. In no case is the individual man who is finite and limited in his or her being can claim to be the *ātman* which is infinite and unlimited. But the fact that the finite human being embodies the infinite shows that the infinite can coexist with the finite without being identical with the latter.

The Upaniṣads do not overlook the fact that the finite world is itself the field of action of the Infinite Being. That is to say, the Infinite Being needs the finite being for its manifestation and action. This is evidenced in the Upaniṣadic idea that *Brahman* is very much present in the world (*jagat*) itself as the latter is essentially non-different from the *Brahman*. The world is limited and finite so far as its apparent nature is concerned, but in essence it is *Brahman* itself.

The idea of the human being as an embodiment of the *ātman* is the underlying theme of the Upaniṣadic metaphysics. Human beings are never looked down upon as mere physical beings in the Upaniṣads. They are treated as the bearers of the immortal soul which is the infinite and universal principle underlying the universe. Thus man and the universe are united by the principle of the *ātman*. The *ātman* that is in the universe

6. *Chāndogya Upaniṣad*, VI.12; XIII.1-3.

is also in man, according to the Upaniṣads.[7] That is to say, the principle that is impregnated in the universe is also present in the human being thus making man the 'son of immortality' (*amṛtasya putraḥ*). This spiritual view of man is a remarkable feature of the Upaniṣadic metaphysics of man. Without this, much of the Upaniṣads will be speculative metaphysics sans practical relevance.

The Human Mind, Soul and the Body

The Upaniṣadic idea of a human being is the idea of a complex totality of the *ātman* (the soul), the *manas* (the mind) and the *śarīra* (the body). This totality or the complex whole is marked by the presence of the universal principle along with the conditioned and the particular features like the body and the mind. The body is the totality of the sense-organs, both gross and subtle, which are assigned specific functions within the system. The Upaniṣadic analysis of the physical features of the body is very subtle in view of the fact that there is a scientific understanding of the minute functions of the sense-organs (*indriyas*). The sense-organs have specific functions like seeing, smelling, tasting, touching and hearing. Each *indriya* is given an independent function within the system. Taken together they make the bodily system work unitedly.

The Upaniṣadic concept of the body is such that there is no trace of it being downgraded in terms of reality and importance. The human body is the best embodiment of the soul, since in man alone is the soul fully revealed. This must be taken as a positive way of looking at the body which is very often reviled in religious literature.[8] The human body is

---

7. Ibid., IV.10-15; *Śvetāsvatara Upaniṣad*, VI.11.

8. Orthodox literature on religious practices call for the mortification of the human body. Upaniṣads are an exception to this.

in that sense the house of the soul on the ground that the soul has chosen it as its fittest instrument. It is, however, true that the body has not been made into an instrument of pleasure and lust in the Upaniṣads because the body is the basis for spiritual realization and not for earthly pleasure. There is an inherent balance between the physical and the spiritual in the Upaniṣadic philosophy.[9]

Mind occupies a significant place next to the body. It is the complex of mental functions like thinking, experiencing, remembering and knowing, etc. These functions are carried on by the mind which is an inner organ according to the Upaniṣads. The mind acts on the sense-organs which in turn receive the sense-impressions from the outer world. The sense-organs are the channels which receive the impressions of the objects and the mind thereafter unifies them into a unitary experience. Thus experiences are made available to the soul which receives them under the different categories like seeing, feeling, imagining, etc. Though the soul is unaffected by the sense-experiences themselves, it is still under their influence till it is able to differentiate between its own nature and the external world. The soul has the capacity to rise above the empirical world because of its own non-empirical nature. Thus the body-soul distinction is inherently a metaphysical principle which is underlying the Upaniṣadic metaphysics.

The soul is different from the mind for the reason that the mind is limited and finite while the soul is infinite and unlimited. The finite mind is capable of receiving the experiences but cannot conceptualize them without the soul which is the seat of thinking and other creative activities. In the famous Upaniṣadic allegory of the chariot,[10] the soul is

9. *Kaṭhopaniṣad*, I.iii.10-12.

10. Ibid., I.iii.3.

the owner of the chariot, the intellect the charioteer, the mind the reins, the sense-organs the horses and the body the chariot. In this allegory the soul gives direction to the body which is driven by the mind along with the sense-organs. The soul is very much at the helm of affairs since it controls the body with the help of the mind. This shows that the Upaniṣads clearly point out that the soul has to be included in the complex of the human person because without it the person is just a mind-body complex. But being endowed with a soul, the person rises above the body-mind dualism and gives a clear unity to the person.

One can notice here the fact that the soul is different from the body and the mind because the latter are physical in nature, while the soul is immaterial in nature. The Upaniṣadic mind is not spiritual as in Descartes and other dualist thinkers. Here the mind is an organ of the physical type and is taken as a part of the subtle body (*sūkṣma śarīra*). The soul is categorically different from the body and the mind, it being of the nature of consciousness (*prajñānam Brahman*).[11] The *ātman* is consciousness itself and there is no question of it being in any way physical at all. The conscious soul is capable of associating itself with the mind and the body, without being dissolved into them. The mind is proximate to the soul but it cannot be identified with the soul. Therefore, the mind must remain within its physical limits, though it can aspire to get closer to the soul.

The Upaniṣads have introduced the notion of the five sheaths or the *pañcakośas*[12] which are as follows: the *annamaya kośa* (the bodily sheath), the *prāṇamaya kośa* (the sheath of life), the *manomaya kośa* (the mental sheath), *vijñānamaya kośa* (the

11. *Aitareya Upaniṣad*, III.i.3.

12. *Taittirīya Upaniṣad*, Part II.

sheath of consciousness) and the *ānandamaya kośa* (the sheath of bliss). All these five sheaths form an ascending series starting from the body and culminating in the *ātman*. Each sheath is important and constitutes an important part of the whole. In each higher stage we encounter a new reality. From the body life evolves, from life the mind, from mind consciousness and from consciousness the supra-conscious state of bliss. One can find here the evolution of the supra-mental consciousness in an evolutionary process[13] from the sheath of the body. In this scheme of things neither the body nor the mind nor the *ātman* can be dissociated from one another. They together constitute the whole reality both at the individual plane and also at the plane of the cosmos. Mind is the intermediary between the body and the higher plane of supra-mental consciousness.

Language and Mind

Language emerges out of the mental plane according to the Upaniṣads. At this plane, the linguistic faculty grows as part of the mind. *Vāk*[14] or language is concomitant with the mental faculty because where there is mind there is language, and vice versa. The fact is that without there being a mental faculty there can be no linguistic faculty for the reason that to use language is to involve thinking. Language is the vehicle of thinking and is thus an indispensable means of communication. The Upaniṣadic thinkers have recognized that the linguistic ability to communicate and formulate ideas is ultimately a gift of the human soul. This is so, because without the soul being naturally endowed with this gift, the mind itself cannot be accompanied with a language. Language is the subtle faculty that brings in a rich harvest of abilities all packaged into one

13. See Sri Aurobindo, *The Life Divine*, vols. I and II (Sri Aurobindo Ashram, Pondicherry, 1972).

14. *Kena Upaniṣad*, I.2.

faculty of thinking. Hence language and mind cannot stand apart in this complex whole, they penetrate each other.

For the Upaniṣadic thinkers what is important is that mind and language are both subservient to the soul in that both get illumination from the latter. The soul gives direction to the mind and meaning to language in that it injects the thought-components into language. Language throbs with the soul's stirrings by virtue of the fact that the linguistic expressions are carriers of the meanings first arising in the soul of man. Language is lifeless in the absence of the soul. Thus language is the means of expressions of the soul. The *ātman* takes the help of language to express itself, that is, its inmost conscious nature.

Language is identified by its expressive power and the power of communication. That is why language has to have symbols with meaning. The Upaniṣads recognize the systematic structure of symbols and their meaning especially in the Vedic language called Sanskrit. This language is the vehicle of the Vedic meanings expressed in the Vedic symbols. The sentences are conceived as meaning-units out of which the word-meanings are carved out. Śaṅkara in his commentary on the Upaniṣads holds that the sentences and words express meaning as the *sphoṭa*.[15] The *sphoṭa* theory came into existence much later but it can be guessed that the Vedic grammarians already knew that language has an expressive power which is an underlying reality. Language in any case has an underlying grammatical structure that accounts for its meaning. In this sense, the Upaniṣads can be credited with the knowledge of meaning as the semantic content of language.

15. See Swami Gambhirananda (tr.), *Eight Upaniṣads: With the Commentary of Saṅkarācārya*, vol. I (Advaita Ashram, Kolkata, 1957; rev. edn., 1989), p. 53 fn.

However, it cannot be said that the Upaniṣadic thinkers were concerned with grammar in the modern sense of the term. They were more concerned with the fact that language is the vehicle of thought and meaning and that it has an inner dimension that accommodates the powerful expressions like *ātman, Brahman,* etc. which have an extraordinary meaning not to be found in the ordinary language. That is why they were struggling to keep the extraordinary meaning within the bounds of language, though they ultimately failed to do so. The *ātman* or the *Brahman* remained beyond the expressive power of language.[16] Language is fully competent to express the thoughts about the world and its various aspects, but it fails to express anything about the *Brahman* which is beyond the world.

Limits of Language and Mind

The Upaniṣadic thinkers are concerned with the limits of language and mind because they are aware that language and mind cannot reach the transcendent reality.[17] This is because the transcendent reality is such that it is beyond the expressive power of language. The *ātman* or the *Brahman* has no features which can be described in language except negatively. The negative attributes are not such that they can grasp the *ātman* in its true nature. The *ātman* is beyond all the known attributes like being in space and time, being grasped by the sense-organs and being located here and now. Thus all attributes expressible in language are automatically withdrawn with regard to the ultimate reality, the *Brahman.*

The *ātman* cannot be described in language because it is not one of the objects which can be grasped in language. The

16. *Kaṭhopaniṣad,* II.iii.12; *Kena Upaniṣad* I.3.

17. *Taittirīya Upaniṣad,* II.4.

empirical objects are naturally expressible in language because the words are so designed that they can take us to the objects directly or indirectly. But the *ātman* is not an empirical object nor is it having attributes which can be called empirical. So there is no way we can grasp the *ātman* through language. The inexpressibility of the *ātman* in language may entail its unknowability, but this need not be the case because the Upaniṣads promise that the *ātman* can be grasped through higher intuition. According to the Upaniṣads, those who claim that they know the *ātman* through language and mind really do not know it, but those do not know it really know.[18] This paradoxical way of putting it expresses the idea that the *ātman* cannot be known in the way we know the world.

The Upaniṣads do not assign to the mind an all-powerful role so far as the knowledge of the *ātman* is concerned. Mind is as much handicapped as language is with regard to the *ātman*. Mind is incapable of grasping the *ātman* because of its inherent limitations. It can grasp an object given in space and time but it cannot grasp something that is beyond space and time. Mind is itself partly physical and so cannot apprehend anything that is completely non-physical. Mind is itself illuminated by the *ātman* and so is dependent on the latter for its powers. Therefore, it cannot apprehend the source of its power itself.[19]

The intellect which is one aspect of the mind is taken more positively so far as the knowledge of the Self is concerned. The intellect when sharpened enough, gives rise to the knowledge of the *ātman* by virtue of its proximity to the Self. The intellect has the power to rise above the limitations of the mind to know the Self. It is, however, not clear whether the

---

18. *Kena Upaniṣad*, II.3.

19. *Kaṭhopaniṣad*, II.iii.12.

intellect is so enlightened that it can overcome all the limitations of the mind. In any case the knowledge of the *ātman* is guaranteed in the Upaniṣads for the very reason that it is the Self that illumines the mind and the intellect. How can the self that is conscious not be unrevealed to itself?[20]

Language comes under sharp scrutiny in the Upaniṣads because language can never reach the Self, that is, cannot reveal the Self because it is handicapped by the very structure of language. Language has a natural origin in the world and can be counted as a natural phenomenon. Therefore it cannot reveal the Self which is supra-natural. The Self is outside the natural world that is governed by the laws of Nature by virtue of the fact that the Self is not one of the entities in the world.[21] The self is the transcendent reality that cannot be counted as one among the entities of the world. The Upaniṣads are of the view that the Self is the universal principle of all existence and so cannot be counted as anything within the natural world. Language itself falls within the natural world and so cannot express anything that is beyond the bounds of natural language.

However, the ineffability of the Self does not mean that it is unknowable. The Self is knowable to the man of spiritual vision. It is beyond the language we naturally understand, but language can be extended through myths and symbols and thus can be used to express the Self as it is done in the Upaniṣads themselves. The Upaniṣadic sentences have the power to express the nature of the Self in an indirect and symbolic way. Thus Upaniṣads are critical about the natural language itself and not about the symbolic language which is the language of the Vedas.

---

20. *Muṇḍaka Upaniṣad*, II.ii.3.

21. Wittgenstein, *Tractatus Logico-Philosophicus*, tr. D.F. Pears and B.F. McGuinness (Routledge and Kegan Paul, London, 1961), 5.632.

The Language of Metaphysics: The Mahāvākyas

The Upaniṣads have developed a language — for the expression of the *ātman* — which is known for its symbols, allegories and paradoxical sentences. They have tried to convey the deep thoughts about the *ātman* in this symbolic language. However, in this language there are some privileged sentences called the *mahāvākyas*[22] like *tat tvam asi, aham brahmāsmi,* etc. which directly give us the knowledge of the *Brahman*. These sentences are also called the identity sentences which show the identity between the *Brahman* and the *jīva* in such a way that there is ultimately only one Reality and not two. These sentences are in a sense very important in that they give us knowledge of the identity of the *Brahman* and the *jīva*.

The sentences of the Upaniṣads in general have the deeper import of conveying the meaning of words like *Brahman* and *jīvātman*. They convey the deeper fact that the ultimate Reality is of the nature of consciousness and that it is the *Brahman* which is conscious. The Upaniṣadic sentences have a privileged status in the sense that they reveal the nature of the *Brahman*. It is not that the Upaniṣadic sentences are the unfailing means of knowledge of the *Brahman* because they can be superseded by the direct experience of the *Brahman*. It is admitted by the Vedāntins in general that the *śruti* or the verbal testimony cannot stand as the final means of knowledge of the *Brahman* because it can be superseded by direct experience (*anubhava*).[23] The Upaniṣads have recognized the importance of *śruti* because it is the only non-empirical means of knowing the *Brahman*. Other *pramāṇas* like *pratyakṣa* and *anumāna* fail to give us

22. *Mahāvākyas* are identified as identity statements. See D.M. Dutta, *Six Ways of Knowing* (University of Calcutta, Calcutta, 1972), pp. 319-30.

23. *Muṇḍaka Upaniṣad*, I.i.4-5.

knowledge of the *Brahman* because they cannot take us to the real nature of the *Brahman*. It is only the *śruti-vākyas* that can get us nearer the truth. The *Brahman* cannot be finally known except by one's direct realization. Therefore there is so much emphasis on the direct experience of the *Brahman*.

The language of metaphysics is always different from the language of ordinary objects. It is the language of the metaphysical objects which can explain the reality of the Absolute, *Brahman*, God, etc. The metaphysical terms carry the non-natural meaning which takes us back to the ultimate nature of things. The speciality of the metaphysical language lies in its introduction of non-natural meaning. It may fail to have the cognitive meaning of the natural language sentences, but it does not lose all meaning altogether. It has a deeply embedded meaning which cannot be ruled out because of the fact that metaphysics reveals new aspects of reality which natural language cannot.

The language of metaphysics in the Upaniṣads is unique in the sense that it uses words that have a deeper meaning than can be deciphered by the ordinary hermeneutics. The standard meaning of the words is completely subverted for acquiring a new meaning. For example, the word *ātman* does not mean the self of a person. It means the universal Self which is present in the whole universe. Similarly, the words like 'exists,' 'goes,' etc. used with reference to the *ātman* do not have the conventional meanings. They have to be understood in the context of the Upaniṣads so that we are not misled by the surface grammar of these words. Metaphysics has the right to introduce a new meaning of the words because it conveys a new meaning with old words. Every metaphysics goes beyond the conventional meaning of the words and thus acquires a new meaning and a new context. Hence it cannot be said that the only meaning available is the conventional one.

The Limits of Natural Language

The Upaniṣads remind us of the fact that the natural language suitable for describing the natural world is seriously handicapped to express the higher Reality, that is, the *ātman* or the *Brahman*. The *ātman* is a transcendental and non-natural reality and hence must remain outside the domain of the natural language. Natural language is such that it is confined to the natural world and is so constituted that it can only represent the natural objects in the world. The reality that is non-natural like *ātman* does not belong to the natural world. *Ātman* is the ultimate ground of the world and so cannot be natural in itself. It transcends this world as it is infinite while the world is finite. Thus there is reason to believe that the Upaniṣads have rejected the natural language for describing the nature of the *Brahman*. They repeatedly say that language cannot reach the higher realm of the *ātman*.[24]

The Upaniṣads, however, recognize that there is a reality beyond the world such that we can have an access to it through *tapas*, meditation and the practice of discipline (*brahmacarya*).[25] The higher reality is knowable, though not through the ordinary means of knowledge. The empirical means of knowledge are restricted in their scope and so cannot give us knowledge of the higher reality. Language being an empirical means cannot take us very far. Hence, we have to transcend the natural language according to the Upaniṣads. The spirit of transcendence is the underlying theme of the Upaniṣads.

---

24. *Kaṭhopaniṣad*, II.iii.12.
25. *Kaṭhopaniṣad*, II.iii.9.

It is recognized by transcendental philosophy in general and the Upaniṣadic philosophy in particular that there is a reality beyond the limits of the language, i.e. language of the natural kind. The reality beyond the limits of natural language is, however, such that it reveals itself, not only through language but also through other means. This revelatory character of Reality is emphasized by Wittgenstein in the following way:

> There are, indeed, things that cannot be put into words. They *make themselves manifest*. They are what is mystical.[26] (italics original).

This emphatic statement reiterates the Upaniṣadic idea that the *ātman* which is the ultimate ground of all existence does remind us of the fact that even though the ultimate reality cannot be captured in language can reveal itself because the *Brahman* reveals itself in various ways.

The idea that Reality reveals itself is Upaniṣadic because of the fact that they alone talked about the *ātman* being self-evident and self-revealing (*svayamprakāśa*).[27] The *ātman* is self-revelatory by its very nature because the *ātman* is consciousness itself and so cannot be hidden. Besides, the *ātman* is Existence itself because of the fact that it is the ground of all existence and not one of the existent things.

Heidegger,[28] like the Upaniṣadic thinkers, goes beyond the ordinary ontology to invoke the Being as the ground of all existence. For him, the Being speaks to us through language

---

26. Wittgenstein, op. cit., 6.522.
27. *Muṇḍaka Upaniṣad*, III.ii.3.
28. Martin Heidegger, *Being and Time*, tr. John Macquarrie and Edward Robinson (Basil Blackwell, Oxford, 1978), Introduction, pp. 21-63.

which is the "house of the Being" itself. The Being is the reality that transcends the ordinary categories and speaks to us by the means of the language of myths and symbols. Heidegger's idea of Being comes closer to that of the Upaniṣads because the *Brahman* is the Being of all beings. The Being cannot be put into words just as the beings can, because the Being is also the Being of language. Language cannot speak about its own Being but can very well reveal it by its own existence. Language is too earthly to describe the Being, but it can, however faultily, reveal to us the Being because the Being speaks to us in the silence of our innermost self. The Being is revealed in silence.[29]

The Upaniṣads are not alone in going beyond language to search for the Being which is the underlying principle of all existence. They take us beyond language in their search for the highest Truth which is located in the hearts of men and is the most ancient of all Truths.[30] Truth is embedded in the world itself, all that we can do is to discover it from the mass of things created by our ignorance.

The Idea of Truth

The Upaniṣadic idea of Truth is most interesting because of the fact that nowhere is there such a concept that evokes wonder and puzzlement. For the Upaniṣads, Truth is not a semantic property of language as it is taken to be today. It stands for Reality itself. Truth and Reality are the same for them. One who is devoted to Truth is also devoted to Reality, if by the latter we mean the higher Reality like *ātman* or the *Brahman*. It is therefore declared: "*Brahman* is *Satyam*" which

---

29. Ibid., See also J.L. Mehta, *The Philosophy of Martin Heidegger* (Banaras Hindu University, Varanasi, 1967), pp. 521-31.

30. *Bṛhadāraṇyaka Upaniṣad*, V.5.1; *Muṇḍaka Upaniṣad*, III.1.6

means *Brahman* is Truth. This idea of Truth is out and out metaphysical and hence there is very little epistemological content in it.

Truth and falsity are contradictory of each other because where there is Truth, there is no falsity, and vice versa. The Upaniṣads call Truth the Light and Immortality because for them what is true is real and what is real is immortal and beyond the shadow of death. Truth is Knowledge, Wisdom, and the highest Bliss. These ideas remind us of the fact that the Upaniṣadic idea of Truth is not narrowly defined. It is given the highest importance in the metaphysical deliberations. The Upaniṣads carry the metaphysical message that Truth alone matters in the pursuit of highest knowledge, since Truth, Knowledge and Reality converge in the ultimate analysis. What is called Truth is also the highest Knowledge, since what is known is necessarily true. Besides, what is known is also real. Thus there is a metaphysical identity between the Known, the Knowledge and Truth. From this point of view, we cannot create a gap between Truth and Reality.

The Upaniṣads are known for their tilt towards the monistic theory of Reality. The Advaitins call it the non-dual theory of Reality, according to which there is no difference between the *Brahman* and the world in the ultimate analysis. This non-dualistic tendency is eminently present in the central Upaniṣadic idea that there is one and only one Reality and that is the *Brahman*. This idea is further reinforced in the Upaniṣadic dictum that *Brahman* is knowledge and Bliss (*vijñānamānandam brahman*).[31] From this point of view, the *Brahman* is not only the source of all consciousness, but also of all existence. By calling the *Brahman* Bliss, what is indicated is the fact that in the realization of the *Brahman*, one is assured

31. *Bṛhadārṇyaka Upaniṣad*, III.ix.28.7.

of the highest bliss. Bliss is the supreme form of *ānanda* which is the culminating state of the *Brahman*-realization.

Concluding Remarks

The Upaniṣadic idea of language and mind provide the firm foundations for the later Vedāntic theory of *śabda-pramāṇa*. The Vedāntic thinkers across all schools, dualistic as well as non-dualistic, have accepted *śabda*[32] as a source of knowledge. They have admitted that by understanding the language of the Upaniṣads we can understand the highest Reality. Thus the Upaniṣads have laid the foundations of the theory of *śabda-pramāṇa*.

Besides, the Upaniṣads have laid the foundations of the theory of language as limited in its expression of the highest Knowledge and Truth. They have shown the way how a theory of Truth can be built for proving that Truth can never be part of language and must remain ineffable. The Heideggerian and the Wittgensteinian idea of silence regarding the ultimate Truth can be traced back to the Upaniṣads.[33]

---

32. D.M. Datta, op. cit.

33. Wittgenstein, op. cit., 7.

4

Limits of Mind and Universe of Language

Godabarish Mishra*

na so 'sti pratyayo loke yaḥ śabdānugamādṛte ।
anuviddhamiva jñānam sarvam śabdena bhāsate ॥

There is no cognition in world that is not associated with language. The cognition is, as it were, stuck to the speech and hence cognitions of all types are revealed by speech.
— *Vākyapadīya* of Bhartṛhari, Brahma Kāṇḍa, Verse no. 123

The basic argument is that mathematical understanding . . . is beyond the scope of any computation. Take any computer activity, no matter how cleverly it can perform elaborate functions; there is no understanding present in that activity. Understanding requires awareness. — Roger[1]

Introduction

UNLIKE in the West, where mind and self are equated, and mind and body are differentiated, Indian philosophy differentiates self from the mind and treats mind as material

---

* Professor, Department of Philosophy, University of Madras, Chennai - 600 006 (India).

1. Quoted by Kapila Vatsyayan in her article "Alternative Paradigms of Knowledge," *On Mind and Consciousness*, ed. Chhanda Chakraborti et al., IIAS, Shimla, 2003, p. 66.

like the body. The very word *padārtha* involves both mind and language and forms the genesis of philosophical thinking. What I mean to say is: the linguistic constituents of the term *padārtha* are *pada* which means "word," and *artha* which means "meaning"; only a mind can determine or comprehend the relationship between these two. What is pre-eminently discussed as metaphysical category is *padārtha*, along with its dynamics consisting of knowability and namability (*prameyatva* and *abhidheyatva*). The first one indicates the involvement of mind and the second that of language. In all schools of Indian philosophy, we find discussions about the number and nature of *padārthas* and why and how they are accepted. The *prameya* aspect of the *padārtha* makes it necessary to involve epistemology, tools of knowledge, in which the mind has a pre-eminent place and *abhidheya* aspect implies language which is an instrument of knowledge showing the higher level reality of the object.[2] We can have another way of analyzing the dimensions of language and meaning. Word and meaning are inseparably related.[3] Language, in this sense is not language if it does not have any meaning to convey or if its units do not have any referent.[4] In these two components of a category, i.e. *padārtha*, having *pada* and *artha*, it may be said that the *artha* has a pre-eminent position since meaning (*artha*) needs a word (*pada*) and not vice versa. But it is not so because the

---

2. Language is only an indicator or implier of the object, but it is a significant implier. Say, for example, water the word is not water the object.

3. Reference may be made to the first verse of *Kumārasambhava*, wherein Kālidāsa compares the inseparability of speech and meaning with Pārvatī and Parameśvara who are taken to be inseparable. Kālidāsa's *Kumārasambhava*, 1.1.

4. Even the meaningless expressions like *dittha* and *davittha* are meant to imply the meaning of meaninglessness.

word *pada* does *not* stand for *any word*, meaningful or otherwise, it stands *only for meaningful words*. Hence the relation is taken to be eternal and inseparable. This is the view of the majority of the schools of Indian philosophy and on this common idea stands the whole spectrum of language analysis in the Indian context. This paper seeks to show the relationship between language and mind as conceived in Indian philosophy and how in Advaita it is possible to transcend both to attain a higher level reality, which is spoken of as liberation.

Mind or Antaḥkaraṇa

There are three distinct views regarding the mind in Indian tradition. 1. The Nyāya-Vaiśeṣika holds the view that the mind is a substance (*dravya*), and as such material in nature. 2. The Sāṁkhya school is of the view that it is a real entity, which is the product of *pradhāna* or *prakṛti* and hence like *prakṛti*, it is also real. 3. For Advaita, it is material but not real. It is not an independent reality. The only entity that exists independently is the Self or *Brahman*. The entire world is a product of *māyā*, which does not have independent reality; it depends on *Brahman* for its existence. In keeping with *māyā*, the effects of *māyā* are also unreal — those are not independently real. Māyā is material; so is *manas* (mind). Any material object would have to have a size, a dimension. We talk of three dimensions: *vibhu* — the all-pervasive, infinite; *aṇu* — the infinitesimal, atomic; and *madhyama* — the medium dimensional. The mind is spoken of as medium dimensional and is subjected to changes, and these changes are called *vṛttis* — modes or modifications of the mind. Advaitins try to prove the existence of the mind in several ways.[5] On the evidence of *śruti*, they

5. In the *Chāndogya*, we come across the description of the mind as one which is generated from the finest part of the food. Śaṅkara in his commentary on this passage says that by food alone, one →

quote the *Bṛhadāraṇyaka Upaniṣad* which says, "this (reality) can be understood by the mind alone."[6] In *Kaṭhopaniṣad* it is said that, "the objects are superior to the sense-organs, the mind is superior to the objects, the intellect is superior to the mind, and the self is superior to the intellect."[7] Nyāya-Vaiśeṣika proves the existence of the mind by means of an inference. In the absence of mind, in spite of all other factors, we do not attain any cognition at all. This is enough evidence to show that there is something called mind. Experientially too, the mind is directly known, and so there cannot be any question about its existence. It is *kevala-sākṣī-bhāṣya*, directly perceived by the witness-self. Śrīdhara in his *Nyāyakandalī* says, "The contact connecting the objects, the sense-organ and the soul, depends upon some other cause, in producing the effect — because even when the former connection exists the necessary effect, i.e. cognition, does not appear, and this instrumentality upon which they depend is that of the mind."[8] The *Nyāya-sūtra*, 3.2.28, holds that the mind is more like the soul than

→ increases the power of his mind and when a man does not eat, his power of speech and mind are decreased to the minimum. And when food is taken, the power gets increased. Hence, the mind which is a product must be of the nature of food and therefore material. In the *Bṛhadāraṇyaka,* it is said that if the mind is elsewhere, one fails to see or hear and hence it is the mind through which one sees and hears. In his commentary on this, Śaṅkara says that lack of perception is due to the diversion of the mind from that sense-organ to other things. Hence knowledge is entirely dependent upon the attention bestowed by the mind on the object of perception. In the *Kaṭhopaniṣad* we come across a parable that mind is the internal sense-organ which is directed by the self and which directs the sense-organs.

6. *manasaivānudraṣṭavyam.* — *Bṛhadāraṇyaka,* 4.4.19.
7. *indriyebhaḥ parā hyarthāḥ arthebhyaśca paraṁ manaḥ manasastu parā buddhi buddherātmā mahān paraḥ,* — *Kaṭhopaniṣad,* I.iii.10.
8. *Padārtha-dharma-saṁgraha,* 1916, Sec.10, p. 199.

other substances, though it does not have consciousness as its characteristic. Hence for both the schools, the mind is unconscious. In the *Praśastapāda-Bhāṣya*, *manas* is explicitly mentioned as a sense-organ which is instrumental in bringing about a direct experience of pleasure and pain and acts as the mediating organ in the experience of direct perceptual cognition. Having this in mind, Gaṅgeśa in his *Tattva-cintāmaṇi* enumerates six senses, the traditional five and the mind. But it lands in several difficulties. Each of the sense-organs works as the instrumental cause, but the mind is not such a cause for any type of perception — it is a common cause for all types of perceptions. The mind seems to be the liaison between the senses connected with the objects and the self. In this sense mind is not a sense-organ. But for inference, memory and imagination, the mind is directly involved and hence is an instrument.

In Sāṁkhya, the first product is *mahat* or mind, which gives determinate knowledge.[9] Sāṁkhya believes that the mind is a sense-organ. Vijñānabhikṣu holds that *manas* is a sense-organ and an organ of cognition as it perceives the senses of pleasure and pain, and it is an organ of action as it acts like other *karmendriyas* as the cause of knowledge. In the *Sāṁkhya Kārikā*, it is said that the external organs are capable of comprehending the present object only, while the internal sense can comprehend even past and future objects. The problem here is that there is nothing called bare present, bereft of past and future. What perhaps is meant here is that in perception, external organs are directly involved; whereas in inference and verbal testimony, it is the mind that plays a significant role. Here we can see the role of the mind in the sense that in the

9. *budhyā niścita evārthe ahaṁkāra mamakārau jāyate* — *Sāṁkhya-pravacana-bhāṣya*, tr. R. Garbe, Harvard Oriental Series vol. II, 1895, p. 23.

understanding of language it is the mind which is necessary.

In the *Pañcadaśī*, Vidyāraṇya says that there is *pramāṇa-vyavasthā* in the case of the senses. The self is the ultimate pre-supposition for any cognition — it is necessary but not directly involved in the process of cognition. It only illumines the objects of experience. It cannot give specific determinate cognition. But there is the co-ordination of cognition of objects and also the cognition of goodness or badness of an object. What is the entity that gives this cognition? This cognition does not stem either from self or from the sense-organs. Hence mind (*antaḥkaraṇa*) has to be accepted as a third entity involved in the process of attaining cognition.[10] The self cannot know anything by itself; it cannot have *viśiṣṭa-jñāna* by itself. The *viśiṣṭa-jñāna* involves three factors — *tripuṭī* (*tripuṭī-jñāna*) *pramātā*, *prameya* and *pramiti*. The mind and the sense-organs also cannot give us *viśiṣṭa-jñāna* by themselves since they are material by their very nature. The self becomes the knower because of the sense-organs and the mind that functions as the *upādhi* (limiting adjunct). Then only *Viśiṣṭa-jñāna* is possible as in the case of the sun's rays burning a piece of cotton when they pass through a lens. An ordinary piece of iron does not burn the finger, but when it is hot, it burns. In the latter case, we would not be able to differentiate between iron and fire which pervades the piece of iron completely. So also when the *antaḥkaraṇa* is in close proximity with the self, the consciousness pervades it completely to such an extent that the insentient mind (*jaḍa-antaḥkaraṇa*) cannot be different from consciousness. The *antaḥkaraṇa* is capable of reflecting consciousness, of being pervaded by consciousness — as even a material mirror can reflect light. The consciousness reflected by *antaḥkaraṇa* is called *cit pratibhāsa* or *pratibimba* or *cit-chāyā*.

10. *guṇadoṣa-upalabdhi anyathā anupapatyā tatkāraṇatvena mana eva abhyupagantavyam.*

As a mirror invariably reflects the object in front, so does the *antaḥkaraṇa* reflect the self invariably. Vidyāraṇya calls this as *sahaja*-relationship between self and *antaḥkaraṇa*. The self is referred to by words like *bimba*, the original or a prototype. What is the relationship between *cit* and its *upādhi*? There is a false identification between the two. The identity between two different entities is always false. It is because the very concept of two-ness is based on the fact that there is a difference between objects. This false relation is called the *tādātmya* relation. For Advaita, there cannot be any change in the essential nature of a thing. If there is a change the object is no more there. As a result of this *tādātmya*, there is a climb-down or fall as it were in the case of consciousness. Because of this, the consciousness which is one and relationless, seems to have become limited and relates to the *antaḥkaraṇa*. The *cit* and *antaḥkaraṇa* blend together like heat and the piece of iron and this is a complex entity. The self gets itself individuated as a result of its relation with *antaḥkaraṇa*. Out of this (*tādātmya*) identification of the self with *antaḥkaraṇa*, the notion of 'I' — ego emerges. The self which is universal gets particularized now.

It has to be kept in mind that there cannot be any genuine relationship between the *cit* and *antaḥkaraṇa*, since both are totally opposed in nature. Consciousness by itself is not the ego. Nor can the *antaḥkaraṇa* claim to be 'I.' The ego emerges as a result of consciousness — internal organ blend. Unless there is a fall in the case of consciousness, the ego cannot arise. In Advaita, consciousness by itself is not the knower, nor can *antaḥkaraṇa* be the knower. As a result of this blend, the ego arises and that is the knower, the *pramātā* or *jñātā*. The *antaḥkaraṇa* which carries the reflection of consciousness is the *pramātā*. The relation of identity between consciousness and mind is natural (*sahaja*), as a result of which the state of a knower arises. We can never know when consciousness gets associated with *antaḥkaraṇa*. For Advaita, it is *anādi*, beginningless. But there is an end to it since the state of *jīva* comes to an end in liberation. The sense-organs are also *upādhis*. In the second state there is also an identification with sense-organs. In the first stage, the notion of 'I' arises and in the second the concept of 'my' arises in the form of my ears, my eyes, etc., which manifests in the statements like 'I am blind' and 'I am deaf,' etc. In the third state, there is the identification with the body, which is expressed in the form of 'I am fat,' 'I am fair,' 'I am male.' In the fourth stage, there is the identification with external objects, right from one's personal possessions to one's own country. This latter variety of identification is not that strong because as we go outer and outer, the identification becomes thinner and thinner.[11] Once there is identification there is empirical life. Strictly speaking, in Advaita, consciousness alone exists. But various states of things are spoken about and this is a case of error, which is *bhrānti-janya*. In the self there is no trace of duality; it is attributeless, without characteristics (*nirviśeṣa*). But because of its association with *antaḥkaraṇa*, etc. it looks as if it has qualities. There is a false identity with the body (*deha-abhimāna*) and then one owns up the qualities of body and the sense-organs and their qualities. One plays a role without the awareness that he is playing the role and this identification with the role leads one to empirical existence. This role identification is born out of basic identification between consciousness and mind.

Mind as a Sense-Organ

We have already seen the division of opinion that exists with

---

11. The complete or strong identifications are called *sakala adhyāsa* and the partial or weak identifications *vikala adhyāsa*.

regard to the mind as a sense-organ. Some say that it is a sense-organ and others say that it is not. For Advaita, the world of manifestation and non-manifestation is because of the imagination of the mind. Gauḍapāda holds that the mind is material and is a part of the body which is perishable. Śaṅkara is not very explicit about the status of the mind as a sense-organ. But he holds that all empirical experience is because of *antaḥkaraṇa* and it is the foremost limiting adjunct of the self. From an empirical level, *antaḥkaraṇa* is created like any other object of experience. In the scheme of creation, Śaṅkara feels that among the subtle elements, ether was created first and then all other elements in their subtle form came into existence.[12] Whether mind is an *indriya* or not has been the disputable point of discussion in the post-Śaṅkara Advaita. Vācaspati Miśra holds the view that the mind is a sense-organ like any other sense-organ. He is of the opinion that according to Śaṅkara, it should be so because Śaṅkara gives the justification from *smṛti* that mind is one of the eleven sense-organs.[13] According to *vivaraṇa*, mind is not a sense-organ. It is because sense-organs make the other objects known, but are never self-revealing. At best they can be known through inference or verbal testimony. If the mind is a sense-organ it cannot be an object of *pratyakṣa*. Mind is perceived by the witness-self of *sākṣī*. Dharmarāja, the author of *Vedānta-paribhāṣā* says that the mind is not a sense-organ. What is to be understood here is that the mind is not a sense-organ like that of the Naiyāyikas. Suryanarayana Sastri reviews this problem and says that the texts are inconclusive and are

12. On the scriptural evidence "Food (earth) when eaten becomes threefold; the gross becomes faeces, its middle portion becomes flesh and its subtlest portion mind" Śaṅkara admits that mind is a subtle matter.

13. Bhāmati on 2.4.7.

susceptible to being interpreted either way.[14] The two verses of *Kaṭhopaniṣad*, as referred to above, do not indicate that the mind is not a sense-organ, but that it is more subtle than the external senses.[15] It can also be said that knowing a thing by the mind does not make the mind an *indriya*. The mind is an auxiliary to *pramāṇa*. It is the locus, not the instrument of valid knowledge.[16] The mind, in Advaita, is a name for the state of consciousness of which pleasure and pain are two different aspects. The physiological counterparts of these psychical states such as touch, taste, sound, smell, and sight are all explainable and these sensations are presented to the mind in the ordinary way. A sensation indicates a cognitive state and refers to the given object as the cause of the sensation. We cannot point to anything and say that it is painful or pleasurable in the same way in which a red rose is the object which produces the sensation of redness in us. Thus pain and pleasure are more feelings than sensations and hence it is not justified to assume the mind as the internal sense-organ producing the sensation of pain and pleasure.

Mind and Language

In continuation with what I have attempted earlier in this section, I would like to deal with the relation of language with the mind. A glimpse at the Upaniṣadic corpus reveals

14. *Vedāntaparibhāṣā*, tr. S.S.S. Sastri, Adyar, 1942, p. 11.
15. Professor Hiriyanna says "The object of these two *mantras* is merely to indicate that the person is beyond everything else, for there is nothing to be gained by knowing that anyone of the others among the series is subtler than the other. Consequently, not much value need to be attached to the exact place which any of the phenomenal entities ought to take in the series." *Kaṭhopaniṣad*, tr. M. Hiriyanna, Vani Vilas Press, Srirangam, 1915. p. 74. footnote. 1.
16. S.S.S. Sastri, *A Critique of Difference*, University of Madras, 1936, p. 3.

this very relationship. In the *Taittirīya Upaniṣad* we come across the passage which says that whatever is thought in mind is spoken in words.[17] In the *Bṛhadāraṇyaka*, it is said that "he made a conjugation of mind and speech."[18] In the school of grammar, language gets a pre-eminence. Bhartṛhari says that it is language which determines the knowledge or understanding. In Mimāṁsā, the opposite is being accepted, in the sense that after the perception of the object, the words are remembered.[19] These two views expressed in Pūrvamīmāṁsā as far as the meaning of a sentence is concerned may throw some light on the relation between the mind and language. The Prābhākara School views that the sentence is the unit of the language and each word in it conveys the word-meaning and their mutual relation. Prabhākara propounds an interpretation of meaning which involves action. When a person asks somebody to 'bring the cow,' the child nearby first learns the meaning of a word 'cow' not by looking at the object when the word is uttered, but by watching the usage and activity of elders or by associating the word with action as in the sentence referred to above. If the doctrine that the injunctive sentences and their meanings are primary in the Vedas is accepted, then the doctrine that in ordinary speech also the meanings of the words are first learnt when associated with verbs enjoining action is considered to be a necessary corollary. This doctrine of Prabhākara is called *anvitābhidhāna-vāda* or that a sentence consists of words meaningfully connected with a verb. In other words the child would learn through action and practices. The followers of Kumārila are of the opinion that a word conveys only its meaning and the

17. *yaddhi manasā dhyāyati tad vāca vadati — Taittirīya Śruti.*

18. *sah manasā vācam mithunam samabhavat — Bṛhadāraṇyaka.* 1.2.4.

19. *arthajñānottaram śabdajñānam bhavati, arthadarśanāt param śabdasmaraṇam bhavati.*

mutual relation is conveyed by the word-meanings, and not by the words. They further say that the word is not the cause for the cognition of the sentence (*na padam vākyārthabodhe kāraṇam*). Kumārila and the Vedāntins are of the view that when an elderly person points to the object cow and tells the child 'this is a cow,' the child learns the meaning of the word. The doctrine of Kumārila is known as *abhihitānvayavāda* which means that a sentence is a meaningful connection of uttered words with independently obtained meanings. The difference is that: according to Prabhākara, the noun must have already been connected with a verb before it is uttered in order to form a meaningful sentence. Kumārila holds the view that the noun and verb are uttered with separate meanings and then connected to form a sentence. Now taking this into account we may see that they both view the relation between the language and the meaning in different ways. The co-ordination between the mind (understanding) and object (meaning) is proposed in two ways.

In Vaiśeṣika, the mind is a substance (*dravya*) different from self which is another *dravya*. *Dravya* is one of the categories, i.e. *padārtha* which means that it provides a meaning to the *pada* or a word. Here is a case where Vaiśeṣikas make a reference to both the mind and the language. The emphasis on meaningful language is of some significance here. According to them, anything that does not provide a meaningful expression ceases to come within the ambit of human experience. Vaiśeṣikas believe that substance exists along with its quality.[20] According to them, *ātman* is a substance having subtle qualities like intelligence. Both the schools admit that the relation between a word and its meaning is a matter of

20. *guṇavattvam kriyāvattvam vā dravyasāmānya lakṣaṇam* — *Tarka Saṁgraha*.

convention (*samaya*). In grammar, we come across the eternality of the words but those are treated as non-eternal because of being generated by the organ of speech. Patañjali and Kātyāyana are in agreement with the idea that the relation of word and meaning is eternal (*siddha*) and not created by us. It is like: when a person wants to get a pot, he goes to the potter and asks him to make a pot. It is not the case with grammarians since nobody goes to them to get words. Both Jaiminī (*sūtra* 1.1.5) and Kātyāyana hold the view that the relation between word and meaning is non-derived, which means that the relation is not created by human convention (*apauruṣeya*).[21] Bhartṛhari advocated the theory of *sphoṭa* saying that each linguistic unit — a letter, a word or a sentence — is a *sphoṭa* and it is manifested in each singular unit of speech. At the level of *sphoṭa*, a linguistic unit and its meaning or the thought are one and undifferentiated. For Bhartṛhari, there cannot be any difference between cognitive episodes and verbal thoughts.

Before I discuss the implication of mind and language in Advaita from the varieties of views already proposed, I would like to deal with Indian aesthetics which gives an intermediary view. The aesthetic experience is based on the world of sense and the relational world of word and meaning. Besides the words and their relations in a sentence, it is the *tātparya* or *dhvani* (import or suggestion) that helps us to understand the meaning immediately. Similarly, in aesthetic experience, it is an immediate apprehension characterized by a harmonious experience of the self, by a realization of self-consciousness, and by a transience of the self and the not-self.[22] Through the process of *sādhāraṇīkaraṇa* or universalization of the latent

---

21. *autpattikaḥ hi śabdaḥ arthena sambaddhaḥ.*

22. *Sāhityadarpaṇa* of Viswanatha, p. 72.

emotion or *bhāva* the experience becomes non-relational. When we enter into a poetic world, we become a part of it and begin to relish it.[23] The distinction between subject and object are transcended, resulting in the identity of the two in terms of reality or consciousness. In his *Locana,* the commentary on the famous *Dhvanyāloka,* Abhinava says that immediate apprehension of the aesthetic state refers to words. However, these words function differently, both transcending ordinary usage and non-aesthetic experience since they are surcharged with aesthetic imaginations. Aesthetic experience is then the direct experience of a universal emotion involving one's own consciousness.

From here we would go on to see the limits of mind and the Universe of Language. What I mean by "the Universe of language" is the periphery of language or the sphere of language in its understanding and usage. As is known, Advaita advocates a reality which is beyond mind and speech. Advaitins are vociferous about the fact that it is the Upaniṣadic revelation (*śruti*) that constitutes the sole means of knowing *Brahman,* which culminates in liberation. Starting from Śaṅkara and in and through the post-Śaṅkara tradition, it is admitted that the authority of *śruti* is not inflexible. But *Brahman* is beyond words and mind. This brings us to the dilemma as to how to account for knowledge without mind, and understanding without language. Here Advaitins invoke the *avasthātraya* and state that the whole discourse about the liberation takes place in the *vyavahārika* state, whereas liberation takes the person to the *pāramārthika* state. *Śruti* does not bind whoever has reached the unexcelled state of *Brahman.* Once truth is known, the Upaniṣads tell us, the Vedas become non-Vedas (*yatra vedāḥ avedāḥ bhavanti*). As far as I am aware,

23. *Abhinavabhāratī,* 1.280.

no other religion in the world has a revelation that openly cancels its authority out.

Since, in Advaita Vedānta, the whole world is ultimately false (*jagat mithyā*), *śruti* as a part of the *śabda-prapañca* is also false. Still, *śruti* has the capacity to denote what is true. Nobody argues that the word 'water' cannot, indeed, indicate its referent, i.e. water. *Śruti* can very well fulfil a similar purpose, with the notable difference that its referent is super-sensuous. Whether an object lies within or beyond the sphere of the senses, once it is known, the words that have brought about its knowledge are no longer useful. It is in that sense the *śruti* declares that with the dawn of knowledge, the Vedas become *avedas*. Vivekananda once said that these texts were not written for the intellect or for the understanding through a process of rational enquiry and analysis. He was firmly rooted in his opinion that it was only the Vedas which assert the need for going beyond them as per the Vedic dictum mentioned above. They are written for the adult who is in the childhood state of his religious growth and hence he must outgrow reliance on them.[24]

---

24. *Complete Works of Swami Vivekananda*, Advaita Ashrama, Calcutta, 1992, 5.311.

5

Language and Consciousness
The Advaita Perspective

*Meera Chakravorty**

LANGUAGE in human civilization remains potent in all its inventiveness, utterly unique in the evocation of the hues of comprehensional spectrum. Current philosophical and scientific discussions on consciousness are noteworthy for a vision that has moved many a philosopher and scientist to achieve understandings which are often very trying. These two points can be cited both to support the creative character of the language study and the difficulty involved in the understanding of the phenomenon like consciousness. In the light of this observation, one may raise the question what is the real interesting import of studying the relation between language and consciousness, since it becomes evident from the numerous sources that the phenomenon of consciousness has not been so far definitely defined. The fundamental problem in defining consciousness can be attributed to what to 'include' or in most cases what to 'exclude,' in one's definition. Objective methods developed and relied upon throughout the scientific era are and have been used to try and define consciousness which lies deep within the subjective

* Professor, Department of Sanskrit, Bangalore University, Bangalore, India.

domain. Controversy over particular definitions and theories typically relate to what should be included in one's analysis of the topic.

Up till now, language has been left with the poets, authors, philosophers and a host of other areas. We have scarcely seen the approach of language to a satisfactory theory of exploration of consciousness. Yet, such a theory is certainly needed. Consciousness affects us all. Whoever wants to understand and analyse it, cannot avoid the question of its essence and nature. Consciousness is one of those phenomena that we understand as long as we are not asked, but that we cannot rest content with an answer of this kind, and we cannot abandon the question of the concept of consciousness if we want to speak of it. And this question is not so easily answered as may appear at first sight. Consider a note to Royall Tyller's elegant translation of Murasaki Shikibu's, The Tale of Genji. It explains that 'hahakigi' (broom tree) is a plant from which brooms were indeed made and which had the poetic reputation of being visible from afar and disappearing as one approached. Consciousness has been as enigmatic as the "hahakigi" as mentioned earlier, that slips away even as one tries to grasp it. Such instances might make one think that the relation between language and consciousness can be relatively and generally understood. But it is equally hard to think of this relation. From the Advaita perspective, the understanding of consciousness remains puzzling and a phenomenon about which there is less analytic consensus. No widely accepted definition exists. Often, it is not possible for one to demonstrate decisively its way of interactions. It may be possible to ask questions about it without there being any obvious best answer. How is its universality to be reconciled with particularity? What methods help this enquiry most profoundly? All these uncertainties mean that mapping this relation finds the enquirers more often with their backs to one another, staring out at different obscure horizons. Hence, any understanding may only adumbrate some general contours. The philosophical difficulties have been there all along relating consciousness to language. How will language express consciousness? Whether this expression is perfectly compatible or whether there is any disjuncture that causes theoretical stumbles, cannot be decided with certainty.

Looking at this relation, however, the phenomenon of consciousness appears to suggest that at certain levels it is not a problem. That language does convey the experience grasped by the conscious mind though there is, to be sure, a mind/body distinction in the offing which may or may not appear to be ontological in accordance with the perspectives of different schools of Indian thought. If there is a supposition that mental things are (by assumption) a species of material things, it may not follow that mental concepts are a species of material concepts. There can after all be many ways of thinking about the same thing; for instance, the concept 'water' is distinct from the concept of H_2O used by the language of science. But water is H_2O nonetheless. Similarly, perhaps, the concept of brain-state and the concept of a conscious phenomenal state are different ways of representing the same configurations of one and the same phenomenon. At this level, the intuition of mind/body distinction may appear as a sort of hypostatic illusion in which a difference between kinds of concept is mistaken for a distinction between kinds of things. Controversy over a particular theory relates to what should be included in this analysis, for instance, the problem of consciousness in Advaita suggests that materialism cannot be absolutely true at all.

The problem in Advaita, states Śaṅkara, commenting on the relation of language to consciousness at a given specific level, is, that it is a matter not requiring any proof that the object and the subject which are signified by the terms *yuṣmat* and *asmat*, qualified by the intention object and subject respectively (also referred to as "not self" and "self" respectively) and which are opposed to each other like light and darkness, cannot be identified. Hence, it is but natural though wrong to superimpose upon the subject which is of the nature of consciousness and which is referred to as *asmat*, the object which is spoken of as *yuṣmat*, i.e. the attributes of the object. It is equally wrong to superimpose the subject and the attributes of the subject on the object. Astonishingly, all this appears quite natural. The explanation given is that this is owing to wrong knowledge. And this is precisely why one does not distinguish the two entities and their respective attributes while one carries on the worldly life by saying 'I am' (*aham asmi*), 'this is mine' (*idam mama*) and so on. Now, if 'I' stands for the Self, the transcendental subjectivity, how can it be identified with anything that is transcendent to it, be it mind or the sense-organs or the body or any external object? It means that the Self without remaining aloof becomes worldly and is entangled in the affairs of the world giving rise to the problem of "enworlded" subjectivity. Hence, the usage of language as 'I am,' 'This is mine,' and so on.[1]

One may say that the problem is not really with regard to consciousness; there is a widespread conviction that materialism appears to be false. It is rather with consciousness that there appears to be a widespread intuition that

---

1. Śaṅkara, *Brahmasūtrabhāṣya*, Chowkhamba, Delhi, 1966, *atyantaviviktayoḥ dharmādharminormithyājñānanimittaḥ satyanṛte mithunikṛtya, ahamidam mamedamiti naisargiko 'ayam lokavyavahāraḥ.*

materialism is unintelligible, and this intuition survives the recognition that conceptual dualism is compatible with metaphysical monism. Hence, the use of language appears bizarre. For instance, if one may ask, how can pain (which hurts) possibly be the same thing as insensate molecules rushing around in nerve fibres, it is a quite a different kind of question from why should one believe that pain is the same thing as insensate molecules rushing around in nerve fibres. The second kind of question arises about water and H_2O, the usual chemical evidence is germane. By contrast, the intuitive objection to mind/body materialism is that it raises questions of the first kind but does not answer them.

The challenges presented by consciousness impede our ability to develop a coherent linguistic expression of consciousness directed to the experiences mentioned above. Language plays a critical function in communication as well as in our capacity to think in certain ways. However, language has primarily an 'either'/'or' orientation. This causes the inner and the outer worlds to be exclusively perceived in an 'either'/ 'or' orientation. Explaining revolutionary concepts and ideas to ourselves and to others has to be done through the inadequate language. In writing, this is evident in the placing of parentheses around a common word. For instance, we write self with 'S' capital and use parentheses to indicate a difference. This implies that the author wishes to express an altogether different meaning and it is hoped that the reader will know what the author means. Metaphors are yet another way to describe the indescribable. It is equally important to understand that revolutionary concepts and ideas must be expressed and shared through inadequate words.

Like phenomenology Advaita wants to describe consciousness as it is in itself, experienced as experienced, hence, prior to the impositions that intellect/mind makes. This process creates a bizarre position. Bringing in the analogy of light and darkness in his introduction to Advaita philosophy (*Brahmasūtrabhāṣya*), Śaṅkara the expounder says that the terms *yuṣmat* and *asmat*, by which the understanding of consciousness referred to as Self and that of not-Self are meant respectively, remain at constant conflict (*virodha*) since they are dissimilar in nature.[2] To understand this in proper spirit one needs the Vedāntic studies, he says. When the Self and the not-Self become mixed up it results in a never-ending chain of false knowledge. According to him, this false knowledge is the cause of all spatio-temporal life of actions of human beings as much as it is the cause of bizarre usage of language. For instance, when one says *mama putra*, my son or *mama bhāryā*, my wife, etc. (as mentioned above), the question is who is this 'I' in *mama*?

Explaining this position further of the false knowledge referred to as *adhyāsa*, Padmapāda, a noted scholar of Advaita, mentions that the not-Self as Ego is always designated as the Self, while the Self is beyond any such spatio-temporal designation; still it is designated as *yuṣmat* (object) on the logical concept that the Self (*asmat*) is reflected on it. The Self and the not-Self though appearing as different on the face of them are really always appearing as identified due to an *adhyāsa* between them. The *adhyāsa* is referred to as superimposition of one onto the other like for instance 'the sky is blue,' etc. although what is experienced appears to reach towards a contour of sense experience deeply known in the body, but unavailable in language except through the mind's mediation.[3]

---

2. Ibid., *yuṣmadasmatpratyayogcārayoḥ viṣayaviṣayinostamaḥ-prakāśavadviruddhsvabhāvayoritaretarabhāvanupapatyau siddhayam...*

3. Ibid., *apratyakṣe 'api ākāśe balastala-malinataddyadhasyanti ...*

Even the most intellectuals begin as novices enthralled by the senses through which the world is made known to them. The subsequent discerning alert drives towards representation, entangling sense and mind in a knot, and poses the problem underlying language composition. How to make a third thing, a linguistic one, in which the senses represent mind and mind re-creates the senses? Every achieved experience is built on the paradox by which an object reproduces, on the virtual plane of language, sense and mind moving inextricably together, as they do in every act of consciousness.

How to follow an understanding of consciousness without reducing it to 'pure mentality'? The method of Advaita consists in a rigorous enquiry into the given world as presented to consciousness. The given world as presented to consciousness comprises not only the outer world of external objects, but also the inner world of cogitations of the mind. Strangely, at times, the world within which we have evolved appears not ours for long, not as we have known it. This difference has to do with the way they relate to experience and perception. The inner world of mind comprising various mental operations is as much transcendent to the Self (also referred to as pure consciousness) as the outer world is. Thus, the experience of the inner world is formed by extending some state of perceptual classification or re-creation into the frame provided by a general experience. However, if one wants to draw this distinction one cannot by appealing to the way they relate to perception/experience by using language like 'perceiving,' 'experiencing,' etc. because, 'perceiving,' 'experiencing' and the like are themselves phenomenal concepts.

To identify phenomenal concepts with the ones that bear such and such a relation to perception is to presuppose the very distinction that one is trying to explicate. The point is that if one wants to explain phenomenal concepts by reference to examples that are themselves by assumption phenomenal, it would be like running in a circle. If there is a problem about how to distinguish phenomenal concepts from others, there is the same problem about how to distinguish perceptual concepts from others; e.g. how to distinguish really seeing a piece of silver or diamond (the advertisement of diamond branded as Nakṣatra) in the advertisement, a mental event that has phenomenal perceptions from seeing one only subliminally, a mental event that does not. Prakāśātmayati, yet another scholar in Advaita, explains this through an example "This is Devadatta whom I had seen earlier" (*so 'ayam devadattaḥ*, etc.). Here, there is remembrance of a previous object/person in the then space and time, etc. is due to, he says, *smaraṇābhimāna*, or in mental form, while the person present now here is not.[4] This may suggest that the world within which we have indulged may not be ours for long, nor as we have known it. What kind of language will impel us to portray this contour? It will be painstaking transmutation and elaboration in language of what the expectant mind attentively receives.

In view of the above one may be, at times, led to believe that the mind can be traced in dialectic motion; in and out, back and forth, may be a desire that our sense questionings should be ready to see changes. For instance, according to New Physics, we are in a participatory world in which both the subject and the object are thought to interact. In that case, the world may, as the poetess Jorie Graham says, also desire, as we receive its conflicting aspects, that we should be ready

4. Vidyaranya, *Vivaraṇaprameyasaṁgraha*, Chowkhamba, Delhi 1965. *tasmādārthamatraviṣayajñānajanya smṛtirārthamātrameva viṣayīkaroti, na pūrvajñānenaviṣayīkṛtam jñānamapi anyathā nīlajñānat pite 'pi smṛtiḥ syāt. . .*

to understand, in our view, its 'incoherences' in our reciprocating consciousness. Investigating the relationship between mind and the world, the emerging trend in New Physics may not allow any strict division between subjective and objective, but point to the third possibility of the omnijective aspect in our understanding. Advaita speculates that the evidence of consciousness is apodictic. It holds that whatever is affirmed by consciousness through its "intentional" performance can never be rejected and that whatever is denied by consciousness through its intentional performance can never be accepted. Consciousness reveals objects on its own; it also reveals them through the ego or the mind. The intentional performance, says the Advaita, is not ascribed to the pure Self or Consciousness, but only to consciousness associated with ego or 'I' which is transcendent to consciousness. While language, in fact, is not particularly helpful in distinguishing the Self from the ego, the word 'I' is used to refer to both of them. For example, when we say, 'I know this,' 'I resolved to do that' and so on, the 'I' in all these statements refers to the ego, which performs various mental operations. Yet, understandably, the use of language intends to make some sense of these mental operations.

The dialectical back-and-forth operations may appear too unusual a form for the myriad and flexible motions of the mind, at times freezing the mind's action. The multiple aspects of consciousness take the challenge of representation through not only its dialectics, or its reflexibility, or its memory, but also through its simulacra of the world. At such contexts, the difficulty of adopting the principle of syntactical relations can be seen with limitations in grasping the inscape of an image. The subsequent experience extending to a far-focused glimpse of the phenomenon, and the attempt to fix the form in memory, followed by an evaluation of the truth or falsity of representation may be judgemental. However, there is a strong tendency to see the objective world and the mind as incongruent, the one resisting any fixed interpretation by the other, e.g. 'the sky is blue.' Where is the sky to be blue can be a pertinent question in this context.

The influence of objective favouritism has led to the tendency to define consciousness by its observable (objective) attributes. It is taken for granted that consciousness in our waking experience is always conscious of something that can probably be studied, quantified and tested by using language. Therefore, consciousness is generally defined according to its observable attributes, dependent upon the brain and requires social intercourse bound by language equated with rational thought. As in the case of the waking experience, in the dream experience too, Advaita describes consciousness to be intentional, because here too it is related to 'objects.' The waking state, however, will repudiate this along with its diction associated with the 'objects.' Similarly, the experience of social phenomena now will become unreal and its descriptions disjointed phrases.

The experiences of 'deep sleep' (*suṣupti*) as distinguished from the waking and dream experience are different though. When a person wakes up from deep sleep and reflects on the nature of the experience he had, he says, that at that time he was not conscious of anything whatsoever. Nevertheless there was the presence of consciousness at that time, though there were no objects, no phenomenon related to it. Further, if consciousness were also absent at that time, recollection to the effect 'I was not conscious of anything then,' or 'I slept well,' etc. will be impossible. Consciousness remains here as the impersonal Self whose 'I' enunciates natural process, refusing the subjectivity. It may appear like representing the way in which the thoughts of a single mind counterpoint each other. Or we conjecture that consciousness is used to hold in mutual suspension a number of simultaneous phenomena and chooses to render some and not others.

There is a rather convincing way to admit the possibilities that consciousness reveals objects if they are presented to it, and if not, consciousness remains without such presentation and hence needs no use of language. Or, if it could be emphasized, there seems to be a sort of explanatory gap between these states, one perhaps without precedent in the history of understanding of consciousness. The point is that if it is possible to explain why water is H_2O, why is it not possible to explain, 'This is mine.' So there are, after all, cases where bona fide identifications result in an explanatory gap identified by language relations. While it is true that there is no phenomenon without consciousness, there is no linguistic evidence to say that there is no consciousness without the phenomenon.

Just as there is consciousness of the presence or absence of something, even so there is consciousness of the presence or absence of the ego or the 'I,' as the case may be. It follows that the ego or 'I' which is known as sometimes present and sometimes absent is transcendent to consciousness. On the basis of the distinction between consciousness and the ego, Advaita holds that not only the intended act, but also the act of objectivation, identification, fulfilment and constitution (cf. Husserl) belong to ego (or the mind) which is transcendent to consciousness. It justifies this position on the ground that these cogitations are known in the same way as the external objects and their qualities are known, and that what is known must be transcended to the knower. When one sees an object, the object seen is transcended to the seer, for example, by the terms, 'I see the red flower,' the quality or action that is perceived cannot be the quality or the action of the perceiver, but of the object in which it inheres. The same principle holds good in case of the cogitations which one is aware of as expressed in terms like, 'I am happy,' etc. Desire, resolve, doubt, faith, want of faith, unsteadiness, shame, intelligence, fear — all these are but the mind.[5] What is emphasized here is that all cognitions or mental operations are but states of mind and that they are not, just because consciousness is aware of them, supposed to be constitutive of consciousness.

If the distinction between *yuṣmat* and *asmat* is, what is referred to in a way, the mind/body dualism and then if it is asked whether intuition of an ontological difference between mind/body can be viewed as a misapprehension of this, then it has got to be drawn in some other way, perhaps in a way that does not assume that the phenomenal and the material refer to different kinds of things. When different concepts refer to the same thing, no intuition of distinctness need be felt. There is arguably a point made in saying that mind/body dualism is true of mind and body concepts but not of minds and bodies. For example, there is no tendency to mistake the difference between the concepts 'water' and H_2O for a distinction between H_2O and water, or if there is, it disappears on brief reflection. However, there is a difference between the water/H_2O case and the mind-state/brain-state case. We may explain why something with the 'microstructure' called H_2O has the properties that water does. If water is indeed H_2O, it follows, given the rest of our science, that water is liquid at room temperature, that it is transparent, that it is heavier than air and (uncoincidentally) that it converts to

5. *Bṛhadāraṇyaka Upaniṣad*, 1.5.3., Chowkhamba, Delhi, 1965.

hydrogen and oxygen under electrolysis. In that slightly tortuous sense, our science explains why water is H_2O.

But nothing of the sort holds in the mind/brain case, and that it does not is a traditional source of puzzlement. For instance, if it is assumed that certain brain-state is found, *de facto*, to be correlated with a certain phenomenal state: such and such going on in one's visual cortex correlates with having an experience of a blue flash, etc. then there is no arguing with induction. But one might wonder nonetheless why the brain-state has that phenomenal counterpart rather than some other; just as one might wonder, in much the same way, why there is correlation between being H_2O and being a liquid at room temperature rather than a correlation between being H_2O and being a gas at room temperature.

Further, the point the philosophers have been worrying about is that although it is possible to explain why water is H_2O, it is extremely difficult to explain what Advaita tries to say in statements like, 'That are Thou' (*tat tvam asi*), referring to the 'enworlded' subject consciousness as one and the same as the 'unenworlded'/pure consciousness. If there is no intuition of distinctness about *tat* being *tvam*, it is not because they are referred to by two different pronouns. Rather, it is because one antecedently understands how, in a given case, *X* and *Y* could turn out to be the same identity. Whatever makes one feel that the unenworlded 'leave out,' it cannot be the former images what it refers to but the latter does not. But truly, nobody has the slightest idea how that could be so. And because nobody does, it is also the case that nobody has the slightest idea what kind of empirical research might throw light on the issue.

Rather than attempting to draw a definitive linguistic relation with consciousness at this time it would be more necessary to survey the variety of linguistic expressions which have been rendered throughout history on consciousness. Quantum physics, mythology, esoteric teachings, religion, biology, philosophy, mysticism, poetry, etc. all hold valuable clues which may help explain the linguistic relation regarding consciousness. Attempting to strip consciousness of its inherent subjective nature may not be possible. Instead of reducing phenomena to their elemental properties it may be desirable to move towards expansionism having multiple levels for more significant results. This does not mean to seek absolute inclusion in favour of reductionism. The choice between surrounding the study of consciousness with a frame of reductionism versus the longer frame of multi-disciplinary approaches may help us to address the problem.

References

Ariew, Roger and Garber Daniel, tr. ed., *Philosophical Essays*, Indianapolis: Hackett, 1989.

Balasubramaniyan, R., "Advaita Vedānta on the problem of Enworlded Subjectivity," in *Phenomenology and Indian Philosophy*, Delhi: MLBD, 1992.

Bancroft, Mark, *Problems in Defining Consciousness*, Enspire Press, 2004.

Bleicher, John, *Contemporary Hermeneutics*, London: Routledge and Kegan Paul, 1980.

Chattopadhyaya, D.P., Embree Lester, J. Mohanty, eds., *Phenomenology and Indian Philosophy*, Delhi: Motilal Banarasidas, 1992.

Fodor, J., *On Consciousness*, UK: LRB, 2002.

Gambhirananda, *Brahamasūtrabhāṣya*, tr., Kolkata: Advaita Ashrama, 1965.

Kumar, Pushpendra, *Linguistic Thought in Ancient India*, Delhi: Nag Pub., 1984.

Morris, Mary and G.H.R Parkinson, *Philosophical Writings*, London, 1973.

Papineau, David, *Thinking About Consciousness*, Oxford, 2002.

Radhakrishnan, S., *Indian Philosophy*, London: Allen and Unwin, 1923.

Remnant, P. and J. Bennett, tr. ed., *New Essays on Human Understanding*, Cambridge, 1982.

Tyler, Royall, tr., *The Tale of Genji*, Penguine, 2000.

Veuller, Helen, *On Never*: *Graham Jorie*, London: LRB, 2002.

6

Advaitic Language of Sublation

*U.A. Vinay Kumar**

Introduction

IT is trendy these days to say that 'to be is to be the value of a variable.' So, a proposition 'This is a table' is symbolized as ($\exists x$) Tx, or 'Table exists' is symbolically written as (Tx). In the former symbolism, x, the variable has to be given the 'value' — which in this case happens to be 'table.' In such a symbolism, the variable-value 'table' has to be 'instantiated,' which instantiation is again purely imaginary. Added to this, the meaning 'proximity' that could be attributed to the word 'this' seems to be completely lost in the din of symbolism. In the latter, semantically there seems to be some kind of a tautology — x is T.

However, without prejudice to the general utility of logical symbolisms or logical understanding, it can be said that the *ultimate* court of appeal for the *truth* of a proposition is not the logical truth-value or logical network, rather it is the experience. Logic, or its proposition(s), does not really bother about *what there is*. Rather logic is eager to see to it that the network it creates is (tautologically) true. Or, if a singular proposition is involved then it would speak of its possible

* Reader, Department of Philosophy, Goa University, Goa – 403 206. India.

truth-values. In this sense, logical truth can be said to be vacuous; whereas, a direct experiential set-up points to an object-situation. So long as this object-situation persists with its contents — desirable or otherwise — experience would wield the conclusive authority over the truth of the propositions that the experience generates. The propositions that emerge from experience may be called as cognitive propositions since they have — or are supposed to have — express cognitive content. *Experiential content* as the determinant of truth-value of a cognitive proposition may be in a way equated with the *numerical value* of a solution of material science problem. Numerical value fixes the final answer to the abstract calculations that are made through symbolisms.

In logic, the symbolism ($\exists x$) or (x) presupposes the existence — or at any rate — the implicit possibilities of existence of an external object *other than the experiencing subject.* But then one could ask: is there an 'external object'? If there is one, then, how does one come to know of/about it? How does one know the object to be real as opposed to merely imaginary? Over the years, realism and rationalism, and their innumerable persuasions, belonging to both Indian and Western traditions, have tried to answer this problem, and have done so in many different ways.

In this paper I am mainly concerned with the logic and language of a special Advaitic device called sublation. In this paper I confine myself to Śaṅkara and Dharmarāja. Sublation or *bādhā* is an experiential episode that enables the experiencing subject to draw conclusions about the permanent falsity of an entity *via* the falsity of the corresponding cognitive content. Obviously an examination of this concept has also to look into the linguistic formulations of these episodes, since an experiential episode always requires an articulating mode, such as language. I use the term Advaita/Advaitins in this paper mainly with reference to the above-stated thinkers.

The concept of *bādha* or sublation informs us that, that which is sublated/sublatable is unreal; thus, any entity, real or imaginary, if sublated, or is sublatable, then it is unreal; obviously its linguistic counterpart in a proposition makes the *whole* proposition susceptible to error, hence the falsity of the proposition (*in toto*/partially). [We shall see later in greater detail whether it is proper to say that the *whole* proposition becomes prone to falsity/error just because some part of it is falsified.] And, alternatively that which is unsublated and/or unsublatable is real, its linguistic counterpart in a proposition is also conceded as true. The term 'real' is purported to mean 'existence in triple time,' *trikāla-abādhita*, and 'unreal' to mean 'non-existence in triple time,' *trikāla-bādhita*. There is also an intermediary class, which is sometimes 'red' and some other times 'unreal.' Outwardly the whole thing looks simple; and gives an impression that there is one-to-one correspondence between sublation and unreality, and unsublation and reality. Yet it will soon become clear that the matter is extremely complex, and that deciding the reality-status through sublation is fraught with difficulties.

While it is common that from the experience of cognitive entity one can necessarily move to its propositional (linguistic) articulation one cannot necessarily move from formal propositional statement to the actual existence of its cognitive counterpart, for, the latter *could be* imaginary. Thus, mere propositional statements give only a contingent situation which may or may not have a corresponding cognitive experiential situation. The movement from cognition to propositional articulation includes the movement to reality-status and the truth-value status, of the cognitive content and its linguistic form.

The cognitive propositions being in precedence over merely formal propositions with respect to cognitive content, and they being in a necessary relation to cognitive language, one could pertinently ask for an elaboration of the role of language in all our cognitive dealings. Our life is almost fully pervaded by cognitive content and cognitive propositions. Every cognitive proposition directly attempts to connect two things; the subject of experience — the agent who is experiencing (mind, soul, etc.) — on the one hand, and the object of experience on the other. The subject tries to 'comprehend' the object. At once language comes a-calling. For, without language, comprehension of an object is, or at least seems, impossible. Thus, cognitive content and the language are the twin things that occupy us. Though there is this necessary relation between the experience and language, they are not identical, and hence they are not one entity.

If so, what is the role of language in all these affairs? Does it play a postman?

(i) A postman is presumed to faithfully deliver the goods and go. He does not tamper even a bit with the content. His *handling* of the goods is only incidental, and *does not affect* the content in any way.

(ii) Or shall we say that language is sometimes *like,* and some other times *unlike,* a postman? And what it means to say language is *not like* a postman?

The ensuing analysis of the concept of *bādhā* is expected to help us decide on this question.

I

Cognitive Content and Propositions

In Advaita, almost all (cognitive) propositions are treated as of substantive-adjective (predicate) relation type. Therefore, any formalism that one wants to arrive at in this case has to bear in mind the cognitive nature of the propositions. Advaitins consider most sentences (*vākyas*) as an adjective is predicated of substantive (*uddeśya-vidheya-sambandha* or *viśeṣya-viśeṣaṇa-sambandha*).[1] However, there is one notable exception to this characterization. Advaitins consider "some *vākyas* as not expressing this general subject-predicate or substantive-adjective relation."[2] The class of identity propositions is the exception. The identity propositions cannot be interpreted in a substantive-predicate way.

In contrast, Bertrand Russell refutes the claim that all or most propositions are of subject-predicate form. This he does by citing the vast class of asymmetrical propositions, as for example, "*A* is greater than *B*." But the Advaitins, according to D.M. Datta, will prefer to force the asymmetrical propositions of Russell into the very form of ordinary substantive-quality way.[3] The way they do this constitutes

1. D.M. Datta (1972), pp. 317-18 "(The Advaitins) . . . contend that though most sentences can be considered as propositions, in which an adjective is predicated of a substantive, there are a few *vākyas* which cannot be taken as expressing this general subject-predicate or substantive adjective relation . . . ."

2. Ibid., p. 318.

3. D.M. Datta, (1972), p. 318 "The motive that inspires Russell to maintain that the subject-predicate form is not universal, is to refute absolutism, which he thinks is based on the fundamental misconception that all judgements predicate some quality or qualities of Reality . . . (he does this by) showing that all judgements do not contain a subject and a predicate. . . ."

another interesting matter.

In non-identity propositions, always, the meaning is said to be relational — thus we have *saṁsargāvagāhī vākyas*; whereas the identity propositions express a non-relational meaning, which is not constituted by the relations of two or more elements. Such a sentence is called *akhaṇḍārthaka-vākyam* — a sentence with an indivisible or unitary or non-relational meaning. These *akhaṇḍārthaka-vākyas*, in appearance, are very much similar to the subject-predicate type of propositions. However, they are, in reality, not belonging to the subject-predicate type. (Henceforth I use the term 'proposition(s)' or 'cognitive proposition(s)' for 'cognitive proposition(s),' unless I have stated otherwise.)

Now the question is: Is there any cognitive content in such identity propositions? In asking this question we should not forget that there is another equally tricky situation presented by the 'contradictory' content. One could claim that under the class of cognitive propositions, the *akhaṇḍārthaka-vākyas* may be construed as forming one extreme-end of the hierarchy while the other being constituted by a-cognitive entities without even an express-status to them in a proposition, such as, for example, 'son-of-a-barren-woman,' (*vandhyāputra*), which have no ontological existence, or being, *ab initio*. Does this then imply "infinite" cognitive content at one end and 'zero' cognitive content at the other?[4]

In both these proposition-cases the truth-claim has to be decided on the basis of cognitive content or its absence; equally so the middle-range cognitive propositions. This follows from our earlier assertion that cognitive content determines the status — reality and truth. Cognitive content *is* the meaning.

---

4. Compare Fregean Hierarchy, A.K. Sen, (1998) p. 187.

If so, absence of cognitive content in any proposition makes it meaninglessness. In this way, if the cognitive content is assigned the status of an arbiter to decide the truth-value of a cognitive proposition, then the absence of cognitive content in a proposition that contains the term "son-of-a-barren-woman" as in —

"'Son-of-a-barren-woman' does not exist" (SoBW) [1]

will not make it false, but meaningless, even though the "proposition" is construed to be true. This is a fictitious problem created by the imaginative faculty and injected through language. And this is an uncalled-for imagination. For an Advaitin, this problem would not have arisen at all. After all no one would seriously assert a proposition with "son-of-a-barren-woman" as a subject or as a predicate.[5] Moreover, from a purely logical point of view no one can say [1] is or is not

5. Svāmi Saccidanandendra Saraswati (1998), pp. 110-11; 2.2.5.28.58. In the context of refuting the Vijñānavādin, Śaṅkara argues that the awareness and the object of awareness have to be, of necessity, different. This is because, he says, the difference between them is also an object of awareness. One could argue against this by saying "what is the object of awareness now looks *like/as if* being outside, even though it is merely an internal object." One who argues this way is overtly and subjectively desirous of denying the external (*bahirvat*) reality. Such subjectivity has no place in arguments. If he were not desirous that way, how could he use such a word — "x looks *as if* it exists outside" at all? After all — "A [absolute] non-entity that 'x' is, cannot be visible at all in the first place." So there is no question of speaking about its existence either inside or outside. No one speaks thus: "Viṣṇumitra *looks like* a *vandhyāputra* (son-of-a-barren-woman)." SoBW, being totally non-existent, can neither be likened to something nor be accessible for likening. In Śaṅkara's example, something, Viṣṇumitra, a real entity, has been likened to that which is not accessible for likening, SoBW, when in fact we cannot

→

true, unless one actually begins to look into the semantics of the subject term 'SoBW.' But then that will involve getting *inside* the term, a conceptual dissection. As such getting into the term is all that is available for anyone to decide the truth of such subject-terms as for example 'SoBW,' 'Square-circle,' etc. Otherwise no one — not even the greatest of the logicians/ scientists — can a priori rule out that they do not exist. And this is what even an Advaitin does. If the subject-term (or predicate-term as the case may be) has no corresponding cognitive content, the proposition ceases to be of meaning, since cognitive content is meaning, although it may be relational. That is why the term 'SoBW' is, cognitive content-wise *tuccha,* where *tuccha* denotes *lowest* in the cognitive hierarchy. As such there is no significant mention of it in any proposition, because the discussion on mere imaginary propositions is not encouraged. For our understanding, however, we can add that the proposition [1] may be termed as *tuccha vākya* — the lowest proposition of non or a-cognitive sort. The understanding that results from [1] is merely verbal just as Matilal has pointed out.[6] This could be a classic instance for an Advaitin where language fails — i.e. it makes us go away from cognitive content. Language that was summoned to reflect our cognitions faithfully, like the proverbial 'hedge started grazing,' began reflecting itself! The same can be said of what are imaginary entities like *gagana-kusuma, śaśaka-sr̥ṅga,*

→ seriously use SoBW either as a subject or as a predicate.

sarvalokaprasiddhām bahiravabhāsamānām saṁvidam pratilābhamānāḥ pratyākhyātukāmāśca bāhyamartham 'bahirvat' iti vatkāram kurvanti/ itarathā hi kasmāt 'bahirvat' iti brūyuḥ? na hi viṣṇumitraḥ vandhyāputravat avabhāsate iti kaścit acakṣīta . . .

6. Matilal (1997), see "2.2 Empty Terms, and 2.2 Reference and Existence" in "Problems of Philosophical Logic in Navya-Nyāya" pp. 77 f.

'unicorns,' 'golden-mountain,' etc. The rule is semantics that enables the logical dissection of the concerned term. The falsity has to be semantically and logically justified. Cognitive nullity is the final determinant of reality-status and truth-value in this case. Not always language at outer level reflects reality.

While the propositional truth-value mainly hinges on the cognitive content, we can ask — upon what does the reality or unreality of the cognitive content hinge? Now, to say that propositions determine the reality/unreality of the cognitive content is to put the cart before the horse. Or to cite the experience itself as the deciding factor is to beg the question. Yet there is no other Court of appeal available to us apart from our experience. The only alterations in this Court of experience one could possibly make are to take either a partial or a holistic view of human experience. The Advaitins opt for the latter, i.e. they take a holistic view. Their holism takes into account not merely the waking state experiences but also the illusory experiences falling within the ambit of waking state, and dream-experiences during sleep, and also what lies outside the purview of wakefulness and dreams in sleep, i.e. deep sleep. It is by the keen analysis of these common human experiences that they have arrived at the criterion of reality called the *abādhitattva*, the non-sublation theory of reality, which seems to subsume under it different logics.

Now we shall examine the origin of the concept of *bādhā* in Śaṅkara.

II

Sublation of Predicate-content

The origin of sublation as criterion of reality (and consequently truth) may be traced to the metaphors used by Śaṅkara in his preamble to the *Brahma-Sūtra-Bhāṣya*. Śaṅkara, while discussing the *adhyāsa* (superimposition) between self and the non-Self, first defines *adhyāsa* in a particular manner and cites two metaphors —

(i) *śuktika hi rajatavadavabhāsate*[7]

"*Nacre* itself appears like silver" (NS-type)

(ii) *ekaścandraḥ sadvitiyavat*[8]

"Same moon, i.e. the single, self-same moon, appears to be with another (moon)" (DM-type) (*both tr. mine*)

The most common meaning of *adhyāsa* being mistaking one thing as what it is not,[9] Śaṅkara speaks of three things implicitly or otherwise, that may be called as *conditions of adhyāsa*. That is, the conditions those are to be satisfied in order for one to know that there is *adhyāsa* committed by him. They are:

(a) Necessity of *simultaneous apprehension* of both the entities involved in *adhyāsa*,

(b) *Necessary unreality* of one of the two entities, including *necessary reality* (*relative reality or absolute*) of the other, and

(c) The *simultaneous knowledge* of these two facts in order that there is the right knowledge.

[One may notice some amount of ambiguity regarding the terms 'apprehension' and 'knowledge' as used above in (a) and (c).]

We should note that the *adhyāsa* or superimposition has to be known as an error committed presently, and to be known presently by the person himself. Others' knowledge of this error in no way helps the individual in question to realize the

7. Svāmi (1998), Adhyāsa Bhāṣya vol. I.

8. Ibid.

9. Ibid., p. 10.

said error. The hypothesis of the possible falsity of an experience *as stated by others* can only help one under error form such a hypothesis. Yet it is he himself — that is the person under error — *who has to realize* it. Therefore, the conditions of *adhyāsa* are essentially:

(i) The conditions of occurrence of *adhyāsa,* and

(ii) The conditions of its simultaneous understanding.

Otherwise, if it was mere explanation of the occurrence of *adhyāsa,* then since the same could perhaps be well illustrated by NS-type illusion easily, without DM-type illusion, NS-type illusion alone could be sufficient.

In an illusion case of NS-type, later-falsity of 'silver' clearly satisfies (b). Thus, one knows that the 'entity' (or merely the 'predicate'?), which was perceived earlier as silver is unreal. Since no one can have the cognition of the form *"This nacre* is/ was *silver,"* NS-type illusion apparently fails to fulfil the first condition of *adhyāsa* of simultaneous apprehension of the two entities involved in *adhyāsa.* To avoid this contingency the existence of an abstract substratum could be posited. Even then NS-type illusion does not and *cannot* ensure *sensory-perception* of such a substratum. Therefore, so long as such perception does not come forth, a skeptic (or a Berkeleyan perhaps) could always hold that there is no — and cannot be — such a substratum. To avoid this further contingency (in addition to the simultaneous knowledge of error) there ought to be at least one example of sensorily simultaneous — but at the same time erroneous — perception; so that people would at least grant the possibility that there could be simultaneous knowledge and error occurring in an individual. Moreover, meaning in any non-identity proposition being relational, there ought to be *something* to which the silverness at t_1 and nacreness at t_2 are attributed. Therefore, to satisfy this, Śaṅkara brings in a DM-type illusion. This illusion presents two sensorial moons — one real, and the other illusory. However, let us term the earlier referred to abstract substratum as 'this,' where the term 'this' primarily denotes the existence of an *external object/locus*, proximate or otherwise.

In the NS-type illusion there is surely *no simultaneous* knowledge of the two entities in the sense that the silver that I *presently perceive is not*-silver. That is, there is neither the simultaneity of knowledge of 'silver' and '*nacre*,' or of the 'silver' and 'not-silver.' The occurrence of 'knowledge' of false silver *later* or the *presumption* of the falsity of the silver-experience coming forth due to such frequent illusory experiences in our day-to-day life *cannot* act as an appropriate substitution to simultaneous knowledge of two entities, which is a necessary condition for *adhyāsa* to take place as stated above in (a) or (c). The abstract substratum "this" could always be skeptically dismissed after all. So, as mentioned earlier, to ensure at least a psychological possibility of such simultaneity (i.e. simultaneity of two sensory entities, one real and the other unreal, and also their simultaneous apprehension/ knowledge) Śaṅkara brings in the DM-type illusion. This type of illusion clearly takes care of the third condition. There is knowledge/apprehension, whatever you wish to call it, of *both the entities simultaneously*. Since we already *know* beforehand that the second moon that *is presently seen* out there is after all *not* there — yet *is being perceived* by the sense-organs *here* (external locus) *and now* — it is unreal and is also sensorial and simultaneous to the sensory-perception of the real moon.

The analogous application of this idea of *adhyāsa* to the first order cognitive propositions having 'I' as the subject-term, as in 'I am this (body)' *ahamidam*, should result — (Śaṅkara wishes) — in the falsity of all relational substantive–adjective propositions with the sole exception of identity proposition *aham brahmāsmi*. In other words, the cognitive content of the respective terms should all be sublated, retaining the *Brahman*-content alone. For this purpose one must start *perceiving* their (those I-proposition's) cognitive content counterpart of 'I' *as such*. This application leads one to many logical difficulties.[10]

The DM-type illusion, though primarily important to make the point of simultaneous apprehension of falsity, is limited in its sentential analysis because, as stated already, almost all propositions, with the sole exception of identity propositions, are analysed into subject-predicate type. [For an exhaustive treatment please see Kumar (2006) ICPR volume.]

Thus, NS-type of illusion constitutes the core as it explicitly involves both S-P analysis [Subject-Predicate analysis] (which is apparently complex in DM-type otherwise), and positing of an abstract (i.e. un-predicated) unchanging *external* substratum.

The silver-predicate gave room for nacre-predicate; thereby nacre-predicate falsified the proposition.

"This *is* silver (asserted at t_1)" [2]

It is false to the limited extent of predication. Let us note that the 'isness' in [2] is attached to the substratum and not to the predicate. Cognitively speaking, the previously perceived silver turned out to be unreal; hence it is now construed as illusory silver. We shall denote such illusory objects or predicates by indicating them in single quotes. So we have 'silver,' which is, now needless to say, unreal/false. Although I had seen silver (actual from my viewpoint) at t_1, I now realize that what I had seen is really not there (from the object-point of view). Along with this perception I also start thinking that

10. Kumar (1988).

the silver I had seen *was not there even at that very time* t_1, because I now refuse to attribute any cognitive content to it. Therefore, can we say the proposition [2] is false or should we confine to the falsity of predicate and predicate-content alone? Suppose [2] is construed as false, then will this construal make the 'externality' of the locus vanish? If 'externality' to the persistent locus is refused, how on earth am I now able to say I am perceiving nacre *exactly at the same place* where I had seen 'silver' earlier? On the other hand, if reality and truth to the external 'this' is granted then there would result Dvaita, dualism — of 'This' and 'I'.

In ordinary terms, nacre sublated the silver, where 'sublation' simply means replacement of certain cognitive contents by some others in the same locus where they existed earlier. The term replacement *does not* indicate any active *dis*placement by nacre-predicate or nacre-object by thrusting itself upon the 'silver'-predicate or 'silver'-object, as for example in chemistry, as a gas-molecule does to a water-molecule.

However, from this fact of illusion one can validly infer that some predicate-contents are subject to this kind of sublation/change. Let us note here that 'this,' the alleged substratum, is not a cognitive-content in the normal sense. Rather it is only an inferred entity. This is so far as Śaṅkara goes.

III

Sublation and Removal

Having seen the sublation of a predicate-content, which for all practical purposes meant a mere change from one predicate to another, propositionally, and one predicate-content to another, experience-wise, we shall now see the *Vedānta Paribhāṣā* view of sublation.

For *Vedānta Paribhāṣā*, sublation is not a mere change from one predicate-content to another; otherwise a situation of flux, in the same locus as in a movie for example, could be termed as sublation, which it is not. In a movie, the *screen* is the *locus*, in which *different* images are perceived every second. This 'change' of images cannot be termed as sublation. For that matter any real-time change *cannot* be termed as sublation. Rather, sublation involves the destruction of a predicate-content along with its material cause, which is materially responsible for the emergence of the said predicate-content in the first place.[11] As such, Advaita seems to claim that the material cause of *all* predicates is some or the other kind of *avidyā*, ignorance. The case where the destruction of predicate-content is not accompanied by the destruction of its material-cause is to be merely construed as removal.[12]

Vedānta Paribhāṣā further says that the cause of sublation is the intuition of the real nature of the substrate.[13] This intuition is to be understood as the ontological negative of *avidyā*. Thus, because of this mutual ontological opposition between the said intuition and *avidyā*, the intuition at once removes/negates the nescience or *avidyā* which is, as noted earlier, the material cause of (unreal) predicate-content. By extension, one could understand that when there is the intuition of the final real nature of the ultimate substratum, all predicate-contents are destroyed along with the *mūlavidyā* (primal nescience), which is the material cause of them. Any ad hoc intuition of the purported real nature of the entity, as, for example, nacre in

11. Sastri (1984), *VP*, I.109, p. 46. *kāryavināśo . . . kaścidupādānena saha,/ . . . bādhaḥ/*

12. Ibid., . . . *kaścittu vidyamāna eva . . . nivṛttiḥ.*

13. Ibid., *VP*, I. 109, p. 47: *(bādhasya) kāraṇamadhiṣṭhānatattvasākṣātkāraḥ, tena vinā upādānabhūtāya avidyāya anivṛtteḥ/"*

'silver,' can be construed in two ways according to *Vedānta Paribhāṣā*.

When the primal material cause, *mūlavidyā*, is understood to persist in a change, one should understand that there is a change from ordinary illusory 'silver' to nacre. This purported change can be understood *with* or *without* reference to a lesser nescience called *tulāvidyā*, modal nescience. Then,

(a) If the change is understood *without* reference to *any* material cause, including *tulāvidyā*, then the *change* of predicate-content is to be understood as removal.

(b) If the change is understood with reference to *any* material cause such as, for example, *tulāvidyā*, then the *change* from 'silver' to nacre, i.e. from one predicate-content to another, is to be understood as sublation.

Then, we obtain the following logical possibilities with regard to sublation:

(i) When we understand that *all* predicate-contents, including illusory and worldly, are destroyed along with their material cause — which is supposedly the *mūlāvidyā* — there is sublation of all predicate-contents by the *Brahman*-intuition. [S-1] This is Primary Sublation (PS).[14]

(ii) When mere *illusory* predicate-contents are destroyed, one could understand it to be (a) sublation, only if one takes into account the destruction of *their* material

---

14. Ibid., *VP*, I. 111, p. 47, *evam ca śūktirūpasya śūktyavacchinnacaitanyaniṣṭhātulāvidyākāryātvapakṣe śūktiriti jñānena tadajñānena saha rajatasya bādhaḥ/mūlāvidyākāryatvapakṣe tu mūlāvidyāyā brahmasākṣātkāramatranivartyatayā śūktitvajñānena anivartyatayā tatra sūktijñānāt nivṛttimātram mudgaraprahāreṇa ghaṭasyeva* ||

cause, *tulāvidyā*. [S-2] This sublation of illusory 'silver,' etc. by the nacre, etc. is to be understood as Secondary Sublation (SS), as it does not refer to the destruction of primal nescience, and refers only to modal nescience, *tulāvidyā*;[15] [(b) removal, when no reference is made to *any* material cause].

One can reasonably assert that there cannot be sublation involving only *some* of worldly predicate-contents [as for example nacre-predicate (i.e. nacre), that we encounter in day-to-day life], because world-predicates are supposed to be the product of primal nescience in totality. Such a nescience can be destroyed only by *Brahman*-intuition. And *Brahman*-intuition cannot make distinction between one product of primal nescience and another for the purpose of destroying/ not destroying them. For this purpose there cannot be distinction between ordinary illusion and world as illusion either. Therefore, either there is the entire world sublated, along with illusions intrinsic to it, by *Brahman*-intuition, or none at all, and no *Brahman*-intuition.

Hence

(a) *Brahman*-intuition always results in PS.

(b) Ad hoc reality-intuition always results in SS.

(c) No reality-intuition results only in Removal.

In the view of the removal, the causes are not the intuition of the absolute or relative reality of the substrate.[16] Rather it is merely the origination of an opposed psychosis and the removal of defect. Further, while SS can be understood as Removal, PS cannot be understood as removal at all.

---

15. Ibid.

16. Ibid.

For Eliot Deutsch,[17] the sublation *requiring* the destruction of *avidyā*, the material cause, and points to a 'disvalue,' according to him. Thus, 'silver' is a disvalue. However, this disvaluational process does not and cannot mean a conscious disvaluation as Deutsch seems to think in an implicit manner when he says — "the judging process itself is . . . an axio-noetic sort. 'X, because of *a, b, c* . . . is to be rejected and replaced by *Y*'. . .." This is because the ability to subrate is not commanded by the agent, at least in the ordinary illusory experiences. On the contrary one could concede conscious disvaluation of the world-predicates in favour of *Brahman*, since in the ordinary course *Brahman*-intuition is not forthcoming without conscious human effort. Further when disvaluation or valuation takes place it always implies the reality of its object *even after* such valuational process takes place. But *Brahman*-intuition is supposed to negate the world-predicates in triple-time, in such a way that there remains no trace of the things that are disvalued. Or else Deutsch's subration can only be construed as SS.

Coming back to our analysis; what is of utmost importance is to examine the ontological negation [ON] (thus unreality), and the consequent logical negation [LN] (thus falsity), that are attributed to a predicate-content in the cases of sublation. Construal of a case as sublation necessarily means ON of the predicate-content in triple time and the corresponding LN in triple time too. Correspondingly, the 'silver' seen earlier has no ontological status in all the three times — hence unreal in all three times, and nor can the proposition at t_1, 'This is silver,' be attributed truth even at the time t_1 — that is at the time of the experience — when at time t_2 the 'silver'-predicate corresponding to a merely fictitious 'silver' is understood as

17. Deutsch (1968), pp. 16-17.

being unreal. In other words there never *was* 'silver' existing in the purported locus, not to speak of its patent absence *now*.

Then, what is the truth-claim of the proposition 'This is silver [as made at t_1]' as a whole, that is, including the term 'this'? The 'whole' therefore refers to 'this' and 'silver.' That is, whether the purported negation has to extend not merely to the predicate 'silver' in triple time but also to the subject term in triple time, now? If such a triple-time ON and/or LN is done then there would be no difference between the entities *vandhyāputra* on the one hand, and 'this' and 'silver' and 'This is silver' ('This is silver' a cognitive false identity gives an entity, which only on distinction becomes two. Distinction has to be made to show the *adhyāsa*. Distinction would then retain 'this' as a separate entity. On the other hand, if distinction is not made then *adhyāsa* cannot be demonstrated, and more importantly, there would be no difference between *vandhyāputra* and 'silver'), on the other. Obviously this cannot be so, for *vandhyāputra* can never yield any experience in triple times, as it — in a manner of speaking — stands sublated forever, and whereas 'this' and 'silver' *are not* so. If '*vandhyāputra*-status' is accorded to 'silver' then emergence/ experience cannot be accounted for. If it is not accorded the said status, then 'silver' and such other predicates will have to be assigned some or the other ontological status, i.e. a neither/nor situation. [One can here ask pertinently, does the time involved in our experience get sublated? Normal illusion-cases do not lend support to the view of time-sublation. This is because some kind of memory of time seems to persist even of the illusory objects.]

Taking the alternative of assigning an ontological status, it is said: When a shell is perceived, albeit delusively, as silver, the silver-content can be neither unreal, nor what is elsewhere real, e.g. in the shop or treasury; for, such content would be imperceptible, no contact therewith being possible. Nor can it be real, as, then so sublating cognition can arise in the form, 'this is not silver, but nacre.' Hence a content has to be admitted, which, being in contact, is not unreal, and yet, being sublatable, is not real; it is novel, indeterminable and produced in the shell substrate even in the absence of the (*real*) silver atoms; the production is brought about by nescience, defect (in the sense of sight or in the *manas* or in both) and residual impression (*saṁskāra*) of former veridical experience of silver. This standpoint can be understood as world-standpoint, that is, the logician is looking at the complete reality and propositional hierarchy from the present world-point of view and is trying to account for the entire phenomena. In its process a hierarchy of realities is created. The other alternative can be called the *Brahman*-standpoint. Even when the logician is in the world, he refuses to go away from two-valued logic. In the act he directly posits himself to be in the *Brahman* locus and tries to explain the matter. In such a schema the world has to be assigned the status of *vandhyāputra*. Taking either of these standpoints is logically fraught with insurmountable difficulties. These two standpoints, broadly speaking, are responsible for the divergence of the post-Śaṅkara thinkers.

From the world-standpoint, 'silver' is indeterminable either as real or as unreal. We shall call it *sadasad*, that is, neither *sat* nor *asat*, as indicating its ontological status in the reality hierarchy. Can the same be said of 'this'? That is, can the pure 'this' also be a *sadasad*? Obviously it cannot be so because it (this) is a pure *Brahman*. On the contrary, from the *Brahman*-standpoint, if proposition [2] is absolutely negated, including the 'this,' then such a *Brahman* is also negated. It is here that Mind and Language are highlighted to escape from the difficulties.

IV

Asat, Jagat, and Sat

If we carefully work out the above matter concerning world-standpoint we shall at once see that the world-predicates are conceived in analogous terms to the illusory 'silver'. If so, the whole actual world is nothing more than constitutive of world-predicates. Should we — or should we not — add the locus 'this' to this external world? Presuming that at the time of PS all external world predicate-contents are destroyed along with their material cause — the primal nescience — *mūlavidyā*, what would happen to the substrate term "this" and its corresponding content 'this'?

By no stretch of imagination could one conclude that the term 'this' itself denotes a predicate term, and its corresponding ontological content in a predicative manner. Such a presumption would make a mockery of the language as then one would have to say that 'a predicate is predicated.' (*Note*: Śaṅkara in fact makes the *adhyāsa*-proposition by using the term 'this' (*idam*) as a predicate term when he says *aham idam*. But then this *idam* or 'this' is only denotative of predicate that is attached to 'I,' and does not refer to an external independent locus. Similarly by extension, 'I am (this) body' would imply that the *predicate 'I' is predicated by 'body-predicate'*! Sublation of all predicates would automatically lead to total annihilation. Predicates everywhere! No wonder Śaṅkara has been branded a *pracchanna bauddha*!)

And we do not have the choice of calling the sublation of the world apart from PS either as SS or as Removal, because then it would mean that PS which occurs due to *Brahman*-intuition has not taken place yet — that is, only some other secondary *avidyā* has been removed along with the world-predicates; and if it is removal it only means that some psychoses opposed to the world-predicate psychoses have emerged, in which case the same have to be specified. This would lead to infinite regress. This fallacy will ultimately take the toll on the so-called pure 'I,' the *Brahman*. That is, there will be a backward chain of psychoses opposed to the ones that are just then sublated. This means that there is no guarantee that the ones that have come afresh will also not be sublated in future.

Analysis of Perception (*pratyakṣa*) in *Vedānta Paribhāṣā* holds the key. According to *Vedānta Paribhāṣa*, all world-predicates are products of nescience associated with the residual impressions generated by experience with the form 'this.' But impressions where? Obviously impressions are those *as found in the mind* (*antaḥkaraṇa*, or *manas*). Therefore, world-predicates are attributed to the 'this.' And that 'this' in turn is to be traced to the mind for its (this's) origination. The attempt of *Vedānta Paribhāṣā* is to somehow avoid an independent external locus-hood to the 'this.' By avoiding the external locus-hood to the term 'this' the Advaitin hopes to avoid his biggest headache of duality of all sorts. The Advaitin does not want to assign any reality status to the world apart from the *vandhyāputra* status. At the same time he has to successfully explain the emergence of experience of the so-called illusion — 'silver' and later 'world.'

But can he succeed in avoiding external locus-hood to "this" altogether?[18] Let us understand *Vedānta Paribhāṣā* attempt.

18. A conjunctive ($p.q$) is true if both p and q are true. Compare this with the proposition 'This is 'silver." Now this is obviously *not* a conjunctive proposition as ($p.q$). If one takes the view of identity — or false identity for that matter — between 'this' and 'silver' then, if 'silver' is false (unreal), then 'this' is also false (unreal). This means that "This is 'silver' would be false (unreal) wholesale, →

Generally there is no problem understanding the *asat*, or unreal entities, as remaining permanently sublated. Under this category two sub-categories are identified. First, the class of propositions containing entities like sky-flower (*gagana kusuma*) or hare's horn (*śaśaka śṛṅga*), which are called as *vikalpa*. In these fictitious entities at least some imaginary predicate–content is possible. They, however, remain sublated, since they are imaginary by definition ". . . the apprehension of the word 'hare's horn' is a *vikalpa*, which is different from knowledge. Apprehension of such cases of pure fiction is different from knowledge whether it be of the real or of the illusion. What constitutes this difference is the absence of any substratum to which the cognition may refer."[19]

The second class containing, for example, *vandhyāputra* or 'son-of-a-barren-women,' is defined as "incapable of being: hence not capable of being experienced in all times whether past, present or future. These are absolute *asat*, or *alīka*, which form absolute non-existence, i.e. *atyantābhāva*. In this class, there cannot even be an imaginary predicate-content, let alone substratum."[20]

→ without any room for the truth (reality) of 'this.' Thus part-falsity or part-unreality has no room at all."

However this understanding leads to (i) the difficulty of logically identifying nacre in the same locus as that of the earlier "silver," and (ii) the elimination of cognitive-content in normal 'I-propositions,' i.e. if 'I am body,' etc. are finally sublated at the time of *Brahman*-intuition, then by using the above logic of identity between the subject and predicate, the subject 'I' will be negated, which will lead to nihilism, unless some other 'I' is brought in to protect the thought from nihilism. [Recall the second condition of *adhyāsa* (b), which says, necessary reality of one entity and necessary unreality of the other.]

19. Devaraja (1972), p. 131, fn 13.

20. Narain (1964), p. 151, op. cit.

If predicates are predetermined with respect to the cognitive content of two distinct sorts (a) that of subject 'I,' and (b) that of 'this,' such as, for example, in 'I am happy' and 'This is silver' respectively, then it follows logically that such a predetermination will continue to be so since there is an inseparable unity between them. (Chomskian creativity can be taken care of, easily.) In that case the 'I' that is usually made the subject of propositions cannot anymore remain unsublated, if and when the predicates are. This is because they are inseparable. Then do we have any subject term 'I' which withstands the sublation of associated predicates? Possibly none, none at all at least in the waking state. So what has been thus far construed as the subject ('I') and understood cognitively in a way because of its identity with cognitive predicates also gets sublated. Is there anything left? If the sublated 'I' is *antaḥkaraṇa*, which is playing the trick, first how did it do so? Under the spell of false identity of *Brahman* with *antaḥkaraṇa*, as in red-hot-iron ball, for example *antaḥkaraṇa* behaved as if it is the 'I'. However the guise is removed in *suṣupti*. *Sākṣin* awareness shows us that there is yet another 'I' which is *not predicated* at all. There is no 'this' representing any object. The 'this' is negated with the sublation of predicates. Language ceases. Mind ceases. Experience alone remains. There the witness is.

Conclusion

The above discussion makes it clear that at least at one place language acts like a not-so-trustworthy postman. The case in reference is *tuccha vākya*s wherein *tuccha* concepts are involved. If mind and language are identified then the 'mind' — the postmaster — may be the real culprit! There is no cognitive content with regard to the *tuccha vākya*s or *tuccha* concepts, yet language delivered a false packet. A *tuccha vākya* cannot be, in its undissected form, attributed with truth-value false in the normal sense of falsity, wherein possibility of falsity should imply the possibility of truth also. Therefore a *tuccha vākya* is meaningless inasmuch as the *tuccha* term is.

The postman, in the normal course brings all articles faithfully, as addressed to the addressee; delivers and returns. The addressee has to read and understand the content. In the normal course the postal articles may contain matters pertaining to 'others' and/or the 'addressee himself.'

The addressee may realize one fine day that, despite the fact that the postman was doing a good job, the *addressee himself was not*. That is the addressee himself was not able to understand the hidden message. All these would happen the day *suṣupti* is understood as *sākṣin*, the Witness. The hidden message is: 'all postal articles that are delivered are to be discarded.' As also, the real addressee is not *antaḥkaraṇa* or mind — complex (*jīva*), rather it is the *sākṣin*. But then *sākṣin* does not need any postal articles.

References

Datta, D.M. (1972), *Six Ways of Knowing*, University of Calcutta, Kolkata, First Published (1932).

Deutsch, Eliot (1969), *Advaita Vedānta: A Philosophical Reconstruction*, East-West Center Press, Honolulu.

Devaraja, N.K. (1972), *An Introduction to Śaṅkara's Theory of Knowledge*, Motilal Banarsidass, Delhi, 2nd rev. edn.

Kumar, Vinay, U.A., (1988) "Existence of Self and *Adhyāsa* in Advaita", *Journal of Indian Philosophy*, Netherlands 16 (1988), pp. 201-15.

———, U.A., (2006), "Adhyāsa (Superimposition) Revisited", in *ICPR Volume in honor of Prof. Ganeswar Misra*.

Narain, K., (1964), *A Critique of the Madhva Refutation of the Śaṅkara School of Vedānta*, Udayana Publication, Allahabad.

Śastri. S.S.S. (ed. & tr.) (1984), *Vedānta Paribhāṣā* of Dharmarāja Adhvarin, the Adyar Library and Research Centre. The Theosophical Society, Adyar, Chennai, First Published 1942.

Saraswati, Svami, Saccidanandendra (1998), *Brahma Sūtra Bhāṣya of Śaṅkara* (Original with Kannada tr. Both original and tr. in Kannada Script) in 2 vol. Adhyatma Prakasha Karyalaya, Holenarasipura, First Published, 1951.

Sen, Amit Kumar (1998), "Logic with Truth Value Gaps", in *Indian Philosophical Quarterly*, vol. XXV, no. 2, April 1998, pp. 185-90.

7

Thought and Language
The Bhartṛharian Perspective

Tandra Patnaik*

LANGUAGE presupposes thought and thought also presupposes language. But what bothers the philosopher most is regarding the priority of one over the other. This paper tries to place Bhartṛhari's views in the backdrop of one of the central issues of modern philosophy of language — whether thought is independent of language or thinking is language-determined. Bhartṛhari's *Vākyapadīya* can be claimed to be one of the oldest treatises meticulously dealing with this issue. I shall discuss his views on the topic from two angles — (i) thought and language as components of linguistic communication and (ii) thought and language as conceptual entities and their relative priority. On the first issue he conceives a two-dimensional relation between language and thought. And on the second, he prefers to prioritize language, dismissing thereby the popular and commonsensical theory that language is just a vehicle of thought. In this context, I shall also like to compare notes with some relevant modern views on these issues. Sometimes such comparative study is necessary because the present is always enriched by the past, and the past is better assessed by its capability to face the challenges of the present.

* Professor (retired), P.G. Department of Philosophy, Utkal University, Vani Vihar, Bhubaneswar, India.

I

Before I explicate Bhartṛhari's views on the theme, I must clarify that no discussion on any aspect of his philosophy is complete without reference to his multilayered method of analysis of the phenomenon, called *śabda* (generally, translatable as language). Broadly speaking, he explicates language from three angles — (i) *śabda* as a *tattva*, i.e. the metaphysical principle; (ii) *śabda* as an object of *loka-vyavahāra*, i.e. as it is used; and (iii) *śabda* as *śāstra-vyavahāra*, i.e. as an object of analytical or grammatical study. Here, my focus would be on *loka-vyavahāra*, though occasionally I have to refer to the notion of *śabda* as a *tattva*.

Bhartṛhari conceives language that we use in our day-to-day life as communicative in nature, for he uses the term *vyavahāra*, very often to mean 'the use of words to communicate one's thought,' 'verbal usage' or 'exchange of ideas.' He also projects language as an act. It is an activity in human beings. The Sanskrit term for this is *śābdana*, which B.K. Matilal very aptly translates as 'languaging.' As an act, it involves the speaker's expression of his intention through the utterance-act, and the hearer's ability to grasp what is being expressed along with the intention of the speaker. He explains this process of linguistic communication by introducing a distinction between *sphoṭa* and *nāda*. In case of expressive words [as opposed to the meaningless sounds] one has to distinguish two elements — one is the root cause of manifestation (*nimitta*), and the other is the applied (*prayujyate*), when manifested to convey meaning. (*Vākyapadīya* 1.144). In other words, every linguistic communication has two aspects: (1) the element that causes manifestation, that makes the implicit potency explicit through the (sentential) utterances, and (2) the element which being actualized conveys the meaning to the hearer. The former is called *nāda/dhvani* and the latter *sphoṭa*. Bhartṛhari pinpoints that the process of linguistic communication necessarily involves three basic elements — (i) the speaker, (ii) the hearer, and (iii) the common ground for inter-subjectivity. For, in his opinion communication is not a process of directly transferring the contents of thought from the speaker to the hearer. The competence to express the thought and grasp the meaning exists as an inherent power within human beings. It is a property shared by both. So the expressive word (that the speaker intends to communicate) is made explicit through a "stretch of sounds" (I use this term following Matilal, because, it helps us to clarify that, according to Bhartṛhari, sentences, and not the words are the primary units of communicative meaning); this is *nāda/dhvani*. This audible stretch of sounds that is presented sequentially, syllable by syllable, is the cause (*nimitta*) of the manifestation of the meaning to be communicated. The hearer too, grasps the stretch of sounds along with their multiplicity and sequentiality. But unless the hearer understands the stretch of sounds as representing a unitary and sequenceless meaning, linguistic communication is not achieved. This sequenceless meaning-unit is *sphoṭa*. As Bhartṛhari clarifies, "Since *nāda* (sound pattern) arises in sequence, *sphoṭa* which has neither the former nor the latter stage and which is sequenceless (*akrama*) is apprehended through *nāda* and appears to be having sequence as well as parts." (*Vākyapadīya* (*VP*) I.48). Thus the meaning-unit or (*sphoṭa*) is a partless and indivisible whole. In contrast, the discerning elements like grammatical and syntactical divisions are very much prominent when the meaning the speaker intends to communicate is presented through the stretch of sounds. If utterance represents speech and the meaning expressed is taken to be the non-verbal element present in the mind of the speaker, then it is obvious that Bhartṛhari maintains a duality between speech and thought. Both the elements are autonomous, yet not autonomous to the extent of excluding each other. But he would claim that in the ultimate sense these two elements are indistinguishable, as is evident from his explanatory note on the verse 1.144, where he clarifies: "In the sequenceless nature of the *vāk* (speech) [which also means *sphoṭa*] both the powers, the power to be articulated in sound (audible form) and the power to convey meaning, lie intermixed." It is clear from this statement that Bhartṛhari does not identify *sphoṭa* with the *artha* or meaning. Rather, Bhartṛhari believes that *sphoṭa* along with expressing the meaning expresses itself. While elaborating this he says, "just as light/fire (*jyoti*) resides in the *araṇi* (churning) stick and being manifested becomes the cause for manifesting other objects; *śabda* resides likewise in the mind (*buddhi*, the inner faculty) and being manifested becomes separately the cause for manifesting itself as well as the meaning" (*VP* I.46). In the quoted passage we note that he uses the terms *śabda* and *sphoṭa*, almost interchangeably. And both the terms seem to refer to a principle that includes both, the sequential form of words and the meaning. So henceforth I shall use the term language-principle to refer to *sphoṭa*. I intend to come back to the question of the principle called *sphoṭa* a little later.

We have noted that Bhartṛhari maintains a distinction between the 'meaning to be expressed' and the 'meaning actually expressed' through articulated stretch of sounds, though ultimately he seems to reject their autonomy. This may give rise to a paradoxical situation. But Bhartṛhari sees no paradox in his position. He may still hold that at a certain level there is an undeniable interdependence between language and thought. The implications of such a viewpoint will be clear if we examine Bhartṛhari's analysis of the processes of linguistic communication. Exploring the process of linguistic communication from the speaker's angle, he pinpoints three discernible elements in an utterance, viz. the sound pattern/form of words (*vācaka*), the meaning expressed (*vācya*) and speaker intention (*vivakṣa*). *Vācya* is the meaning to be expressed and *vācaka* is the meaning expressed through the stretch of sounds. In a broad sense, *vācya* stands for the meaning-content (*artha*) and *vācaka* for the stretch of words. (*VP* I.50). For certain practical reasons the distinction is to be maintained. If meaning would have been conceptually inseparable from words then the same meaning could not have been expressed in different forms of sentences: or we could have translated the meaning of a sentence from one language to another. But we must remember that the speaker's utterance is always presented sequentially, syllable by syllable. The moment one syllable is uttered it is replaced by another syllable. So how does the speaker manage to convey the meaning that has a unitary sense? Bhartṛhari's answer to the problem is interesting, yet profound. He would say that the level of utterance is just one part of the linguistic expressibility. So he introduces the notion of a three-tiered process of linguistic communicability. In this scheme the level of utterance is only the last stage of the process, which he calls the *vaikharī vāk*. The level of utterance points to a deeper level of thought. It is the pre-verbal stage identified as the *madhyamā vāk*. This pre-verbal stage is roughly comparable to the modern notion of an episodic but unexpressed pre-verbal thought. It is a thought with the same verbal content. If we take thought to mean what the sentence purports to communicate then we can say language presupposes thought and thought is operative through language. But uttered speech with discernible elements and the pre-verbal stage with the supposed distinction (though pre-verbal) between the word and the meaning, refers to an ultimate stage where the distinction between *vācya* and *vācaka* is obliterated. This stage is called the *paśyantī vāk*, a purely non-verbal stage of language. This is the stage of *sphoṭa*, the language-principle from which meaning, as if, bursts forth (for, that is the etymological significance of the root *sphuṭ* from which the word *sphoṭa* is derived) along with the phonetic and syntactical elements. The potency of language is like a peafowl's egg. All the colours of a full grown peafowl are potentially there in the egg. These colours are manifested when the peafowl comes out of the egg. Similarly the *sphoṭa* or *śabda* is the potential stage in which the linguistic form, along with its power to mean is already there in all languaging beings (*VP* I.51).

But is it not a problematic stance adopted by Bhartṛhari? If languaging rests on unity then why does he maintain a duality in the initial stage between thought and language? Bhartṛhari assumes such distinction as a convenient ploy, for otherwise languaging cannot be an act of communication. He says, "Just as the mind of the speaker first turns to the words, in the same way, the attention of the hearer also is directed towards them" (*VP* I.53). So he believes that even if the duality between thought and language is suppressed in the ultimate level, the residual force of the differentiation is not totally abandoned. So the moment a speaker desires to say something the duality is again operative. "It is this merging and emerging of word, which is looked upon as its activity" (*vṛtti* under *VP* I.51). But, a relevant question may be raised at this point — if the element of differentiation is so important for communication what is the need for Bhartṛhari to conceive of a non-differentiated language principle, called *sphoṭa*? Most of the theories explain linguistic communication in terms of the duality between the expressed meaning and thought to be conveyed or expressed. So it is relevant in this context to examine how the modern Western philosophers have handled this problem. This is likely to help us in assessing Bhartṛhari's philosophy of language, and specifically, his theory of *sphoṭa*.

It is well known that the course of Western philosophy took a linguistic turn in the first part of twentieth century. Now let us see how the renowned Western philosopher of language, Wittgenstein would have reacted to Bhartṛhari's way of looking at the language-thought equation. It is well known that, in his post-*Tractatus* phase he highlighted the functional and communicative dimensions of language. But Wittgenstein, especially in his *Philosophical Investigations,* does not feel the necessity of assuming any such duality between language and thought. So he would suggest to us to confine analysis of the concepts of 'language' and 'meaning' within the limits of utterance. He admits that we do talk of such mental concepts as 'meaning,' 'belief,' 'understanding,' and 'intention' in the context of linguistic expression, but they are nothing more than 'grammatical fictions.' He even goes to the extent of labelling such mentalistic hypothesis as a 'general disease of thinking.' Explaining his position on this issue, Pitcher (1977, p. 275) says: "once we have an overall view of a variety of situations in which the terms 'meaning' and 'understanding' are used, and of the various criteria of their use, there is nothing more to know about what meaning and understanding are. To know their meanings, Wittgenstein would say, is to know their use." He rather adopts a form of linguistic behaviourism as far as analysis of meaning is concerned. So for him, an independent level of mental activity need not be presumed. Subsequently, Paul Grice and John Austin explicitly propagated a communicative theory of language, thereby adding new dimensions to the study of language so far neglected in the Western tradition. They conceived language to be an audience (hearer) directed activity. Both of them emphasized that the speaker's intention to express his thought plays an important role. But Austin prefers to explicate the speaker's intention as well as its impact on the hearer in terms of the rules of language. Full credit must be given to Austin for admitting that using language is equivalent to engaging in an activity. He also successfully draws attention to the fact that apart from the fixed meaning-content, the speaker can also express his intention in uttering a particular utterance, which he preferred to call the 'force,' as opposed to the 'meaning' of a sentence. But very much like Wittgenstein, he avoids treading into the level of thought. So he felt that intention has nothing to do with the level of thought. For Austin, the 'intended meaning' or 'force' is ultimately dependent on linguistic and institutionalized conventions. Both, Grice and Austin also seem to neglect the hearer's role in their explication of the communicative theory of language. John Searle's (1969) account of speech acts, however, takes care of the hearer's 'understanding.' But, very much like Austin, he too, proposes to explicate the hearer's understanding in terms of the constitutive rules (convention) of language. He talks of 'force-indicating devices,' such as performative verbs and sentential moods to explain the speaker's intention (force). So these philosophers prefer a form of reductionism, i.e. reducing thought to language, as they interpret the intention of the speaker as well as the understanding of the hearer in terms of linguistic behaviour. Besides, the question as to how the meaning is conveyed from the speaker to the hearer virtually receives no attention. Most probably it is taken for granted that knowing the rules and syntax of language is enough to guarantee the transference of meaning from the speaker to the hearer. Bhartṛhari would have outright rejected this type of reductionism. He definitely believes that language is an act, but as a communicative act it must have to be connected to the level of thought at some level or other. So, thought, at no cost, can be reduced to language as long as we are talking of the speaker's intention to indulge in speech-act and the hearer's desire to understand the utterance.

Now I intend to throw some light on another Western viewpoint, which is more recent. This theory, broadly known as Expressivism is the standard view upheld by the philosophers of language and the philosophers of mind as well. In this case, unlike the theories discussed above, the autonomy of thought and language is maintained, but primacy is attached to thought over language. According to this theory the primary function of language is to enable speakers to convey the content of their thought to the hearer. In other words, it is presumed that the speaker has a thought, with a certain content and he chooses words in such a way that on the basis of these words the hearer is able to recognize that the speaker has a thought with such and such a content. This doctrine is supposed to have its genesis in Frege's famous theory of thought. According to him a sentence expresses a thought. He says: "I call a thought something for which the question of truth arises . . . thought, in itself, is immaterial, clothes itself in the material garment of a sentence and thereby becomes comprehensible to us. We say a sentence expresses a thought." Thus language, for him, is dependent on thought. As he points out: "when one apprehends or thinks a thought one does not create it . . .." Thus it stands as a *transcendental signified*, which remains constant, in spite of varied forms of utterance. However, we must not conflate Frege's theory with Expressivism. Thought, for him has deeper nuances and in all cases does not mean the "content of thought, which the speaker intends to express." So it will be better if we concentrate on Grice's famous theory of thought-based semantics. In his famous paper entitled

"Meaning" (1957) he specifies, "A meant something X is (roughly) equivalent to A intended to produce some effect in the audience by means of recognition of his intention." Such a concept of meaning implies that the speaker has an intention and he wants his intention to be understood by the hearer (audience) on the basis of his utterance. In order for a speaker to express a thought in this way, it is necessary that the speaker and the hearer should *share an understanding of language*. Otherwise the meaning would remain uncommunicated. Thus, the idea of *thought content* and *shared understanding of language* by the speaker and the hearer, are fundamental. But one must explain what kind of thought-contents are shared in communication. If it is inferable from the choice of the words used, then we are turning back to language to interpret thought-content. Searle (1983) modifies his earlier position and in his book, *Intentionality*, presents a different kind of thought-based semantics. He explicates meaningful linguistic utterance in terms of the intentional states of the speaker's beliefs, desires and intentions. Searle (1983) applies this notion of 'intentionality' to explain the phenomenon of language. The basic features of his theory are — (i) all our activities (including languaging) are governed by intention, (ii) our assertions and beliefs are supposed to match the word, and (iii) the world represented by a contentful mental act, must be conditioned by the criterion of satisfaction (broadly implying truth conditions). Applying these features to his theory of meaning, wc may say that the speaker, for example, in saying 'it is raining' intends to say so, and has the utterance 'It is raining' having the condition of satisfaction with mind-to-world direction of fit that 'It is raining.' In this case the meaning of utterance is determined by the content of intention with which an utterance is made. But, one may very significantly ask Searle — can such thought-contents exist independent of their linguistic expressions, if we are assuming that language is primarily communicative? Besides, both, Grice and Searle interpret thought-content in terms of episodic thoughts, not thought in general. So we are bound to fall back on linguistic utterances to interpret such episodic intention of the speaker. We may sagely claim that unless the Bhartṛharian position is admitted, that is, thought anchors language and language anchors thought, the theory of thought-based semantics remains inexplicable. Again, a very crucial limitation may be noted in most of the versions of Expressivism. The way this theory is formulated, it appears that it may have no difficulty in handling the simpler forms of language like, 'It is raining,' in terms of the beliefs, intentions and truth-conditionality or condition of 'satisfaction.' But what about the complex expressions (which do not cover the 'condition of fit' or the 'condition of satisfaction,' for example, "Meaning expresses a thought"), that we perform with language? In this context, Peter Carruthers (1996) raises a very important question, i.e. "how are we to explain our ability to entertain unlimitedly many *new* thought-contents . . . except *generatively*, in terms of the construction of new linguistic means for the expression of those thoughts, but putting together old parts in new ways?" (p. 85). This problem raised by Carruthers is a central problem that any philosopher of language must address himself to. Unfortunately, the Western philosophers' obsession with the notions of the language of assertion and truth-conditionality (in Searle's case, condition of satisfaction) does not allow them to give sufficient attention to this problem. But in case of Bhartṛhari this problem seems to have an easy solution. In his *Vākyapadīya* he discusses in detail multiple kinds of activities a man can perform with language, including metaphorical, elliptical, satirical and even ornamental expressions. This, to some extent, is clear from the following explanatory note on verse I.13. He says: "On language depends maybe the speaker's intended meaning, the possibility of applying words to things, the ability to combine words into sentences, the connecting of objects with actions, identification of a thing as to be accomplished, or the projection of the content of an awareness as an external object." So he must have sought an answer to the question — how does our language function in limitless ways? And his answer would be that the power to use language in limitless ways is rooted in the dispositional linguistic ability that is present within each conscious human being. And *sphoṭa* is the basic ground of this linguistic ability itself.

Now, we shall attend to another fundamental question that needs to be answered by any philosopher subscribing to the view that language is primarily communicative, i.e. how does the speaker convey the meaning to the hearer? In other words what is the basis of inter-subjectivity of linguistic communication? Bhartr̥hari would say meaning is not an entity to be transported, to put it in a somewhat modern imagery, in the manner we load the contents of one car into another car. Had it been so, the following problems would not have bothered the philosophers of language:

1. The speaker has to express his thought through temporal and instantly destroyed sound utterances having sequence and multiplicity. The hearer, too, receives them in their multiplicity and sequentiality. But the 'sense' communicated is unitary in nature. How does the hearer grasp the unity and sequenceless whole, called meaning?
2. Why in certain cases the hearer fails to get the meaning even after hearing each word carefully uttered by the speaker?

3. In certain cases the hearer can grasp the meaning even if the speaker has not completed his utterance. How is this possible?
4. The speaker's utterance not only conveys the literary meaning, but also the 'implied' and 'implicit' meaning (which in modern philosophical parlance is called 'implicature' and 'impliciture,' respectively). How does the hearer grasp them from the expressed meaning?

Here the notion of *sphoṭa* comes in handy. Bhartṛhari would say, because, both the speaker and the hearer share the common *sphoṭa* the meaning is communicated. The *sphoṭa* is connected with the inherent linguistic potency (*śabda bīja* or *śabda bhāvanā*) present within all conscious human beings. Therefore human beings have a natural linguistic competence. When the speaker intends to say something, he grasps the unit of the meaning first, and then expresses it in sequential form. The hearer, on the other hand, catches the audible and sequential forms of words first and these words evoke his linguistic potency, and this gives him the competence to understand what the speaker intends to say. If the speaker's utterance fails to arouse the linguistic potency, there is a gap in communication. On the other hand, if the hearer is able to grasp the sense conveyed by the speaker then, even an incomplete sentence is enough for the purpose. In this case he need not listen to the whole series of words to assess the meaning. Nor does he require computing them mentally to gather the unitary sense conveyed. To the last question Bhartṛhari's answer is remarkably clear. He says: "It is the word which is the instructor. Speakers follow the power of words and act when urged by a desire to speak, based on the availability of the right word. When the hearer follows the fixed power of words to convey a meaning through reasoning based on meaning, context indication, interconnection, etc. people look upon the capacity of the words as the reasoning of the hearer" (*vṛtti* under I.137). The ability to express meaning and apprehend the meaning is potent in the *sphoṭa*, which also refers to human linguistic potency (*śabda bhāvanā*). The explanation of linguistic communication in terms of *sphoṭa* or *śabda* may not sound very appealing to the Western mind, but their solution to the issue has not been very satisfying either. They, advertently or inadvertently, nurture a dualism between particulars and concepts, reference and predication, the 'that' of the subject and 'what' of the predicate, propositional content and its assertion. In the context of communication of intention, Grice does talk of a 'shared understanding of the language'. But ultimately, such an understanding is grounded on linguistic convention. But linguistic convention alone is not sufficient enough to explain the complexities associated with communication of meaning. Similarly, Davidson (1976) tries to locate the basis of inter-subjectivity in 'shared language,' but this phenomenon, though not implying linguistic convention, is finally set to rest on a system of beliefs and truth-conditions which indirectly means that he does not want to go beyond the language of assertion.

II

Now I shall try to shift the focus of my discussion to another dimension of the thought-language equation. It is not directly connected with communicative meaning. The issue is confined to the conceptual level. We know that language and thought are two important aspects of human existence. So the question likely to puzzle philosophers is about the conceptual priority of one over the other. It is usually believed that it is a one-way relationship. Thought is conceptually prior to language since language serves as the conveyor belt of thought. On this issue Bhartṛhari's standpoint does not have many sympathizers. He claims that thought presupposes language. Of course, in contemporary academic circles the issue has generated much debate in the field of philosophy of mind and cognitive psychology. Philosophers like Jerry Fodor, Peter Curruthers and Sellars support a thesis which may give credence to Bhartṛhari's stand on this issue. However these philosophers mostly look at the problem from the standpoint of philosophy of mind and cognitive psychology. But Bhartṛhari explicates the issue absolutely from a different angle. He states very clearly that as a *śabda pramāṇaka* (which approximately can be translated as analyst of language) he is primarily concerned with language, not the nature of things. "What the word presents is the only reality for us," he announces. Accordingly, *śabda* or Word-principle is the ultimate Reality (*śabda-tattva Brahman*). Therefore he has no problem in explicating thought as well as the objective world, in terms of the *śabda-tattva*. As far as his metaphysical stance is concerned he is a monist. So *unity* is the key principle in his philosophy. Applying this to the level of the language-in-use, he conceives meaning as a unity of three distinct elements, viz. thought, language, and the object meant. His commitment to monism would not allow him to retain the distinction between thought and language. Therefore, he believes that human consciousness is impregnated with the Word-principle. In *Vākyapadīya* he declares:

> It is the speech which prompts all mankind into activity. Without this power man is nothing more than a log of wood or a piece of stone. — *VP*, I.127

To understand Bhartṛhari's position on conceptual priority of language over thought we must refer to the following aphorisms of this treatise:

> There can be no awareness in this world without being intertwined with language. All cognitive awareness appears as if it is interpenetrated with language. — *VP*, I.123

In this aphorism Bhartṛhari uses the word awareness in a distinctively different sense. We as conscious beings are aware of the innumerable factual and mental events and objects surrounding us. The general impression is that we are aware of them because of the perceptual process. But according to Bhartṛhari we are aware of them not due to the perceptual process, because even this process involves cognizing them as distinct and particular things subsumable under some names and forms. That is the reason why he claims that there cannot be any cognitive awareness without being intertwined with words.

In the next aphorism, it is stated:

> If the language-impregnated nature of awareness went away from it, then a cognition would not manifest (any object), for that (language-impregnated nature) is the distinguishing nature of our awareness. — *VP*, I.124

In this verse he uses two terms *prakāśa* and *pratyavimarśa*, which needs further elucidation. Bhartṛhari does not elaborate implications of these terms in his *Vṛtti*. So we have to take the help of later Grammarians like Utpala's interpretation of these terms. Utpala says that the very nature of illumination (*prakāśa*) is *vimarśa*, i.e. discrimination; otherwise illumination would be inert and passive like a material object, such as a mirror or a crystal. To express it in simpler terms the word-potentness of thought functions in two ways; it reveals the content of thought along with discriminating it from other thought-contents. Matilal, while analysing the import of this pair of concepts says, "illumination means removal of darkness but simple removal of darkness does not reveal the object unless one is able to distinguish the outline of the object from its immediate surroundings or environment." Therefore, Bhartṛhari and other Grammarians believe that even in case of bare awareness, our awareness is impregnated with *śabda* or *vāgrūpatā* (word-impregnation). Without such *vāgrūpatā* (word-loadedness), which Bhartṛhari identifies with *pratyavimarśa*, i.e. "determination by word" (which the later Grammarians call *vimarśa*), an awareness is no awareness. Thought, in any form of its manifestation, implies the contents and these contents are constituted of distinct concepts. And without subsuming them under names and forms distinctness cannot be retained. So he says, "What is called awareness (*saṁjñā*) is having the form of speech or word (*vāgrūpatā*). Consciousness in all beings never goes beyond it, that is, it is never different from the fact of having the form of the word." But, from this it does not follow that thought is a form of 'inner speech' as it has been conceived by Sellar, nor does the theory say that being conscious means being constantly in the process of using words. Our thoughts and awareness need not be wordy, but they have the potentiality to be expressible through words. He is not reducing thought into words, but just shows the conceptual dependence of human consciousness on the principle of language. We only become aware of the word-potentness of thought when the words are expressed in sequential and articulate manner to express our thought. In direct contrast to the views of some of the traditional Indian theories like Nyāya and Mīmāṁsā, Bhartṛhari holds that there cannot be any prelinguistic bare awareness, popularly known as *nirvikalpa*. Even the awareness of a child, who has no knowledge of language, is word-potent. In his commentary on I.125, he says,

> Speech (*vāc*) indwells or inheres in all cases of awareness just as illumination does fire and consciousness in mind (*antaryāmin*). The subtle nature of *vāc* (speech) [i.e. *sūkṣmo vāgdharma*] penetrates and permeates even such states as lack of ostensible mental activity (*asañcetitāvasthā*).

Again, he comments:

> Just as *śabda bhāvanā* (residual traces of linguistic ability) where explicit forms are withdrawn (*samartharūpa*) cannot accomplish anything (*kāryam na kriyate*), similarly, non-conceptual (*avikalpa*) cognition is of no use.
>
> — tr. B.K. Matilal, *The Word and the World*, pp.134-35

Bhartṛhari's explication of the conceptual relation between thought and language may have no takers. It may appear unusual and sometimes like a mystical rhapsody. But given his metaphysical position no other conclusion could have been possible. But recent studies in philosophical and cognitive psychology (refer *Language, Thought and Consciousness* by Peter Carruthers) can be taken as ample evidence for the fact that, even after the considerable lapse of 1500 years, Bhartṛhari's philosophy can withstand the test of time.

References

Bhartṛhari, *Vākyapadīya*, Kāṇḍa I, ed. K.A. Subramania Iyer, Poona: Deccan College, 1966.

Carruthers, Peter, *Language, Thought and Consciousness*, Cambridge: Cambridge University Press, 1996.

Grice, H.P., "Meaning," *Philosophical Review*, LXVI, 1957.

Matilal, B.K., *The Word and The World*, Oxford: Oxford University Press, 1990.

Searle, John, *Speech-Acts: An Essay in Philosophy of Language*, Cambridge: Cambridge University Press, 1969.

———, *Intentionality*, Cambridge: Cambridge University Press, 1983.

Wittgenstein, L., *Philosophical Investigations* (tr. G.E.M. Anscombe), New York: The Macmillan, 1953.

8

Bhartṛhari on Word and Consciousness
The Advaita Perspective

*S.K. Moharana**

WORD and consciousness are inextricable from each other and the grammarian as philosopher has deduced from this datum the identity of both. The whole superstructure, erected by the legend Bhartṛhari — the grammarian, stands on the foundational postulate that word in its essence is an indivisible unit and the plurality of linguistic forms and the objective phenomena which are related as denoter and denoted has only a provisional pragmatic validity. However, linguistics and the philosophy of language are relatively recent developments in the West which were discussed in Indian tradition since time immemorial. Beginning with the Vedic hymns, which are at least 3000 years old, the Indian study of language has continued in an unbroken tradition till date.[1] The goal of philosophy in India has never been rationalization alone but spiritualization, a glorious expression of spiritual life deemed to be worthy of human allegiance. The great sage Patañjali and following him the legend Bhartṛhari have found an Eternal Word which runs through each and every ephemeral

* Lecturer in Philosophy, Humanistic Studies Group, BITS, Pilani, India.

1. H. G. Coward (1980), The *Sphoṭa Theory of Language: A Philosophical Analysis*. Delhi: Motilal Banarsidass.

verbal identity. Bhartṛhari equates this Eternal Word with the Absolute Reality, *Brahman*. This is the permanent and imperishable *akṣara*. There are many theorists of language in the Indian tradition. The grammarian philosopher Bhartṛhari is of special importance. The main focus of Indian linguistics is on the relationship of word, consciousness and mind. This is true at least of Bhartṛhari which is vividly portrayed in his masterpiece, *Vākyapadīya*. The principal task of this paper is to explore whether Bhartṛhari was thoroughly an Advaitin in practice. This exploration will be undertaken on the basis of the presence of the disguised Advaitic elements and its roots in the philosophy of Bhartṛhari encoded in his wonderful thesis *Vākyapadīya*. We then attempt to explore the relationship that can be drawn between Bhartṛhari and the Advaitins, such as Śaṅkara and Maṇḍana Miśra, on the nature of word and consciousness.

Bhartṛhari, a Pre-Śaṅkara Advaitin?

Bhartṛhari was not only a grammarian but also an Advaitin. This can be inferred from the title of the first chapter *Brahma-kāṇḍa* of his masterpiece *Vākyapadīya*. The ancient commentators on the *Vākyapadīya* like Helārāja and Puṇyarāja have held that Bhartṛhari supports Advaita philosophy. Again, in modern times a study of his book has led K.A. Subramaniya Iyer to the view that Bhartṛhari was undoubtedly an Advaitin.[2] There is an external evidence of later Advaitins also who counted Bhartṛhari as a knower of *Brahman*. Maṇḍana Miśra, Pratyakṣasvarūpa and others have quoted Bhartṛhari on

2. K. A. Subramania Iyer (1969), *Bhartṛhari: A Study of the Vākyapadīya in the Light of the Ancient Commentaries*, Poona: Deccan College, pp. 230 ff. The sixth view of meaning that is given on p. 230 is Advaitic, Bhartṛhari seems to support it.

certain problems of Advaita.[3] A recent Advaitin, Raghunath Sharma, has written a commentary on the *Brahma-kāṇḍa* of the *Vākyapadīya* and treated it as a classic of Advaita philosophy.[4] Bhartṛhari's exposition of *Brahman* as *śabda* is accepted by Advaita philosophers who have maintained that the knowledge of the absolute *Brahman* is possible through the knowledge of *śabdabrahman*.[5] Bhartṛhari however has ignored the highest mode of speech (*parā-vāk*) and explained only three levels of language, i.e. *paśyantī*, *madhyamā*, and *vaikharī*.[6] *Vaikharī* is the most external and differentiated level, on which speech is uttered by the speaker and heard by the hearer. Its temporal sequence is fully developed. *Madhyamā* represents, in broad terms, the thinking level of the mind. It is the idea or series of words as conceived by the mind after hearing or before speaking out. It may be thought of as inward speech. All parts of speech that are linguistically relevant to the sentence are present here in a latent form. The innermost level is that of *paśyantī*. At this level there is no distinction between the word and the meaning and there is no temporal sequence. Bhartṛhari associates this level of language with the concept of *sphoṭa*. It represents meaning as a whole, existing in the mind of the speaker as a unity. When he utters it, he produces a sequence of different sounds so that it appears to have differentiation. The process of differentiation into sounds proceeds from the *sphoṭa* on the *paśyantī* level of language via *madhyamā* or inward thought to expressed speech on the *vaikharī* level. For the listener, the process is reversed. Although he first hears a series

3. S. L. Pandey (1983) (ed.), *Pre-Śaṅkara Advaita Philosophy*, Allahabad: Darshan Peeth, pp. 30-31.

4. Raghunath Sharma, *Vākyapadīya with the Commentary, Part I* (*Brahma-kāṇḍa*), Varanasi, 1963.

5. *Brahma-bindu Upaniṣad*, 17.

6. Gaurinath Shastri (1959), *The Philosophy of Word and Meaning*, Kolkata: Sanskrit College, pp. 68-69.

of sounds, he ultimately perceives the utterance as a unity — the same *sphoṭa* with which the speaker began. The *sphoṭa* or meaning-whole thus has two sides to it: the word-sound (*dhvani*) and the word-meaning (*artha*). Sound and meaning are two aspects residing within the unitary *sphoṭa*, which, according to Bhartṛhari, is eternal and inherent in consciousness. Meaning is thus not conveyed from the speaker to the hearer, rather, the spoken words serve only as a stimulus to reveal or uncover the meaning which was already present in the mind of the hearer. The unity of name and form, of sound and meaning on the level of the *sphoṭa* in *paśyantī* applies mainly to the Sanskrit language. However, *paśyantī* represents the subtlest manifest level of nature, and must thus be assumed to be closest to nature itself. Experience of sufficiently refined states of consciousness, i.e. direct experience of the *paśyantī* level of language, should reveal that grammar. In parallel to this view, Abhinavagupta, the main classic commentator on Bharata's *Nāṭyaśāstra*, states that it is the poetic experience of *dhvani*, the sound aspect of speech, which brings about the experience of *rasa*. Advaitins, however, have accepted his explanation and related them to their exposition of *parā-vāk*. Thus philosophy of the four-footed speech that is mentioned in the *Ṛgveda* is developed by Bhartṛhari and his school into *Śabdādvaita*. This development has made a great impact on the doctrine of *vivartavāda*. The word *vivarta* was first of all used by Bhartṛhari and was later accepted and developed by Advaitins.

Word and Consciousness in Vākyapadīya

The main ideas of Bhartṛhari are given in the first four verses of the *Brahma-kāṇḍa*. *Prima facie*, it is said that *Brahman* is One only, without a beginning and an end, and is of the nature of the word (*śabda-tattva*). The whole world comes out of the word. Secondly, the word has many powers. The effects of the word are the objects which are non-different from the powers of the word. Thirdly, time is the most fundamental power of the word. Although it is one and indivisible, many divisions are superimposed on it. The word contains all the principles of multiplicity. It portrays itself basically in three forms, i.e. experience, experiencer, and the experienced.[7] All these ideas of Bhartṛhari have shaped the later development of Advaita. For him, there is no Being endowed with Consciousness whose consciousness of himself or of others (*svaparasambodhaḥ*) is not mixed up with the word. If consciousness or awareness of all kinds is thus intertwined with the word, the question then naturally arises as to whether the two are different from each other or are identical. Traditionally two answers are prevalent. One could be that there cannot be any consciousness which has not the form of the Word. In other words, consciousness and the word are two different things though one is never without the other. The other answer could be that what is called consciousness is just this fact of being the Word. The two are identical. Bhartṛhari, it is evident from *Vākyapadīya* I.118 [126], distinctly seems to favour the latter. He keeps up that what is called awareness (*saṁjñā*) which is the fact of having the form of the Word. Consciousness in all Beings never goes beyond it, that is, it is never different from this fact of having the form of the Word. Therefore, when Bhartṛhari says that *Brahman* is *śabda-tattva*, the Word-Principle, he implies that it is Consciousness. The question then is: how does Consciousness, which is transformed into audible words, express itself externally? Or, what is the proper channel through which the Word-Principle is manifested outside? Some later writers like Nāgeśa are of the opinion that the externalization of the inner word takes

7. K.A. Subramania Iyer, *Bhartṛhari*, op. cit., pp. 98 ff.

place through different stages.[8] It is described that the subtle inner Word (*sūkṣma vāk*) becomes the knower (*jñātā*) and then in order to reveal himself, becomes the external word. To say that the subtle Word, which is no other than the Word-Principle, becomes the knower, means that it takes the form of Mind (*manas*) or Intellect (*buddhi*) and ultimately becomes the fully manifested external word. In the process described in these stages, there is mention of *vāyu* or *prāṇa* also. The Pāṇinīya Śikṣā also describes the process. It says that the Self cognizes the objects with the mind and endows it with the desire to give expression to them. The mind strikes at the bodily energy and that energy sets the breath in motion. What is to be noted in the process of the *śabda-tattva* becoming fully externalized word (*vyakta śabda*) is that various things, such as, *ātmā, buddhi* or *manas, prāṇa* or *vāyu, tejas* or *kāyāgni* and *sthāna* and *kāraṇa* (organs of articulation) are involved in it, according to the authors of the Śikṣā. Bhartṛhari also seems to be referring to the process when he says that the power of the word becomes associated with the mind, the *prāṇa* and the organs of articulation and thus becomes diversified.

Advaita Vedānta unfolds an architecture of increasingly abstract, functionally integrated faculties or levels of mind. This hierarchy ranges from gross to subtle, from highly active to settled, from concrete to abstract, and from diversified to unified. The senses constitute the grossest, most highly active, most concrete and most diversified level of the mind, followed by desire, the thinking mind, the discriminating intellect, feeling and intuition, and the individual ego. Vedāntic psychology uses the term 'mind' in two ways: It refers to the overall multilevel functioning of consciousness as well as to the specific level of thinking (apprehending and comparing)

8. Ibid., pp. 148-49.

within that overall structure. Underlying the subtlest level, that of the individual ego, and transcendental to it, is the Self, 'an abstract, silent, completely unified field of consciousness.' Each subtler level is able to observe and monitor the more expressed levels. Empirical evidence suggests that the transcendental is a field that links all individuals, parallel to Jung's concept of the collective unconscious. Pure consciousness, in contrast to the collective unconscious, can be experienced directly.[9] Within this hierarchy of the mind, *paśyantī* of Bhartṛhari represents the finest manifestation of pure consciousness, and *parā* is located in pure consciousness itself. Pure consciousness is universal and is beyond socio-cultural boundaries. Similarly the level of *parā* is also universal. Socio-cultural specification sets in, once that universal level is left and individual language begins on the level of *paśyantī*.

It may however be observed that language is universal only on the level of pure consciousness. Traditionally, that level of consciousness, because it is beyond activity, is regarded of little use to an active life. Pure consciousness, being pure, contentless, can only be described in subjective, individual terms of expressed language. Advaita psychology tackles this problem by not only describing the hierarchy of the mind, but also proposes higher stages of human development, characterized by the simultaneous experience of pure consciousness together with waking or dreaming or sleeping states. Such a state of functioning is called cosmic consciousness. Such a cosmic consciousness can also be traced back to the Vedic theory of music, *Gandharvaveda*.

9. C.N. Alexander (1990), "Growth of Higher Stages of Consciousness: Maharishi's Vedic Psychology of Human Development", in C.N. Alexander and E.J. Langer (eds.), *Higher Stages of Human Development. Perspectives on Human Growth*, Oxford: Oxford University Press.

Gandharvaveda proposes that the primordial sound, *nāda*, is at the basis of all creation, including consciousness, and that the dancer's/actor's body starts moving in the rhythms and movements of nature when all cells of his/her body begin to resonate with that primordial sound. Thus sound is directly transformed into movement of the body. It could well be argued — as a working hypothesis for further studies — that if the composer composes (or the choreographer choregraphs, or the dancer dances or the actor acts) in a state of cosmic consciousness, the result (the composition, choreography, dancing or acting activity) will be fuelled by impulses emanating directly from the universal level of pure consciousness, unmediated by culture or history. Such impulses will then reach the spectator and enable his mind to reach the same underlying, universal level of consciousness from which the aesthetic impulses originated. Creative activity will be culturally and historically mediated when such activity does not originate from cosmic consciousness characterized by a simultaneity of pure consciousness and activity, but if it originates from the ordinary waking state of consciousness which has no systematic, only ephemeral, coincidental experience of pure, or cosmic consciousness.

Maṇḍana Miśra and Bhartṛhari

Maṇḍana introduces *Śabdādvaita* in the course of his interpretation of the significance of the word *akṣaram* contained in the opening verse of his *Brahma-Siddhi*. Though Maṇḍana expounds his views on Advaita mainly depending on the Upaniṣads, the *Brahma-Sūtras*, and the *Bhagavad-Gītā* without owing allegiance to anyone, one can notice the influence of Bhartṛhari, on Maṇḍana in the exposition of *Śabdādvaita* in the *Brahma-Siddhi*. However, he refers to Bhartṛhari's *Vākyapadīya* only in one place in the whole of the *Brahma-Siddhi.*[10] Maṇḍana argues for *Śabdādvaita* on the basis of scriptural authority and also by means of reasoning.

Maṇḍana quotes the *Kārikās* of *Vākyapadīya* I, 82-4, 85-7, 89-91 in his *Sphoṭa-Siddhi. Sphoṭa-Siddhi* happens to be the most eloquent rejoinder to all the criticisms hurled by no less a dialectician than Kumārila-Bhaṭṭa. The refreshing features of Maṇḍana's exposition are, firstly, its purely logical approach and, secondly, its rigorous analysis of the implications of the alternative hypothesis propounded by Kumārila. Kumārila was the most formidable critic of the theory of *sphoṭa,* i.e. a simple unanalysable sentence or word (*śabda*). Later writers have only expounded Kumārila's arguments and no substantial addition has been made.

Patañjali puts the question in the beginning of his *Mahābhāṣya*: What is a word? To a superficial observer the question seems a superfluity. Patañjali defines word as that which has a meaning. But Kumārila puts forward serious objections against this position. Maṇḍana, however, regards this objection of Kumārila as an instance of frivolous sophistry. The question has been definitely raised to spot out the word-element from a complex setting. For Maṇḍana, the merit of the *sphoṭa* theory lies in the fact that it does not seek to twist the verdict of common sense. It is not liable to dispute that we all feel that the word conveys a meaning and is one and the same in spite of this different incidence. This felt unity, unless it is dubbed an illusion, presupposes the unity of the object. The grammarian-philosopher justifiably lays stress upon this fundamental character of our knowledge. He shows that

10. Edited with introduction and Śaṅkhapāṇi's commentary by S. Kuppuswami Sastri, Madras Government Oriental Manuscripts Series, no. 4, 1937.

the philosophers of other schools have failed to account for the felt unity of the word and that their philosophical exercises are not calculated to carry conviction to an unsophisticated and unbiased student of philosophy in spite of the wealth of ingenuity displayed by them.

Śaṅkara and Bhartṛhari

According to Śaṅkara and his followers, *Brahman* appears as the objective world while Bhartṛhari adumbrates that the Word becomes the cosmos. It is therefore worth reckoning that the grammarian believes in the reality of every unit in creation. Though there is a difference and disparity among the units, the grammarian calls our attention to discover the reality in them which in the ultimate analysis is 'an uncompromising unity.' Bhartṛhari is well aware of the position of the Vedāntin who advocates the unreality of the subject, the object and the modal consciousness, but he still believes in the reality of the immanence of the Absolute which, according to the Vedic traditions he has inherited, is Word.[11] One need not, therefore, be carried away to form an impression that Bhartṛhari's monism is the same as that of Śaṅkara on the ground that, while describing the cosmic evolution, he uses the expression *vivartate* which means that the evolutes are all formal transformations (unrealities) and should not be understood in terms of absolute reality.

Bhartṛhari is the forerunner of the doctrine of reflexion (*ābhāsavāda*) sponsored by the Tṛka writers of Kashmir according to whom the cosmic process is neither one of *vivarta* nor of *pariṇāma.* The Tṛka philosophers opine that the Supreme Reality is *prakāśa* or *caitanya,* i.e. Illumining Consciousness which embraces all that fall within the ken of our experience.

11. *Vākyapadīya*, III. 50, Deccan College Monograph Series.

Anything that we call external is a mere reflexion on Consciousness as on a mirror. The image is as much real as the original of which it is the reflexion.[12] The cosmic world is as much real as Consciousness. The manifestation of the cosmic order is traced to the unfettered and spontaneous power of Consciousness. This paramount power of Consciousness does not seek the aid of any other agency for the initiation of the cosmic process. The universe is not, according to them, an appearance conjured up into existence by the operation of *avidyā*. On the contrary, the Tṛka writers assert that the universe is to be understood as an expression of the Supreme Power of Consciousness and, consequently, they proclaim its spiritual character. In the last resort the cosmos lapses into the Supreme Power which is never recanted but remains even after the world is withdrawn into it.

However, as we have already stated, *śabda* to the grammarian stands for 'consciousness' and the Absolute Word is Absolute Consciousness. Every evolute of the Absolute Word on the empirical plane is an expression of Pure or Absolute Consciousness. To Bhartṛhari, the evolutes are as real as the genesis of evolution. The genesis is the Absolute Word in which lie all Powers including Time or *kāla* completely identified with the locus. The status accorded to *kāla-śakti* and to other Powers by Bhartṛhari can hardly be explained with fidelity to him in case any attempt is made to read Śaṅkara's monism in the doctrine of Verbal monism. *Kāla-śakti*, to Bhartṛhari is ultimately real and it has the same ontological status as the Eternal Verbum. But it is known to us that Śaṅkara does not accept the ultimate reality of any power co-existing with the Absolute. Though Śaṅkara speaks of the powers of the Absolute, yet he never admits that they are possessed of a

12. *Tantrāloka*, I.66, the Kashmir Series of Text and Studies.

co-ordinate reality. It needs to be mentioned that the Absolute, to Bhartṛhari, is identified with the *kāla-śakti* and the affirmation of this Power does not land him in any difficult situation and he can still claim that he is out-and-out an upholder of unqualified monism.

To conclude, the Grammarian is a champion of Verbal monism which enunciates the illusory appearance of the cosmic world — a position very much similar to what we find in the system of Śaṅkara. Bhartṛhari appears to be an uncompromising monist and exhibits his unflinching faith in the age-old monistic Vedic traditions, yet he has given a unique shape to his monistic ideas by declaring the dynamic character of the Supreme Reality which in his language is the Absolute Word or the Absolute Consciousness.

9

Language and Mind in Grammatical Tradition

As Gleaned from Patañjali and Bhartṛhari

*M. Srimannarayana Murti**

IT is nothing but truism that through the oral transmission of the language the members of different speech communities describe objects they observe and convey their intentions effectively and elegantly. The oral presentation which is a physical manifestation of muscular effort synchronizes with the psychic processes of the mind proportionately so as to make the communication relevant and meaningful, to provide harmonious living in the society. The Upaniṣadic passage: *yato vāco nivartante aprāpya manasā saha* (*Taittirīya Upaniṣad*, 2.9), transpires that the language is the activity of the *manas*. For example, Śaṅkara's statement: *vākyārthavicāṇādhyavasānanirvṛttā hi brahmāvagatiḥ,*[1] localizes the principle with regard to the investigation of its target, namely the *Brahman*. The analysis of the language is the analysis of the world which is the accepted mode of metaphysical investigation. Thus the linguistic investigation into the language and mind proceeds

---

* Ex. Director, Oriental Research Institute, Sri Venkateswara University, Tirupati, India.

1. *Brahmasūtrabhāṣya*, 1.1.2.

by blending harmoniously the physical and metaphysical perceptions. It can be demonstrated by introspecting with the observations of āyurvedic physicians on *manas, ātman* and *hṛdaya,* in relation to sensory perceptions, knowledge and consciousness.

I

In the *Bhela Saṁhitā,* Bhela — the contemporary of Agniveśa and the disciple of Punarvasu ātreya — recognizes that the *manas* is of two types, viz. *buddhi* and *citta.* The *buddhi* is the physiological component of the *manas* lying between the palate and the top of the head, which is comparable to the empirical mind or the brain in modern physiology and medicine. This *buddhi* is the cognizer of the taste, etc. through the sensory organs.[2] This view is also upheld by Caraka in his *Caraka Saṁhitā.*[3] This *manas* can be said to be centrally located in the head or elsewhere wherever the sensory organ is located, as the mind has to get into contact with the sensory organs for production of cognitive knowledge. Therefore Caraka opines that this *manas* can be held as located all over the body,[4] as

---

2. *śirastālvādigataṁ sarvendriyaparam manaḥ* ।
tatrasthaṁ taddhi viṣayān indriyāṇām rasādikam ॥
samastān vijānāti trīn bhāvāṁś ca niyacchati ।
tan manaḥ prabhavaṁ cāpi sarvendriyamayaṁ balam ॥
kāraṇam sarvabuddhīnāṁ cittaṁ hṛdayasaṁśritam ।
kriyānāṁ cetaresāṁ ca cittaṁ sarvatra kāraṇam ॥
— *Bhela-Saṁhitā, Cikitsāsthāna,* 8

3. *prāṇāḥ prāṇabhṛtām yatra śritāḥ sarvendriyāṇi ca* ।
yad uttamāṅgam aṅgānām śiras tad abhidhīyate ॥
— *Caraka-Saṁhitā, Sūtrasthāna,* 17.12

śirasi indriyāṇi, indriyaprāṇavāhāni ca śrotāṁsi sūryam iva gabhastayaḥ saṁśritāni, — *Caraka-Saṁhitā, Siddhisthāna,* 9.4

4. *tadvad atīndriyāṇāṁ punaḥ satvādīnāṁ kevalaṁ* ।
cetanāvaccharīramayānabhūtam adhiṣṭhānabhūtaṁ ca ॥
— *Caraka-Saṁhitā, Vimānasthāna,* 5.7

for example the cognition of touch is felt wherever the skin is spread. The three *doṣas*, namely *vāta, pitta* and *kapha* cause diseases in the body.[5] The *manas* in the head gets diseases affecting intelligence (*medhas*), remembrance (*smṛti*) and cognition (*jñāna*) and necessary medicaments are prescribed in curative treatment.[6] For example, Vāgbhaṭa in his *Aṣṭāṅgasaṁgraha* mentions that by administering errhine nasal drops (*pratimarśanasya*) like *aṇutaila* the head becomes light and the mind becomes tranquil.[7] The other *manas* which is called *citta* is a transcendental mind located in the *hṛdaya* and controls all *buddhis*, i.e. the cognitions produced by the contacts of the sensory organs with the respective objects of cognition and emotions.[8]

To synchronize in logic the *hṛdaya* is also recognized as of two types, viz. physiological (*dṛśya-hṛdaya*) or empirical, and transcendental (*indriyātīta-hṛdaya*) or metaphysical. The empirical *hṛdaya* is exactly equivalent to the heart in the modern physiology, and the centre and channel for supply of blood through arteries.[9] The variation of heart beat (*hṛdaya-kampa*) is

5. *tatra trayas tu śarīradoṣā vātapittaślēṣmānas te śarīraṁ dūṣayanti,*
— *Caraka-Saṁhitā, Śārirasthāna*, 14, p. 1977

6. A medicament called *Aindrarasāyana* is prescribed for these defects:

cf. *medhāsmṛtijñānaharaś ca rogāḥ śāmyanty anenātibalāś ca vātāḥ* ।
— *Caraka-Saṁhitā, Cikitsāsthāna*, 1.6, p. 2310

7. *prātar datte bhuktavataś cānte śroto viśuddhiḥ śirolāghavaṁ manaḥ prasādaś ca bhavati* ।
— *Aṣṭāṅgasaṁgraha*, 29

8. *sattvādidhāma hṛdayatanauḥ koṣṭamadhyagam,*
— *Aṣṭāṅgahṛdaya, Śarīra*, 4

tatas tam puruṣaṁ yathoktābhyām snehasvedābhyāṁ yathārham upapādayet, taṁ ced asminnantare kaścin mānasaḥ śārīro vā vyādhiḥ kaścit tīvrataraḥ sahasābhyagacchet, tam eva tāvad asyopāvarttayituṁ yateta ।
— *Caraka-Saṁhitā, Sūtrasthāna*, 15.8, p. 656

9. *tatra prāṇavāhānām śrotasāṁ hṛdayaṁ mūlam, mahāśrotaś ca* ।
— *Caraka-Saṁhita, Vimānasthāna*, 5.3, p. 1491.

found in various diseases and necessary medicaments are prescribed in therapeutics.[10] The treatment is however mixed up with religion.[11] The metaphysical *hṛdaya* is identified with *ātman* and its existence is established by inferential logic.[12] This is the seat of consciousness and all types of cognitions.[13] Further the *ātman is* eternal[14] and is different from the body.[15]

II

Tradition ascribes the identity of Caraka with Patañjali, the

---

10. (i) *sa pāṇḍuroga ity uktas tasya liṅgaṁ bhaviṣyataḥ* ।
hṛdayaspandanaṁ raukṣaṁ svedābhāvaḥ śramas tathā ॥
— *Caraka-Saṁhitā, Cikitsāsthāna*, 16, 4, p. 2975

(ii) *muktāvalībhiḥ śitābhiḥ śītalaira bhājanair api* ।
jalārdrair jalajair hastaiḥ svidyate hṛdayaṁ spṛset ॥
— *Caraka-Saṁhitā, Sūtrasthāna*, 14, 4, p. 626

11. *tatas taṁ puruṣaṁ snehasvedopapannam anupahatamānasam abhisamīkṣya sukhoṣitaṁ prajīrṇabhaktaṁ śiraḥsnātam anuliptagātram sragviṇam anupahatavastrasaṁvītam devatāgnidvijaguruvṛddhavaidyān arccitavantam iṣṭe nakṣatre tithikaraṇamuhūrte ca kārayitvā brāhmaṇān svastivācanaṁ prayuktābhir āśībhir abhimantritāṁ madhumadhukasaindhava-phāṇitopahitām madanaphalakaṣāyamātrāṁ pāyayet* ।
— *Caraka-Saṁhitā, Sūtrasthāna*, 15, 8, pp. 656-57

12. *tattadatīndriyānām punaḥ sattvādināṁ kevalaṁ cetanāvaccharīram ayanabhūtam adhiṣṭhānabhūtam ca* ।
— *Caraka-Saṁhitā, Vimānasthāna*, 5, 3, p. 1491

13. *bhedāt kāryendriyārthānāṁ bāhyo vai buddhayaḥ smṛtāḥ* ।
ātmendriyamano 'rthānām ekaikasannikarṣajāḥ ॥
— *Caraka-Saṁhitā, Śārīrasthāna*, 1, 10, p. 1793

14. *ādir nastyātmanaḥ kṣetrapāramparyamanādikam* ।
atas tayor anāditvāt kiṁ pūrvam iti nocyate ॥
— *Caraka-Saṁhitā, Śarīrasthāna*, 1, 25, p. 1829

15. *parihāro nāma tasyaiva doṣavacanasya parihāraṇaṁ* ।
yathā-nityam ātmani śarīrasthe jīvaliṅgāny upalabhyante tasyāpagamān nopalabhyante tasmād anyaḥ śarīrād ātma nityaś ca ॥
— *Caraka-Saṁhitā, Vimānasthāna*, 8, 60, p. 1645

author of the *Mahābhāṣya* and the author of the *Pātañjalayoga-Sūtra.*[16] The *Mahābhāṣya* is a commentary on the *Aṣṭādhyāyī* of Pāṇini and on the gloss called *Vārtikā* of Kātyāyana. The *sūtra* text of Pāṇini became popular as the *Aṣṭādhyāyī,* without its qualificant (*viśeṣya*) specifying the name of the text, and the commentary on it became popular as the *Mahābhāṣya,* without its qualifier (*viśeṣaṇa*) specifying the subject to which it belongs. Perhaps it is because of their universal adaptability and unfailing source of metaphysical inquiry of the known through language,[17] as no cognition can arise in the world without being subsumed in the language.[18]

The opening sentence (*upakrama*) of the *Mahābhāṣya* itself declaims the orientation of the work:

atha śabdānuśāsanam I *athetyayam śabdo 'dhikārārthaḥ prayujyate . . . śabdānuśāsanam śāstram adhikṛtam veditavyam* I

16. Vijñānabhikṣu says in his *Yogabhāṣyavārttika*:
yogena cittaṁ padena vācāṁ malaṁ śarīrasya vaidyakena I
yo 'pākarot taṁ pravaraṁ munīnāṁ patañjalim prāñjalir ānato 'smi II
Nāgeśa and many others subscribe to this tradition.

17 Helarāja, the renowned commentator of Bhartṛhari, observes that the Vyākaraṇa 'linguistics' was a common science of language applicable to all the recensions of the Vedas and also to the philosophical schools; cf. *sarvapārṣadam hīdam śāstram iti, śabdārtho 'rtha iti vā padārthavyavastheyam, HP,* III. *Jāti*.19, p. 32. So he shows in his commentary all the philosophical theories discussed in different schools and draws special attention to the views held by the grammarians; cf. *itthaṁ ca darśanāntaropanyāsapūrvakam svadarśane jātipadārthavyavasthām upapādya vyavahāre bhinnāyā tv ādijāter ryathāsambhavaṁ svagate dharmaś carcyate, HP,* III. *Jāti,* 41, p. 48.

18. Therefore Bhartṛhari rightly observes that there cannot be any cognition of knowledge without being associated with language;

na so 'sti pratyayo loke yaḥ śabdānugamād ṛte I
anuviddham iva jñānam sarvaṁ śabdena bhāsate II
— *VP,* I.115

keṣām śabdānām । *laukikānām vaidikānām ca, tatra laukikās tāvat* । *gaur aśvaḥ puruṣo hastī śakunir mṛgo brāhmaṇa iti* । *vaidikāḥ khav api* । *saṁ no devīr abhiṣṭaye* (*AV*, 1.6.1) । *iṣe tvorje tvā* (*VS*, 1.1, *TS*, 1.1.1) । *agnim īḷe purohitam* (*RV*, 1.1.1) । *agna āyāhi vītaye* (*SV*, 1.1.1) *iti* । *atha gaur ity atra kaḥ śabdaḥ . . . yenoccāritena śāsanālāṅgūlakakudakhuraviṣāninām sampratyayo bhavati sa śabdaḥ* । *athavā pratītapadārthako loke dhvaniḥ śabda ity ucyate* । *tad yathā* । *śabdaṁ kuru* । *mā śabdaṁ kārṣīḥ* । *śabdakāryayam māṇavaka iti* । *dhvaniṁ kurvann evam ucyate* । *tasmād dhvaniḥ śabdaḥ* । *MB*, 1.1.1, p. 1.

The science of language is called *śabadānuśāsana*. It means, as Nāgeśa paraphrases, this science indicates the correct words differentiating from the corrupt ones.[19] A language in its physical structure is composed of independent speech sounds produced by different efforts and contacts in the buccal cavity. An acoustic representation cannot reasonably have intrinsic correctness or corruptness both from the points of view of the speaker and the listener. The position of the tongue in the oral cavity either because of incapacity caused by physical deformity or indolence makes the difference in the production of sounds. The meaning that is attached to it makes a difference. As Bhartṛhari observes, *aśva* is correct if a horse is intended to be conveyed and *aśva* becomes corrupt as the latter is correct in the sense of a pauper, i.e. a person who is bereft of wealth.[20] Therefore the intention of the speaker should synchronize with the physical effort in acoustics to bring out a correspondence with the empirical mind which controls the

19. *asādhuśabdebhyaḥ sādhavaḥ śabdāḥ jñāpyante iti śabdānuśāsanam.*

20. *aśvagoṇyādayaḥ śabdāḥ sādhavo viṣayāntare* ।
nimittabhedāt sarvatra sādhutvaṁ ca vyavastitam ॥
— *VP*, I.176

See also: M. Srimannarayana Murti, "Intention of the Speaker According to Grammarians", *S.V.U. Oriental Journal*, 30, pp. 21 ff.

articulatory processes with the transcendental mind which governs the shape of the psychological processes of the speaker as well as the listener. It means that the acoustic corruption cannot cause damage to the language by itself until it fails to synchronize with the psychic processes. Combining both the features Patañjali offers the definition of 'word.' In its transcendental function of the *manas*, a word like *go* is that which produces in the speaker or the listener the cognition of a substance which is determined by a dewlap, a tail, a hump, hoof, horn, etc.[21] In its empirical function of the *manas*, which controls the articulatory system, a word like *go* is a sequence of sounds which is capable of conveying some significant sense. The word *śabda* can also be used for the indistinct sounds made also by human beings implied in the sentences like *śabdam kuru* 'make noise,' *na śabdam kārṣīḥ* 'don't make noise,' *śabdakāryayam māṇavakaḥ* 'this boy is habituated to make noise,' which are similar to the sounds produced by beating a drum with a stick without any fixed meaning.[22]

To establish continuity and consistency between the operations of empirical and transcendental minds, Patañjali invokes the first *vārttika* of Kātyāyana, namely *siddhe śabdārthasambandhe lokato 'rthaprayukte śabdaprayoge* (Vt. 1)[23] which ordains eternality of the word, its sense and the relation between them, so that the word when heard can bring home the meaning and vice versa through the operation of their natural mutual relation. Of course, Patañjali sharply takes exception that the grammar of Pāṇini can also hold water if

21. *kas tarhi śabdaḥ yenoccāritena sāsnālāṅgūlakakudakhuraviṣāṇinārh sampratyayo bhavati sa śabdaḥ*, — *MB*, 1.1.1, p. 1.

22. *athavā pratītapadārthako loke dhvaniḥ ity ucyate* । *tada yathā śabdaṁ kuru* । *mā śabdaṁ kārṣiḥ* । *śabdakāryayaṁ māṇavaka iti* । *dhvaniṁ kurvan evam ucyate* । *tasmād dhvaniḥ śabdaḥ*, — *MB*, 1.1.1, p. 1.

23. *MB*, 1.1.1, p. 6.

the conventionality is held for the word, its meaning and their relationship.[24] The naturalism (*svābhāvika*) and conventionalism (*kārya*) is another issue which bears no significance in the operation of the *manas*.

Patañjali discusses the operation of the *manas* and *indriyas* while commenting on Pāṇini's rule *parokṣe liṭ*, [Pāṇ. 3.2.115]. The speech community describes with the language the facts it observes and communicates its intentions. The speakers describe in sentences with a finite verb in different tense terminations and the listeners understand the same fact either by perception or by recollection. The continuum of past, present and future are synchronized with temporal states of the speakers or listeners. It can be asked when an action is completed and ceases to exist, how a speaker can describe it and designate it. Bhartṛhari justifies that it is possible because of recollection of the action which he perceived or experienced earlier in the present state.[25] The intentions are communicated by the finite verbs in modal terminations in the form of wish, desire, caution, request or command to be executed by the listeners. In both tenses and modal forms the verbal root (*dhātu*) denotes action (*kriyā*).[26] Of the tenses, perfect is used when the event is related to the past and when the speaker himself is not a direct witness. It is ordained by Pāṇini's rule *parokṣe liṭ* (3.2.115). While commenting on the word *parokṣa*

24. *tatra tva eṣa nirṇayo yadya eva nityo 'thāpi kārya ubhayathāpi lakṣaṇaṁ pravartyam iti* I — *MB*, 1.1.1, p. 1.

25. *kāle nidhāya svam rūpam prajñayā yan nigṛhyate* I
bhāvās tato nivartante tatra saṅkrāntaśaktayaḥ II
— *VP*, III. *Kāla*, 39, p. 54

See also: M. Srimannarayana Murti, "Time According to Bhartṛhari", *Vishveshvaranand Indological Journal*, XIX.i-ii, 1981, pp. 140-146.

26. *kaḥ punaḥ dhātvarthaḥ* I *kriyā* I — *MB*, 3.2.115, p. 120.

(< *para+akṣa*) in the rule, Patañjali discusses about the operation of mind and sensory organs in perception:

> *parokṣa itya ucyate* | *kimparokṣam nāma param akṣṇaḥ parokṣam* | *akṣi punaḥ kiṁ* | *aśnoter ayam auṇādikaḥ karaṇasādhanaḥ sipratyayaḥ* | *aśnute 'nenety akṣi* | *yady evaṁ parokṣam iti prāpnoti naiṣa doṣaḥ . . . athavā nipātanād eva siddham parokṣe laḍ iti . . . kaṭhaṁjātīyakam punaḥ parokṣam nāma* | *kēcit tāvad āhur varṣaśatavṛttaṁ parokṣam iti* | *apara āhuḥ kaṭāntaritaṁ parokṣam iti* | *apara ahur dvyahavṛttam tṛyahavṛttaṁ ceti* | *sarvathottamo na siddhyati* | *suptamattayor uttama iti vaktavyam* | *supto 'haṁ kila vilalāpa* | *mattō 'haṁ kila vilalāpa . . . athavā bhavati vai kascij jāgrad api vartamānakālaṁ nopalabhate* |
>
> *tad yathā* | *vaiyākaraṇānāṁ śākaṭāyano rathamārga āsīnaḥ śakaṭasārthaṁ yāntam nopalebhe* | *kiṁ punaḥ kāraṇaṁ jāgrad api vartamānakālam napalabhate* | *manasā saṁyuktānindriyāṇy upalabdhau kāraṇāni bhavanti manaso 'sānniddhyāt* |
>
> — *MB*, 3.2.115, p. 120.

The word *akṣi* is derived by adding the *uṇādi*-suffix *-ṣi* to the root *aś* 'to reach' in the sense that "by this the *manas* reaches the object."[27] *Akṣi* stands not only for the eye but also all the five sensory organs of smell, taste, touch, colour and sound. *Pratyakṣa* is the cognition obtained through the contact of the mind with the sensory organs and in its turn with the object of perception. The tenses excluding perfect are used to express the cognition of the speakers obtained by perception. The perfect tense is used when the speaker does not have direct contact of his sensory organ with the object of knowledge.

The word *parokṣa* is irregular in formation; it is expected to be *parākṣa* to be regular in analogy with *pratyakṣa* (>*prati* + *akṣa*).

27. *akṣi punaḥ kiṁ* | *aśnoteḥ ayam auṇādikaḥ karaṇasādhanaḥ sipratyayaḥ. aśnute 'nena ity akṣi* | — *MB*, 3.2.115, p. 120.

Therefore Patañjali validates the formation by the usage of Pāṇini himself.[28] Different connotations of actions without involving the contact of the sensory organ with the object in temporal sequence are ascribed to the word *parokṣa* by different interpreters. (1) Some opine that *parokṣa* denotes that which is related to the remote past; say one hundred years, where the speaker cannot have any chance of connecting his sensory organ with the object. It is called historical past. (2) Others say *parokṣa* refers to action which is related to two days or three days ago, where the speaker might not have had his sensory organ in contact with the object. (3) Some say *parokṣa* refers to action which has taken place behind a curtain of straw, where the speaker failed to have his sensory organ get contact with the hidden object. (4) Still some others say *parokṣa* refers to the action where the speaker ignores to take cognizance of the object as in the example: *vaiyākaraṇānāmaṁ śākaṭāyano rathamārgāsīnaḥ śakaṭasardhaṁ yāntaṁ nopalebhe.* Śākaṭāyana, among the grammarians, sitting on the transport highway has failed to cognize a train of carts which was passing before him. It is because he was so engrossed that his mind did not

28. The word *parokṣa* is an irregular *avyayībāva-samāsa* (< *akṣṇaḥ param*), which is justified on the strength of the sanction of the suffix added to the compound (*samāsānta-pratyaya*) *tac* by the *gaṇa-sūtra*: *pratiparasamanubhyo 'kṣṇaḥ* under the rule: *avyayībhāve śaratprabhṛtibhyah*, 5.4.107, *pratiparasamanubhyo 'kṣṇaḥ* (Gaṇa 148). *yasyeti ca* (6.4.148), *pratyakṣam*. — *Siddhāntakaumudī*, 5.4.107

    The change of *para* into *paro* is also irregular which is validated as: *parokṣa ity ucyate kiṁ parokṣam nāma* । *param akṣṇaḥ parokṣam. . . kaṭhaṁ jātīyakaṁ punaḥ parokṣaṁ nāma* । *kecit atāvad āhur varṣaśatavṛttam parokṣama iti* । *apara āhuḥ kaṭāntaritaṁ parokṣam iti* । *apara āhur dvyahavṛttaṁ tryahavṛttaṁ ceti . . . athavā bhavati vai kaścij jāgrad api vartamānakālaṁ nopalabhate* । *tadyathā* । *vaiyākaraṇānām śākaṭāyano rathamārga āsinaḥ śakaṭasārthaṁ yāntaṁ nopalebhe* । *manasā saṁyuktānīndriyāṇy upalabdhau kāraṇāni bhavanti manaso 'sannidhyāt* । — *MB*, 3.2.115, pp. 119-20.

work to come into contact with the multitude of carts.

Following suit Bhartṛhari theorizes the functionality of time as a linguistic category. Linguistically time is defined as the action itself.[29] All the activities that took place before today are non-today and those that will take place after today are non-today future. The present time will not cover any of the activities that happened yesterday and that will happen tomorrow. Thus in the time scale the divisions are as follows[30]:

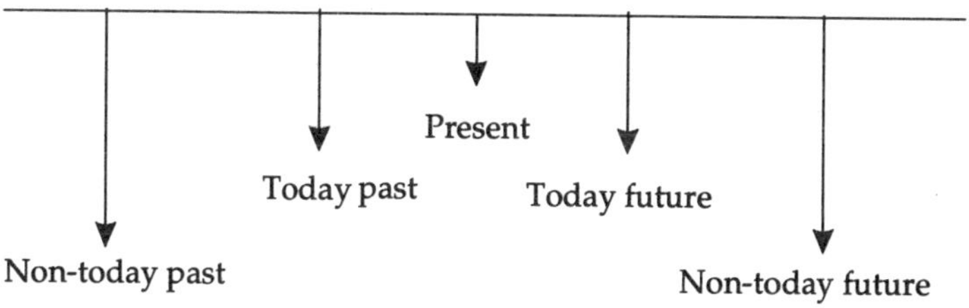

Hence the time divisions are communicated, according to the grammarians, through the tense forms based on the notion of today and non-today. Therefore perfect tense forms can be used in the non-today past unless otherwise the speaker fails to have his mind connected with the object which is in reach of his sensory organs.

III

Patañjali's theory of *ātman* in relation to *manas* can also be obtained by reading together his statements under the rules *karmavat karmaṇā tulyakriyāḥ* (3.1.87) and *parokṣe liṭ* (3.2.115). Examine the following perfect tense forms in the sentences: *supto 'haṁ kila vilalāpa* 'being in sleep I should have wept,' *matto*

---

29. *kriyāntaraparicchedapravṛttā yā kriyām prati* |
nirjñātaparimāṇā sā kāla ity abhidhīyute ||
— *VP*, III. *kāla*, 77

30. M. Srimannarayana Murti, "Divisions of Time according to Indian Grammarians," *The Adyar Library Bulletin*, 46, 1982, p. 21.

'haṁ kila vilalāpa 'being in frenzy I should have wept,' *supto nva 'haṁ vilalāpa,* 'being in sleep I indeed should have wept,' *matto nva 'haṁ kila vilalāpa,* 'being in frenzy I indeed should have wept.'[31] In the dream state or in delirium state the sensory organs do not function properly and in such cases these statements with the perfect tense cannot be justified. Where is the *manas* which caused grief in the dream state or in delirium? The solution is possible only by drawing a difference between *manas* and *ātman*. Patañjali refers to the duality of the heart as empirical and transcendental in the commentary on the rule 3.1.87: *karmavat karmaṇā tulyakriyāḥ,* while justifying the usages *hanty ātmānam ātma* and *ātmanā hanyata ātma.*[32] The dichotomy of the *ātmā* into *antarātmā* and *śarīrātmā* can be resolved by comparing with the classification of *hṛdaya* in the *Caraka-Saṁhitā*. The sentence *hanty ātmānaṁ ātma* 'the heart destroys the heart' is substantiated by admitting two hearts namely *antarātmā* 'the transcentendal heart' and *śarīrātmā* 'the empirical heart,' which in this present context is to be taken as empirical mind. This has been supported in the *Pātañjala-Yoga-Sūtra*: *mūrdhajyotiṣi siddhadarśanam* (3.31) and *hṛdaye cittasaṁvit* (3.33). The *antarātmā* is nothing but the heart which is the absolute consciousness *cit* and the seat of everlasting happiness, what is enshrined in the *Śvetaśvātaropaniṣad* and *Mahānārāyaṇopaniṣad* of the *Taittirīya-Yajurveda* recension.[33]

---

31. *suptamattayor uttama iti vaktavyam* | *supto 'haṁ kila vilalāpa* | *matto 'ham kila vilalāpa* | *supto nv ahaṁ kila vilalāpa* | *mattonv ahaṁ kila vilalāpa* | — *MB*, 3.2.115, p. 120

32. *hantyātmānaṁ ātma* | *ātmanā hanyata ātmeti* | *kaḥ punar ātmānaṁ hanti ko vātmanā hanyate* | *dvāv ātmānau antarātmā śarīrātmā ca* | *antarātmā tatkarma karoti yena śarīrātmā sukhaduḥkhe anubhavati* | *śarīrātmā tata karma karoti yenāntarātmā sukhaduḥkhe anubhavati* | — *MB*, III.1.87, p. 68

33. *eṣa devo viśvakarmā mahātmā sadā janānāṁ hṛdaye sanniviṣṭaḥ* | *hṛdā manīṣā manasābhiklpto ya etad vidur amṛtās te bhavanti* || — *Śvetāśvātaropaniṣad*, 3.17 →

Here to reconcile the identity between *śarīrātmā* and *manas* a clue may profitably be taken from the sayings of Bhagavān Śrī Ramaṇa Maharṣi of Tiruvannamalai in the following verse in which he epitomizes his philosophy of self-inquiry:

hṛdayakuharamadhye kevalaṁ brahmamātram ।
hy ahamaham iti sākṣād ātmarūpena bhāti ॥

hṛdi viśa manasā cinvatā majjatā vā ।
pavanacalanarodhād ātmaniṣṭho bhava tvam ॥[34]

The *antarātman* is nothing but the heart which is the absolute consciousness *cit* and the seat of everlasting happiness. This transcendental heart is located in the cavity situated on the right side of the chest[35] where one would show by putting his hand while referring to himself by the word 'I' in physical demonstration. Like a permanent magnet, it effulges with consciousness. From this transcendental heart passes a beam of consciousness to the empirical mind[36] and activates it as a temporary magnet to get connected to the sensory organs. The sensory organs in their turn get activated only when the *manas* gets into contact with them. When the sensory organ is stretched to the physical object, the consciousness of the sense

---

→ and also:
padmakośapratīkāśaṁ hṛdayaṁ cāpyadhomukham ।
adhoniṣṭyā vitastyānte nābhyām upari tiṣṭhati ।
jvālamālākulaṁ bhāti viśvasyāyatanaṁ mahat ॥
— *Mahānārāyaṇopaniṣad*, 14.2-3

34. *Śrīramaṇagranthamāla* (Telugu version), Sri Ramanashramam, Tiruvannamalai, 1971, p. 76.

35. *hṛdaye cittasaṁvit* । *yad idam asmin brahmapure daharaṁ puṇḍarīkam veśma tatra vijñānaṁ tasmin saṁyamāc cittasaṁvit.*
— *Vyāsabhāṣya* on *YS*, 3.33

36. *śiraḥ kapāle 'ntaś cidraṁ prabhāśvaram jyotiṣ tatra saṁyamaṁ kṛtvā siddhānāṁ dyāvāpṛthivyor antarālacāriṇāṁ darśanam* ।
— *Vyāsabhāṣya* on *YS*, 3.31

organ envelops the object. The *jñāna* requires support of an inanimate object for its manifestation as it cannot be cognized by itself. Through the operation of the *śarīrātman* one would experience pain or pleasure. When language is operated upon there arises a beam of *cit* called *sphoṭa* in the mind of the speaker and *pratibhā* when it flashes in the mind of the listener. If the beam of *cit* in the *manas* is withdrawn and transferred to the *antarātman,* the language and the mind get destroyed. Therefore Patañjali's *vāgyoga*[37] lies in uniting the consciousness located in the *manas* to the full effulgent transcendental heart. In that state the transcendental heart destroys the empirical heart. This is the significance of the sentence: *hanti ātmānam ātma.* The *manas* along with language is the instrument for the destruction of its own self (*ātmanā hanyata ātma*). Bhagavān Śrī Ramaṇa Maharṣi has mystically echoed this linguistic theory of Patañjali in his revelations.

IV

Taking a clue from the *Mahābhāṣya,* Bhartṛhari consolidated his theory of *Bauddhapadārtha* as the basis of understanding *sphoṭa* — the meaning bearer, and *pratibhā* — the meaning of the sentence or the word. Against the conventional theories of sentence called the *anvitābhidhāna-vāda*[38] and the *abhihitānvaya-*

37. M. Srimannarayana Murti, "Vāgyoga of the Grammarian," *S.V.U Oriental Journal,* 39 (1966), pp. 61-74.

38. Consolidating all the views expressed by different philosophers of language, Bhartṛhari observes that the whole discussion can be structured into eight theories:

ākhyātaśabdaḥ saṅghāto jātiḥ saṅghātavartinī ।
eko 'navayavaḥ śabdaḥ kramo buddhyanusaṁhṛtiḥ ॥
padam ādyaṁ pṛthak sarvaṁ padaṁ sākāṅkṣam ity api ।
vākyam prati matir bhinno bahudhā nyāyavādinām ॥ — *VP,* II.1-2

The first three definitions of sentence (*ākhyātaśabdaḥ* (2.7-14), *ādyam padam* (2.47) and *pṛthak sarvam padam* (2.48) are offered according →

vāda,[39] which are based on the presupposition of the divisibility of the sentence and its sense, the grammarians advocated the indivisibility of the sentence with the stance that psychic phenomenon itself is the basis of communication. In other words, the communication of the mental disposition of the speaker to the listener is the purpose of language. All the metaphysical inquiry on the basis of language begins and ends with only psychosis (*vṛtti*) of the intellect (*buddhi*). Hence there

→ to the *anvitābhidhāna* theory. The words in this theory express their respective meanings after they are syntactically related in concordance. The syntactic relation is brought by case relations. In a sentence, we find a sequence of words and also a verb. The concordance can be in three ways. (1) The first word gets connected with all the words and thus the first word itself is called sentence. (2) The verb gets connected with all the other words, as the verb is the main component, because of which the case relations are determined. And, (3) Each and every word is connected with others which are in concordance. The first word normally is the noun in the nominative case and the Naiyāyikas adapted this definition of sentence. Prābhākaras took the verb as the sentence. Puṇyarāja remarks some ancient Mīmāṁsakas adapted the third definition of the sentence.

39. According to the *abhihitānvaya-vāda* the words convey their individual meanings first and then these meanings are connected to form a sentence sense. Hence this interconnection of meanings is called sentence. Here the interconnection among meanings arises either one after the other (*krama*) or simultaneously (*saṅghāta*). Both may also be held, for this interpretation is based on the meanings. This view is held by the Bhāṭṭa Mīmāṁsakas. These two schools of word concordance and word syntax are suggested by Patañjali in the interpretation of the compound *sarvādīni* in the rule *sarvādīni sarvanāmāni* (*Pāṇ.*, 1.1.27). The compound *sarvādīni* can be taken as a *karmadhāraya* type of *tatpuruṣa* according to word-syntax theory. According to this interpretation Bhartṛhari offers the definitions of sentence *saṅghātaḥ* 'aggregate' (*VP*, II. 41-45) and *kramaḥ* sequence (*VP*, II.34-37).

can be no world outside the realm of comprehension. Even if anything exists outside the comprehension, it produces neither pain nor pleasure. Hence the object that appears in psychosis of intellect alone is the meaning and the reality.[40] What we physically experience as the speech and material objects are only an appearance (*vivarta*) of the intellect.[41] The physical components of the speech comprising phonemes, morphemes and sentences are only an appearance, but form a bridge between the speaker and the listener in transmission of the psychic power. The language represents thus the integration of the personality and ability to relate to others of what is contemplated.

The grammarian's theory of sentence is an outcome to overcome the difficulty in the cognition of sentence sense on the presupposition that the sentence and its meaning are indivisible. The sentence sense is indivisible and comprehended at one time without involving any sequence. So also the sentence is indivisible and incapable of classification into words, etc. To circumvent the problem of segmentation of the sentence into components, the grammarian has evolved

---

40. *api prayoktur ātmānaṁ śabdam antar avasthitam/VP*, I.122. Bhartṛhari recognizes the existence of correspondence between the mental object and physical object in the world. But it is only the mental object with which the language is concerned. For Bhartṛhari the relationship of the word and its meaning is that of expression and the expressed and both are mental entities:

    yo vārtho buddhiviṣaye bāhyavastunibandhanaḥ ।
    sa bāhyavastu iti jñātaḥ śabdārthaḥ kecid iṣyate ॥ — *VP*, II.32

41. Puṇyarāja's commentary on *VP*, II.132:
    śabdasya buddhyupārūḍhasya vaikalpikasya yo buddhyupārūḍho bāhyavastunibandhanaḥ bāhyaṁ vastu vikalpajananadvāreṇa nibandhanaṁ yasya sa tathābhūtaḥ । *sa ca vaikalpiko 'rtho bhramavaśād dṛśyavikalpaikākārenābahīrūpo 'pi bahīrūpatayādhyasto 'dhyastam eva vastv avagacchāmi śabdam iti śabdanimittam iti śabdārtha iṣyate.*

the *sphoṭa-śabda*, a new category unknown and unacceptable to other schools of philosophy. The *sphoṭa-śabda* is the expressive word over and above the words which are heard in a sentence. As regards the status of the *sphoṭa-śabda vis-à-vis* the words in a sentence, there are three explanations suggested by Bhartṛhari.[42] Firstly the *sphoṭa* is an indivisible individual (*vyakti*) without any reference to the words (*ananvayaḥ śabdaḥ*), by total denial of any causality between the articulatory words and the expressive *sphoṭa*. Secondly it is a universal (*jāti*) pervading the aggregate of words (*saṅghāṭavartinī jātiḥ*). Thirdly it is only a conceptual reality residing in the mind (*buddhyānusaṁhṛti*). Indivisibility of the sentence is the core principle of the grammarians to bring the psychic phenomena to the forefront subordinating the linguistic criteria.

To bring correlation between the *sphoṭa-śabda*, a mental image, and the physical sounds articulated by the organs of speech, Bhartṛhari gives a vivid account called the *sphoṭa*-theory to explain the process from the conception of the object or idea in the mind of the speaker up to the comprehension of the meaning by the listener. The process of communication has three stages: In the first stage the speaker conceives in his mind the sentence in an indistinct way, soon after the idea flashes in his mind. In the second stage, he constructs in his mind the sentence in a pattern with a specific sequence. And in the third stage he translates the sentence he has constructed in his mind into speech sounds through articulation.[43]

42. Of Bhartṛhari's (cf. fn. 38) eight definitions, the last three, namely *eko ananvayaḥ śabdaḥ* (II.19-27), *saṅghātavartinī jātiḥ* (II.7-8), and *buddhyānusaṁhṛti* (II.30-33) are according to the Grammarians.

43. *vitarkitaḥ purā buddhyā kvacid arthe niveśitaḥ* ।
karaṇebhyo vivṛttena dhvaninā so 'nugṛhyate ॥ — *VP*, I.47

These three stages in the process of communication are called by different names, each one describing a particular characteristic →

The listener also has to pass through these three stages in a reverse order. He listens first to the articulated speech sounds of the speaker. Then he gets a complete impression of the sentence. In the third stage he cognizes a single and indivisible sentence by which he gets the meaning. Bhartṛhari describes these three stages of externalization with three self-explanatory names, *paramopāṁśu, upāṁśu* and *saṁhṛta-krama.*[44] In the *paramopāṁśu* stage the *sphoṭa-śabda* is sill in the mind and the process of articulation has not yet started. These words can be grasped only by the mind of the speaker. And hence the *sphoṭa* is also called *paśyantī.*[45] In the *upāṁśu* stage, the word in the speaker's mind is externalized by the functioning of *prāṇa,* and the articulation of the word begins.[46] But this

→ feature. In the first stage, with reference to the speaker, the word is called *sphoṭa,* and in the second and third stages it is called *dhvani* or *nāda.* The *sphoṭa* and the *dhvani* are the two forms of the word; the *sphoṭa* is the underlying cause of the *dhvani* and the latter is the cause of communication of meaning.

dvāv upādānaśabdeṣu śabadau śabdavido viduḥ ।
eko nimittaṁ śabdānām aparo 'rthe prayujyate ॥ — *VP,* I.44

The *dhvani* in the second stage gets the distinctions of duration called short (*hrasva*), long (*dīrgha*), and extra-long (*pluta*) and it is called *prākṛta-dhvani.*

svabhāvabhedān nityatve hvadīrghaplutādiṣu ।
prākṛtasya dhvaneḥ kālaḥ śabdasyety upacaryate ॥ — *VP,* I.76

The same *dhvani* in the third stage gets the distinctions of rapidity (*druta*), medium (*madhyama*) and slowness (*vilambita*) and it is called *vaikṛta-dhvani.* Therefore the same *sphoṭa* is in fact named distinctively on the basis of the characteristic features acquired in the process of externalization.

44. *upādhimato hy ekasya śabdasya vibhāgā ivāvaśititāḥ saṁhitāsaṁhitayor druta madhya vilambitāsu vṛttiṣu śanairuccairūpāṁśusaṁhṛtakramaṁ ceti, VP,* II.19 *Vṛtti.*

45. *VP,* I.134 *Vṛtti.*

46. *avyaktaḥ kramavān śabdaḥ upāśv abhidhīyate* ।
akramas tu vitaty eva buddhir yatrāvatiṣṭhate ॥ — *VP,* II.19

utterance of the word cannot be heard by others. It is audible only to the speaker. The speaker is conscious of time sequence and the phonological patterns. The vowel sounds take the distinction of short, long and extra long.[47] This is called *prākṛta-dhvani* and *madhyamā vāk*. In the third stage of externalization the word is called *saṁhṛta-krama* because the sentence takes a distinct form and becomes audible to the listener. It is the actual speech sounds pronounced by articulation by the speaker and heard by the listener. Therefore the vowels in this stage take also the distinction as *druta* 'fast,' *madhya* 'medial' and *vilambita* 'slow' on the basis of rapidity, medium speed and slowness respectively in their pronunciation. This is called *vaikṛta-dhvani*,[48] and *vaikharī vāk*.[49] The *vaikṛta-dhvani* is transitory in contradistinction to the indestructible *sphoṭa*. The eternal *sphoṭa*, however, does not differ in its nature from the destructible *dhvani*.[50] Segmentation of the sentence sense into

---

47. *svabhāvabhedān nityatve hrasvadīrghaplutādiṣu* ।
prākṛtasya dhvaneḥ kālaḥ śabdasyopacaryate ॥ — *VP*, I.76

48. *dhvanayaḥ samupohante sphoṭasyātmā tair nabhidyate* ।
śabdasyordhvam abhivyakter vṛttibhedaṁ tu vaikṛtāḥ ॥ — *VP*, I.77

49. *vaikharyā madhyamāyāś ca paśyanyāś caitad adbhutam* ।
anekārthabhedāyās trayyā vācaḥ paraṁ padam ॥ — *VP*, I.134

50. How can the indestructible *sphoṭa* be not different from the destructible *dhvani*? Bhartṛhari resorts to the philosophical doctrine of change called *vivarta*. He defines *vivarta* as "the assumption of one thing as something else without losing its inherent nature (*tattva*) through the apparent diversity of different unreal forms" (*ekasya tattvād apracyutasya bhedānukāreṇāsatya-0vibhaktānyarūpopagrāhitā vivartaḥ*, *VP*, I.1, *Vṛtti*. The *sphoṭa-śabda* which is nothing but the consciousness of the speaker (*VP*, I.122) appears in the form of *prakṛta-dhvani* and *vaikṛta-dhvani* which are destructible (*VP*, I.47 *Vṛtti*). Therefore the indivisible *sphoṭa* appears as divisible in the stages of *prākṛta-dhvani* and *vaikṛta-dhvani* by taking on it the qualities of the sound.

nādasya kramajanmatvān na pūrvo na paraś ca saḥ ।
akramaḥ kramarūpeṇa bhedavān iva jāyate ॥ — *VP*, I.48 →

parts of speech or the sentence into words, morphemes and phonemes is an artificial device employed to the *prākṛta-dhvani* following the principle of co-presence and co-absence (*anvaya-vyatireka*). The limitation to this segmentation is manifold. For example, all the sense that is known from the sentence cannot be distributed as lexical meanings, as certain meanings cannot be assigned to any component. Therefore whatever that is found conveyed over and above the sum total of the lexical meanings put together has to be taken as the sentence sense.[51] For example, the relation of subject and predicate or qualified and the qualificand cannot be attributed to any part. Therefore to show that the sentence sense is preceding all through the segments, Bhartṛhari says that both the words *nīla* and *utpala* in the compound *nīlotpala* or in the phrase *nīlam utpalam* denote blue lotus and observes that it is only the relation of collocation (*samānādhikāraṇya*) which can be established.[52]

→ Just as the reflection of the moon in water appears to be moving because of the movement of water, the *sphoṭa-śabda* also appears to have divisibility, duration and speed.

pratibimbaṁ yathānyatra sthitaṁ toyakriyāvaśāt ।
tatpravṛttim ivānveti sa dharmaḥ sphoṭanādayoḥ ॥ — *VP*, I.49

Here it may be noted that the definition of *vivarta* of Bhartṛhari is accepted and repeated by Prakāśātman with a slight modification in his *Pañcapādikāvivaraṇa*:

ekasya tattvād apracyutasya pūrvaviparītāsatyānekarūpavabhāso vivartaḥ

Padmapādācārya's *Pañcapādika* with commentaries, ed. S. Subrahmanya Sastri, Varanasi: Mahesh Research Institute, 1922, *Varnaka* 5, p. 532.

51. *viśeṣaṇaviśeṣyatvaṁ padayor upajāyate* ।
na prātipadikārthaś ca tatraivaṁ vyatiricyate ॥ — *VP*, III. *Vṛtti* 6

52. M. Srimannarayana Murti, *Sanskrit Compounds — A Philosophical Study*, Chowkhamba Sanskrit Series, 1974.

Bhartṛhari formalizes the *sphoṭa*-theory with illustrations of unrivalled and outwitting poetic imagery. For example he justifies the mental object as the meaning for the mental world called *sphoṭa* with the example of the illuminator and illuminated. An external light as illuminator can illuminate only an external object. In other words the relation of the illuminator and illuminated can exist between two things only when they both belong to the same level. The expressive word called *sphoṭa* is the illuminator and something mental. Therefore it is not even necessary that the meaning of a word should have a corresponding external object. It can exclusively be a mental one, or it may never have an external object at all. But the actions signified by the sentences cannot be accomplished unless the mental objects are superimposed on the external objects and are understood as external;[53] it is also understood as susceptible to action. Following Bhartṛhari, Nāgeśa observes that even if a person uses the word *ghaṭa* intentionally for *paṭa* in the sentence *ghaṭam ānaya* the listener has to decide the meaning of *ghaṭa* as *paṭa*.[54]

As to how an undifferentiated *sphoṭa* appears as distinct sounds he explains with the example of the peacock egg.[55] The peacock has variegated colours and one can observe each

---

53. *yo vārtho buddhiviṣayo bāhyavastunibandhanaḥ* ।
sa bāhyavastv iti jñātaḥ śabdārthaḥ kaiścad iṣyate ॥ — *VP*, II.132

54. *yatra tu tatra vākye ghaṭam ānaya ity ādau ghaṭakarma-kānayanabodhecchayā uccāritatvābhāvā jñāne . . . idaṁ vākyam etadarathapratītīcchayā vaktroccāritam ityākārakatātparyagraho hetuḥ,*
— *Laghumañjūṣā*, p. 524

The lead for this is found in *VP*, II. 285:

atyantaviparīto 'pi yadā yo 'rtho 'vadhāryate ।
yathāśampratyaṁ śabdas tatra mukhyaḥ pratīyate ॥

55. *āṇḍabhāvam ivāpanno yaḥ kratuḥ śabdasaṁjukaḥ* ।
vṛttes tasya kriyābhūtā bhāgaśo labhate kramam ॥ — *VP*, I.51

colour distinctly. But when its seed is fertilized into a zygote we do not find in it the distinction of colours. Again after the development of the foetus into a peacock all the colours are seen distinctly. In the same way the *sphoṭa* which is indivisible appears as divisible by its superimposition on the speech sounds, etc.[56]

As to how the *sphoṭa* is manifested in the speaker and comprehended by the listener, Bhartṛhari takes the example of a picture. A painter observes first the whole object and then each and every part of the object to be painted. After getting a comprehensive knowledge of the object as a whole and of the parts he begins his work. First he draws a sketch on a canvas or paper. Then he paints it with different colours.[57] While painting he sees each and every colour separately. Once the picture is ready the painter does not see the colours distinctly. If each colour is seen separately there is no difference from picture to picture.[58] From the point of view of the listener also the same example holds good. Each colour of the painting is also important for the man of the world to differentiate one picture from the other. However in the perception of the picture he does not see each colour separately but all the colours at a time and the whole knowledge is only one and indivisible. So also the distinct speech units found in the *prākṛta-dhvani* provide a basis for the comprehension of the *sphoṭa*. In other

---

56. *sarvavibhāgodgrāhapratisaṁhāreṇa bāhyo vyavahārikaḥ śabdo 'ntaḥkaraṇe mayūrādyaṇḍarasavat pūrvavibhāgodgrāhabhāvanāmātram avyatikraman pratīyate* — *Vṛtti* on I.51.

57. *yathaikabuddhiviṣayā mūrtir ākriyate paṭe* I
mūrtyantarasya tritayaṁ evaṁ śabdo 'pi dṛśyate II — *VP*, I.52

58. *yathaika eva sarvārthapratyayaḥ pravibhajyate* I
dṛśyabhedānukāreṇa vākyārthānugamas tathā II
citrasthaikasvarūpasya yathā bhedanidarśanaiḥ I
nīlādibhiḥ samākhyānaṁ kriyate bhinnalakṣaṇaiḥ II — *VP*, II.7-8

words all of them together give the indivisible and single cognition of the *sphoṭa*.[59] This *sphoṭa* flashes the meaning called *pratibhā*.[60]

Again to show the *prākṛta-dhvani* as an appearance of the *sphoṭa*, Bhartṛhari draws a distinction between the concrete object and the representational picture of it. The concrete object is that which is experienced by an individual physically while the representational picture is what is painted by an artist. Even though both the concrete and representational forms are very much similar to the knowledge[61] produced in the mind, the physical experience differs. For instance the ups and downs on the spatial mountain cause trembles, falls, hits

---

59. Even though theoretically each word or morpheme in a sentence is held as signifying the whole sentence sense, Bhartṛhari holds that every component is essential. He explains this with the example of memorization of the texts. A text which is to be memorized has to be read time and again. Just as each reading strengthens memory, each component in a sentence supports the final cognition of the sentence sense. The first component gives rise to the cognition vaguely, the second one more clearly, and so on until the last one, helped by the impressions left by the previous cognitions, reveals it in all clarity and distinctness.

    yathānuvākaḥ śloko vā soḍhatvam upagacchati ।
    āvṛtyā na tu sa granthaḥ pratyāvṛtti nirūpyate ॥
    pratyayair anupākhyeyair grahaṇānugais tathā ।
    dhvaniprakāśite śabde svarūpam avadhāryate ॥ — *VP*, I.82-83

60. *vicchedagrahaṇe 'rthānāṁ pratibhānyaivopa jāyate* ।
    vākyārtha iti tām āhuḥ padārthair upapāditam ॥
    idaṁ tad iti sānyeṣām anākhyeyā kadhañcana ।
    pratyātmavṛttisiddhā sā kartrāpi na nirūpyate ॥ — *VP*, II.143-44

61. Puṇyarāja takes it as knowledge: *nīlapītādy nekākāram eva vijñānam upajātam iti* । *vastusthityā tatra jñāna ākārabhedo nāsti*,
    — Puṇyarāja's *Ṭīkā* on *VP*, II.7

and pain while walking.[62] But the same ups and downs in the picture do not produce pain, for there one cannot have strolls or strides.[63]

V

In the final analysis the language is the manifestation of the exhaled breath by an operation of the mind which produces the manifold shapes (*rūpa*) in the buccal cavity and infinite forms of names representing various mental images. While the function of breath is involuntary, the function of mind is voluntary in human beings, as observed by Bhagavān Śrī Ramaṇa Maharṣi. Patañjali in his *Yoga-Sūtras* epitomized this principle that the control of psychosis of mind[64] is the ultimate goal for which the control of breath is the best method. The word *citta* means nothing but that portion of light like consciousness or knowledge which emanates from the transcendental heart and reflects and activates the inanimate mind and in its turn the sensory organs. The whole process becomes established by reading together the texts of *Pātañjala-Yoga-Sūtra, Vaiyākaraṇa-Mahābhāṣya,* and *Caraka-Saṁhitā* — all of which go together according to tradition under the same authorship. Bhartṛhari gave a new dimension to relate the mind and language by philosophizing the *bauddhapadārtha-vāda* and the *vivarta-vāda* to substantiate the transitoriness of the mental world. Thus the control of mind is the ultimate solution for emancipation from pain and pleasure which is nothing but the final goal of human values.

62. *yacca nimnonnataṁ citre sarūpaṁ parvatādibhiḥ* ।
na tatra pratighātādikāryaṁ tadvat pravartate ॥ — *VP*, II.270

63. *parvatādibhiḥ sarūpaṁ nimnonnataṁ citrabhittau dṛśyate, na ca tāvatā tatra pratighātādikāryabhedo jñānantareṇa tatra bhedāvagatir eva ity arthaḥ.* — Puṇyarāja's *Ṭīkā* on *VP*, II.290

64. *yogaḥ cittavṛttinirodhaḥ* । — *Yoga-Sūtras,* 1.2.

References

Caraka-Saṁhitā by Agniveśa, thoroughly revised by Caraka and Dṛḍhabala with *āyurvedadīpikā* commentaries of Cakrapāṇidatta and *Jalpakalpataru* of Gaṅgādhara Kaviratna Kavirāja, ed. Narendranath Sengupta & Balachandra Sengupta, Pts. 1 to 5, New Delhi: Rashtriya Sanskrit Sansthan, Reprint. 2002.

Patañjali's Yoga-Sūtras, (*YS*), tr. Rama Prasada, Delhi: Munshiram Manoharlal, 1988.

Śrīramaṇagranthamālā (Telugu version), Tiruvannamalai: Sri Ramanashramam, 1971.

Vākyapadīya (*VP*) of Bhartṛhari with *Prakīrṇaprakāśa* of Helarāja (*HP*). Kāṇḍa I (1966), III, Pt. 1 (1963) Pt. 2 (1973), Poona: Deccan College.

Vyākaraṇa-Mahābhāṣya (*MB*) of Patañjali, ed. F. Kielhorn [3rd edn.], Poona: Bhandarkar Oriental Research Institute, 1962, vols I-III.

10

On the Nature of Word and our Knowledge of it

*Nirmalya Narayan Chakraborty**

HUMANS are language-using creatures. Words are what we use most. Expressing our own thoughts, documenting other people's thoughts, etc. are done through using words. A person lacking in knowledge of words would not have any knowledge of the surrounding world. Human survival would be at stake in the absence of knowledge of words. Such an important and indispensable element in human existence has been a matter of great debate among philosophers since antiquity. In a way, words are so close to us, yet the moment we try to get a grip over them, difficult questions crop up that are not easy to handle. In the present paper I would like to analyse the classical Indian Grammarian theory of the nature of the word. More specifically, I will follow Patañjali's handling of the issue. Patañjali in his *magnum opus Mahābhāṣya* begins his discussion with a detailed analysis of the purpose and necessity of grammar and in this context he talks about the nature of the word. Since, for Patañjali, grammar deals with the word, a discussion about the purpose of grammar requires knowledge of the nature of the word and the nature of our knowledge of it.

---

* Professor, Department of Philosophy, Rabindra Bharati University, Kolkata, India.

The subject that deals with the laws of the word is called grammar (*vyākaraṇa*). In Indian intellectual tradition it is a common convention that at the beginning of any discussion one mentions four dispositional factors (*anubandha*) the knowledge of which would incline an intelligent person to undertake a study of the topic under discussion. Dispositional factors do not directly form the core of the discussion to be undertaken, but nevertheless they give some idea of the subject matter to be analysed. The importance of the dispositional factors lies in motivating the reader to join the discourse. They are sort of a psychological booster dose to the reader. There are four such dispositional factors: 1. Eligibility (*adhikārī*), 2. Content (*viṣaya*), 3. Relation (*sambandha*), and 4. Necessity (*prayojana*). The person who wants to undertake the study must possess the eligibility to do so. A person who is worthy of undertaking the study of the topic under scrutiny is an eligible person for studying that topic. Whatever is proved in a discussion is the content of that discussion. Relation in the present context denotes the relation between the content and the discipline in which the study takes place. Necessity is the result of studying the relevant discipline. Any reasonable person, before being disposed to do something, must possess the knowledge 'I am capable of doing this.' In Nyāya terminology this knowledge is called *kṛtisādhyatā-jñāna*. Unless one knows that one is able to perform an action, he would not have any disposition to accomplish that act. When one knows that one has the required eligibility to perform the act, then he has the knowledge that with his effort he can perform the task. So the knowledge of eligibility produces the knowledge of *kṛtisādhyatā*. And unless one has the knowledge of *kṛtisādhyatā*, one would not have any disposition to undertake the study. Knowledge of eligibility is the cause of one's disposition to undertake the study. There is another cause of disposition, viz. knowledge of the fulfilment of desire. This is technically called *iṣṭa-sādhanatā-jñāna*. An intelligent person is inclined to perform an act only when he thinks that performance of the act would bring in the desired result. Performing the act is a method by which the desired result will come. If a person does not think this about an act, he will never be inclined (*pravṛtti*) to perform that act. This is where the knowledge of necessity comes in. Once one possesses the knowledge of the necessity of the discipline, he also acquires the knowledge that undertaking a study of the discipline will bring in the desired result. Knowledge of the content also gives rise to *iṣṭa-sādhanatā-jñāna*. In other words, when one knows the content of the discussion, one can decide whether undertaking the study of the relevant topic will bring in the desired result. The direct necessity of a discipline is the knowledge of the content of the discipline. Now this knowledge of content is helpful to the knowledge of the purpose (which is a kind of necessity) of the discipline. Thus the knowledge of the relation between the discipline and its content, between content and necessity and between the discipline and necessity also produce *iṣṭa-sādhanatā-jñāna*. The necessity for which the particular discipline has been written can be fulfilled by that discipline — unless one has thus certain knowledge, one would not be inclined to study the discipline. If the discipline does not have a relation with its content and necessity, that discipline is like a mad person's haphazard comments and so no intelligent person would be inclined to study it. So once we have the knowledge of the content and necessity of the discipline, we can easily have the knowledge of relation and eligibility of that discipline.

Let us discuss a little more the necessity of the discipline called grammar. Patañjali uses the word *śabdānuśāsana* which can be understood as *anuśāsana* of *śabda*. *Śabda* means word (we will shortly discuss this in detail). *Anuśāsana* means governing laws. Grammar is defined as a study of the laws of the word (*śabdānuśāsana*). It is the study of grammar that enables us to have the knowledge of a well-formed word as different from an ill-formed or incorrect word. The laws that grammar talks about are the laws pertaining to the word. The word 'law' could be understood in two different ways. When we speak of the laws of morals, we mean certain rules of conduct that we ought to obey, but not that these laws are always obeyed by everybody in actual behaviour. Human behaviour is not always in conformity with these moral laws. But when we talk of the laws of nature, we mean certain generalizations of natural phenomena and the occurrences of the natural phenomena are always in conformity with these natural laws. The former can be called prescriptive laws while the latter can be called descriptive laws. In which of these senses can we talk of the laws of the word? In one sense we can talk about laws of word as proposed by Patañjali as generalizations of our linguistic use. From Patañjali's allusion to several examples from ordinary and Vedic contexts it is clear that he thinks of the laws of the word as the laws that we follow in our linguistic behaviour. Grammar tries to collect or extract the regularities that are found in using language. Viewed in this way, our linguistic use is always in conformity with the laws of grammar. Thus the laws of the word could be viewed as unearthing the laws in accordance with which we, though directly unaware of those laws, partake in linguistic behaviour. Thus grammar is not a language manual. We do not learn laws of grammar before we learn a language. We come to grasp the laws while learning the language. As we get exposed to a language, we gradually determine the laws governing the uses of the words by observing the behaviour of the native user of that language. But then the laws of the word, the subject matter of grammar, could also be said to have a prescriptive value. Since the knowledge of grammar ultimately leads to liberation, the message contained in the *Mahābhāṣya* is that if one wants to attain liberation, then one must possess the knowledge of the laws of the word. So for every person desiring to attain liberation, knowledge of grammar is a must. The laws of the word have got a prescriptive force in the sense that one ought to know these laws if one wants to attain liberation.

The brahmins are supposed to study and acquire the knowledge of the Vedas along with the six auxiliary subjects without any ulterior motive. There are six auxiliary disciplines (to the Vedas) that one needs to study. These six subjects are: Śikṣā, Kalpa, Nirukta, Vyākaraṇa, Jyotiṣa and Chanda. Śikṣā deals with the rules of pronunciation aiming at correct pronunciation of the Vedic *mantras*. It is only when the *mantras* are correctly pronounced, that they produce the desired results. Pāṇini, Yājñavalkya, etc. have written on Śikṣā rules that are valid for specific Vedas. Here we find discussions of rules of pronunciation of different letters specific to different Vedas. There are other works on Śikṣā where the Śikṣā rules that are described are valid for the specific Vedas. Thus in the works of Śaunaka, Kātyāyana, etc. we find discussion of Śikṣā rules some of which are meant for one Veda, and some others are meant for another. These are known as *Prātiśākhya*. In the Kalpa part we find a systematic analysis of the significance of the *mantras* taken from the Brāhmaṇa part of the Vedas following Mīmāṁsā hermeneutics and description of the performance of the Vedic sacrifices with the help of those *mantras*. Vyākaraṇa, as we have seen just now, analyses the well-formed words into stem and suffix. There is clear evidence that study of grammar started since Vedic period and well before Pāṇini. Nirukta is an appendix to grammar. In grammar some words are introduced but not analysed nor was any formation rule proposed for those words. These are taken up in Nirukta. Knowledge of Nirukta completes the knowledge of grammar. In Jyotiṣa we find a study of determination of time for studying the Vedas and performance of Vedic rituals. In Chanda we find a discussion of the formation rules of *mantra*s in the form of poetry. *Mantra*s in the form of poetry are called *ṛk*. *Mantra*s in the form of prose are called *yajuḥ*. The *mantra*s that are different from *ṛk* and *yajuḥ* in nature and are sung are called *sama*.

It is the duty of a brahmin to study the Vedas along with the auxiliary subjects and the brahmin should perform this duty without any other ulterior motive. Studying and knowing the meaning of Vedas are a must for a brahmin. A brahmin must not expect any worldly gain from this. It is suggested here that a brahmin, like his daily prayer, etc. must study and acquire the knowledge of the meaning of the Vedas everyday. If a brahmin fails to perform this duty of his, then he would acquire vice (*pāpa*). Those who are the best among the eligible persons will be inclined to study grammar, for in any case they need the knowledge of grammar to study the Vedas. One acquires virtue (*dharma*) if one uses the well-formed words following the knowledge of the analytical method of grammar. So the study of grammar leads to gaining virtue. Thus those who are the mediocre among the eligible persons would be inclined to study grammar in order to gain virtue. So the fact that gaining virtue has been mentioned as the necessity of studying grammar is actually addressed to the mediocre eligible persons. Interestingly nothing has been mentioned either by Pāṇini or Kātyāyana as the necessity of studying grammar that is meant for the worst among the eligible persons. The worst eligible people having no faith in the scriptures do not care for the results like attaining heaven, etc. that are obtainable after death. These people always look for mundane results. Patañjali, of course, has talked about the necessity of studying grammar that is addressed to the worst among the eligible persons. From using the word *śabdānuśāsana* one can understand that the necessity of grammar is knowledge of words (well-formed). So it is the word that is the subject matter of grammar. The knowledge of the word is the direct necessity of studying grammar. Thus we can see that the necessity of grammar is knowledge of the word and the subject matter is the word. Though knowledge of the word is the direct necessity of grammar, the ultimate necessity is virtue and liberation.

So the real necessity of grammar is the cessation of suffering. Knowledge of the word itself is not pleasure or cessation of pain. But knowledge of the word is the method of attaining pleasure or cessation of pain. Thus, according to Nāgeśa Bhaṭṭa, virtue and liberation are the necessities of grammar. Study of grammar leads to a knowledge of the word that amounts to knowing the meaning of the word. This leads to the knowledge of the Vedas. The knowledge of the meaning of the Vedas helps one in uttering the *mantras* correctly, which enables one to perform the Vedic rituals properly and this produces virtue. Acquiring virtue leads to heavenly pleasure. From the knowledge of grammar when one acquires the knowledge of the meaning of the word, one also knows the meaning of the Upaniṣads which leads to the knowledge of *Brahman*. One could also claim that by the knowledge of grammar one attains the knowledge of *śabdabrahman* leading to liberation. So even if the knowledge of the word is the direct necessity of grammar, the indirect result of the study of grammar is virtue and liberation. While addressing the worst eligible persons Patañjali talks about the knowledge of meaning as being the necessity of the study of grammar and this would induce people to study grammar.

In philosophical literature *bhāṣya* is defined as that which takes up the words from a *sūtra* and explains their meaning in terms of words that are conducive to the meaning of the *sūtra*. Moreover, a *bhāṣya* explains its own words. The uniqueness of Patañjali's *Mahābhāṣya* is that on many occasions it has given arguments independently of the *sūtras* and *vārttikas* to prove its points. Herein lies the greatness of this *bhāṣya* (*mahā* meaning great). Bhartṛhari regards *Mahābhāṣya* not only as a work on grammar, but also as a collection of the main sources of all the arguments that are available. This book on grammar contains a lucid exposition of many difficult ideas of grammar. The first sentence of *Mahābhāṣya* is *atha śabdānuśāsanam*. Since this is a *bhāṣya*, it explains the meaning of *atha* which it itself has used. Among the many meanings of *atha*, one is 'beginning.' What is beginning is the discipline that deals with the laws of the word.

One must also note that if an author or a speaker gives some hint about what is coming in the discussion or the speech, then it is possible for the reader/hearer to pay attention to the content of the discussion. This statement of the topic by the author/speaker at the very beginning of the discussion is called the promise (*pratijñā*). Without this promise, the reader/hearer is not likely to be attentive to the ensuing discussion and as a result the presentation of the author/speaker would be futile. The author of *Mahābhāṣya* expresses his promise in the sentence *atha śabdānuśāsanam,* viz. he is going to talk about the laws of the word. Thus this first sentence suggests the content and necessity of grammar as well as the promise that is the cause of the attention of the reader/hearer.

The word *atha* also serves the role of invocation. Even though Patañjali does not give any invocation verse at the beginning, he himself has talked about the importance of an invocation verse in *Mahābhāṣya*. So it is not that he is opposed to composing an invocation verse at the beginning of the text, he treats the utterance of the word *atha* as implying invocation.

After deciding that grammar is a study of the laws of the word, the question arises as to which words grammar studies. Grammar does not talk about any and every sound, e.g. sounds of birds, horses and drums. Even humans also can make sounds that do not fall within the scope of grammar. Patañjali thinks that grammar deals with two kinds of words: 1. Ordinary (*laukika*) words and 2. Vedic (*vaidika*) words. *Laukika* means that which is known or used by the people. One must, of course, remember here that only well-formed ordinary words are meant here. So even if people use many ill-formed words, they are not being taken into account. While explaining the meaning of *śabdānuśāsana* it has already been stated that grammar deals only with well-formed words. Obviously the Vedic words are those that are used only in the Vedas.

One could ask here: Given the self-veridical nature and importance of the Vedic sentences, why doesn't Patañjali mention the example of the Vedic words first? Since ordinary words are always used by the people, they are well known to us; they come to us first when we think of words. It is due to our close acquaintance with the ordinary words that Patañjali mentions the example of the ordinary words first. In ordinary Sanskrit language the order of the words in a sentence is not important. *Gaurasti* (there is a cow) and *asti gauḥ* (there is a cow) — both are well-formed expressions. Because of the flexibility of the order Patañjali mentions words as examples of ordinary words. The first example of an ordinary word that Patañjali gives is *gau*. The word *gau* suggests something auspicious and it also has different meanings. Thus one could treat an ordinary Sanskrit sentence as *śabda*. But in cases of Vedic sentences the order of the words is of crucial importance. With the change of the order of the words, a Vedic sentence ceases to be a Vedic sentence. Vedic sentences have a fixed order of words. This is why while giving examples of Vedic words, Patañjali mentions Vedic sentences having a fixed word order and not individual words. This also implies that the utterance of the Vedic sentences following the order that has been maintained in the teacher-student tradition (following the exact method of pronunciation) is important for maintaining the Vedic nature of the Vedic sentences.

It is interesting to note that Patañjali mentions, as examples of Vedic sentences, *śanno devīrabiṣṭaye*, etc. that constitute the *mantra* part of Vedas. He has not given any example from the Brāhmaṇa part of the Vedas. But Patañjali himself accepts both *mantra* and Brāhmaṇa as parts of the Vedas. According to Patañjali, Vedas were authored by different sages. It could be that *mantras* were composed first and then came the Brāhmaṇa. Vedic rituals are performed by uttering *mantras* and Brāhmaṇa sentences are never uttered there. Thus the *mantras* occupy central place in the Vedic ritualistic framework. Brāhmaṇa sentences are explanations of the *mantra* sentences and so they are parasitical on the *mantras*. Hence Patañjali has given the examples from the *mantra* part of the Vedas. Moreover, even if people hold that Vedas lack any human authorship (*apauruṣeya*), it is the *mantra* part that is revealed to humans first and then the Brāhmaṇa part got manifest. Both in terms of temporal sequence and primacy in performance of Vedic rituals the *mantra* sentences have been given as examples of Vedic sentences.

Normally when we talk of the Vedas, we talk of the four Vedas in the order *Ṛg, Yajur, Sāma* and *Atharva*. In various Upaniṣads we find the mention of the four Vedas in this order. Patañjali, disregarding this order, has given examples of Vedic sentences taken from *Atharva, Yajur, Ṛg* and *Sāma*. One could ask about the justification of this new order mentioned by Patañjali. According to grammarians, *mantras* are used in performing Vedic sacrifices (*yajña*). This sacrifice is of two kinds: 1. *Śrauta* and 2. *Smārtta*. The sacrifices that are prescribed in the Brāhmaṇa part of the Vedas are called *śrauta* sacrifices. The sacrifices that are prescribed in *Gṛhyasūtra* are called *smārtta* sacrifices. The sacrificial fire is of three kinds: 1. *āhavanīya*, 2. *gārhapatya* and 3. *dakṣiṇāgni*. These three kinds of sacrificial fire are known as *tretā*. The person who receives this *tretā* sacrificial fire following the Vedic methods becomes eligible for performing *śrauta* sacrifice. A person who, on the other hand, receives the sacrificial fire following *Gṛhyasūtra* becomes eligible for *smārtta* sacrifice, but not for *śrauta* sacrifice. In performance of *śrauta* sacrifice *Yajur, Ṛg* and *Sāma* have utility, but *Atharvaveda* does not play any role. But in constructing the sacrificial altar, the site of sacrificial fire, etc. *Atharvaveda* does have utility. Construction of the sacrificial altar, the seat of the *ṛttvik*, etc. are known as *vihāra*. Before constructing the *vihāra* one has to perform various peace-ensuring rituals so that the sacrifice could be performed till the end without any hindrance. *Atharvaveda* provides us with all these much-needed peace-ensuring rituals. Thus we see the relevance of *Atharvaveda* even before the sacrifice starts. Hence Patañjali has mentioned the example of Vedic words from *Atharvaveda* first. The sacrificial duties of an *adhvaryu* has been mentioned in *Yajurveda*.

He who initiates the performer of the sacrifice (*yajamāna*) into performing the sacrifice is called *adhvaryu*. This initiation act of the *adhvaryu* is of crucial importance in the sacrifice. And the duties of *adhvaryu* have been mentioned in the *Yajurveda*. Also the daily sacrifices like *agnihotra* sacrifice, etc. can be performed by using the *mantra*s from *Yajurveda*. So after *Atharvaveda* Patañjali mentions example from *Yajurveda*. In many sacrifices like *darśapūrṇamāsa* alongside the duties of *adhvaryu*, certain kinds of rites called *hotra* rites (rites related to offering things to the sacrificial fire) have been prescribed. It is the *Ṛgveda* that provides us with these *hotra* rites. Hence after *Atharvaveda* and *Yajurveda* Patañjali mentions examples from *Ṛgveda*. In some other sacrifices, like *agniṣṭoma, jyotiṣṭoma*, alongside the rites of *adhvaryu* and *hotra, audagātra* rites (rites related to chanting *mantra*s before the sacrificial fire) have been prescribed. *Sāmaveda* provides us with these *audagātra* rites. So Patañjali, after mentioning *Ṛgveda*, has mentioned examples from *Sāmaveda*. This explains why Patañjali, ignoring the traditional order, mentions examples from the Vedas in a different order.

There is a debate as to whether *Atharvaveda* is to be regarded as a Veda. Kumārila Bhaṭṭa rejects *Atharvaveda* as a part of the Vedas though later, Jayanta Bhaṭṭa refutes Kumārila Bhaṭṭa's arguments. It is however evident from Patañjali's allusion to the example from *Atharvaveda* that Patañjali regards *Atharvaveda* as a part of the Vedas.

Now we come to the most important question: What is a word? Taking an example of an ordinary word Patañjali asks the nature of the meaning of 'cow.' Patañjali comes up with several possible answers and refutes each of them. Then he puts forward his own thesis. One thing that must be noted at the outset is that the question does not concern the nature of the letters. The letters, being perceptible through auditory sense-organs, are known to us and there is no confusion on our part with this knowledge of the letters with any other knowledge and so there is no room for doubt about our knowledge of the letters. With the absence of doubt there is no space for query and so no possibility of discussion. Hence the question is not about the nature of the letters. However, when we utter the word 'cow,' the word, its meaning and the knowledge of the meaning gets floated in our mind all mixed up.

Once we think of the situation in detail, we see that even the meaning does not get itself manifest in a clear way. The animal cow is a substance (*dravya*) and so in it reside quality (*guṇa*), action (*kriyā*) and the universal (*jāti*). In order to have the knowledge of the substance one has to have the knowledge of the colour in it and the universal residing in that substance. Without knowing all these one cannot have the knowledge of the substance. Patañjali holds that when one knows the substance following the knowledge of the word, one also possesses the knowledge of the quality, etc. that reside in the substance. According to the grammarians, when one acquires the knowledge of the substance, one also gains the knowledge of the word itself where the word is what that refers. As the substance is identical with the quality, etc. it is also identical with the referring word. Of course, the referring word is both different from and identical with the substance, quality, etc. Since the substance is different from and identical with the quality, the referring word, etc. with the utterance of the word 'cow' one acquires the knowledge of the substance along with the knowledge of the meaning, quality, action and the word itself. The knowledge of the word does not appear without the knowledge of these other things. There is an argument (*tadabhinnābhinnasya tadabhinnatvam*) that says that if two or more than two things are identical with something, then those two or more than those two things are identical with each other. When one acquires the knowledge of the substance following the utterance of the word 'cow,' one also gains the knowledge of the quality, action, the referring word and the universal because of their being identical with the substance. Thus since quality, action, universal, word and substance get manifest in a single knowledge appearing as identical, it becomes difficult to distinguish the word from that intermingling. So while Patañjali is enquiring into the nature of word, this word is to be understood as distinguished from quality, etc. So we must focus our attention on the word and not on the quality, substance, etc.

In answer to the question what is the nature of the word 'cow,' one could say that the thing having hump, horns, etc. is the word 'cow.' Patañjali rejects this answer by arguing that the animal having hump, horns, etc. is the substance which is not to be confused with the word. It seems to me that Patañjali wants to drive the point home that the realm of the word and the realm of the substance to which the word refers are different. A word is a linguistic entity. A word is formed and ruled by a set of linguistic rules. The substance, on the other hand, is an extra-linguistic entity. It is formed and governed by a set of natural laws. Grammar applies to words. Natural sciences apply to substances. So treating the animal having hump, horns, etc. as the nature of the word 'cow' is tantamount to changing the subject matter of grammar, for then grammar would be dealing with the substances and not with the words.[1]

1. One is reminded here of Frege's attempt to distinguish meaning (sense) from reference. Frege introduces the notion of sense in order to account for the cognitive difference between two identity →

The second possible answer regarding the nature of word is that the nature of a word lies in the bodily movements done to express the intention of the speaker like twinkling of the eyes, etc. The idea is that various bodily gestures accompany the utterance of words and the essence of the word lies in those accompanying bodily movements. Patañjali criticizes this view by arguing that the bodily movements are to be regarded as actions. These gestures vary from person to person, from time to time and from society to society. The nature of the word is different from these gestures, even though the bodily movements always happen to accompany utterance of words.

One might again argue that the nature of the word 'cow' lies in the colours like white, brown, black, etc. When one utters the word 'cow,' one always thinks of either white or brown or black cow. So, the thought runs that the essence of the word 'cow' lies in these colours. Patañjali rejects this answer by suggesting that these are qualities. These qualities reside in the substance. It is true that whenever we think of a cow, we think of either a white or a brown or a black cow. But the nature of the word 'cow' resides in the word and not in the substance. Grammar deals with word and not with substance. The qualities like white, etc. are qualities of substance and not of the word. Even if the word is a quality, it is known through

→ statements where one expression in an identity statement is substituted by a co-referential expression. Frege goes on arguing that sense is not to be equated with mental ideas either. Although it is not clear that Patatjali refuses to equate meaning (*sphoṭa*) with subjective ideas, a discussion about the ontological status of Fregean sense and Patañjali's *sphoṭa* is worth taking up. For Frege's arguments see his "On Sense and Nominatum" in H. Feigl and W. Sellars (eds.), *Readings in Philosophical Analysis*, New York: Appleton-Century-Crofts Inc., 1949, pp. 85-102.

the auditory sense-organ, while qualities like white, etc. are grasped through the visual sense-organ. So the nature of the word cannot lie in qualities like white, etc. The underlying principle that Patañjali seems to rely on is that if two things are known through different sense-organs, then the nature of the one cannot be identical with the nature of the other. Accepting this principle one could similarly argue that even if the word is treated as substance, it is different from the animal having hump, etc. for while the word is known through the auditory sense-organ, the animal having hump, etc. is known through the visual sense-organ.

The last possible answer to the query about the nature of word that Patañjali mentions is that the nature of word is that which is shared by all the different cows, which is not destroyed by the destruction of the cow, which is universally present in all the cows. It is undeniable then, that when in different instances we use the word 'cow,' there is some commonality that explains our using the same word 'cow' in various cases. And this commonality is not dependent, for its existence, on the existence of individual cows. This common feature is called *sāmānyabhūta*. This means, according to Kaiyaṭa, *sāmānyasadṛśa* (like *sāmānya* or universal). Existence (*sattā*), which is a universal, resides in substance, quality and action. But existence is pervasive in all the universals like cowness, etc. So this existence is not only a universal, it is a great universal (*mahājāti*). In the present context this universal, viz. existence has been mentioned as comparable with the universal cowness. As existence is a universal, similarly cowness is a universal and here lies the nature of the word 'cow.' Nāgeśa, however, explains *sāmānyabhūta* as that which has gained generality. The universal cowness resides in all the cows in a similar way, and so cowness has acquired generality. Patañjali, however, rejects this answer as well. This common universal cowness, according to Patañjali, is nothing but *ākṛti*. *Ākṛti* means ordered parts (*avayava sansthāna*). *Ākṛti* refers to the particular way the parts are organized or staying together. Patañjali's argument seems to be that the reason why we use the same word 'cow' in very many instances is that we perceive the same orderly parts in all those instances. This universal cowness is present in all the different cows simply because all the different cows exemplify the same arrangement of parts. This arrangement of parts (*ākṛti*) lies in the realm of the substance and has nothing to do with the word itself. An explanation of the nature of the word cannot be reduced to an explanation of the ordered parts of the corresponding substance.

The order in which Patañjali refutes several possible answers with regard to the query about the nature of the word is worth noting. First he refutes the attempt to explain the nature of the word in terms of substance and then in terms of action, then in terms of quality and at last universal. There is a justification behind this order in refuting the allegedly wrong views. Substance is the substratum of action, quality, and universal. Substance, in this sense, is primary compared to universal, etc. So first comes the refutation of explaining the word in terms of substance. Action (e.g., bodily gestures) produce qualities in the substance and so in the second place Patañjali examines the view that the nature of the word is the action. Then comes the third alternative, viz. the nature of the word is explained in terms of quality. Last comes the question of universal because universal resides in substance, action and quality. After talking about the substratum of universal, Patañjali critically examines the question of universal at last.

After refuting all the wrong views about the nature of word, Patañjali proposes his positive thesis saying that the nature of the word (e.g., cow) is that by uttering which one has the knowledge of the animal having hump, horn, etc. Simplistically taken this definition could mean that the letters are where the nature of the word lies, for it is the letter that we utter. But this is not what the grammarian view is. This is why, Kaiyaṭa understands the expression 'uttering which' as 'which manifests' and 'manifests' here means becomes known, becomes the object of knowledge. Thus 'gets manifest' and becomes 'object of knowledge' have the same meaning.

The grammarians regard the word (*pada*) or sentence (*vākya*), which is different from the letter, as the referring expression (*vācaka*). If the letter was identical with the word, then the very first letter in a word would produce the knowledge of the meaning and the following letters in the word would become redundant. All the letters, on the other hand, could not be produced at a time and so due to the absence of all the letters at the same time knowledge of the meaning could not be produced. Letters are uttered sequentially and so the letters cannot be present at the same time failing to produce the knowledge of meaning. The letters are uttered sequentially and they are stored in memory giving rise to the knowledge of meaning. This is why grammarians hold that *sphoṭa* which is manifest through the *nāda* or *dhvani*, that is different from letter, is where the nature of the word lies. This *sphoṭa* is something that refers to the word. Nāgeśa explains 'utterance' as when the air rises above from the *mūlādhāra* (the lowest part of the spinal cord) and gets in contact with the vocal parts expressing the *sphoṭa*. So, understood in this way, the nature of the word lies in that the manifestation of which produces the knowledge of the animal having hump, horn, etc.

Various philosophers have given different accounts of how

knowledge of meaning arises out of the word. We use words in order to produce knowledge of meaning in other people. The interlocutor acquires knowledge of meaning from the words uttered by the speaker. According to Nyāya-Vaiśeṣika, all the letters are subject to production and destruction. Following our attempt to utter, a letter is produced and at the next moment it stays on and in the third moment it is destroyed. Some older Naiyāyikas, however, hold that the word exists for four moments. On this view, the collection of the letters, which are subject to birth and destruction, constitutes the word and the collection of words constitutes the sentence. Since the collection is not different from the individual members that make up the collection, a word or a sentence is not different from the letter. Naiyāyikas also believe in an infinite number of letters.

Mīmāṁsakas reject the Nyāya thesis of infinity of letters. According to the former, all the letters are one in number, eternal and omnipresent. The letters get manifest, and not created, when air gets in touch with our vocal organs. The collection of these manifest letters is the word and the collection of words is a sentence. None disagrees with the view that knowledge of meaning is produced from a sentence. In the Nyāya-Vaiśeṣika view, the first letter gets destroyed while the second letter stays. Similarly the second letter is destroyed while the third letter stays on. Thus while uttering the last letter of the word *ghaṭa*, for example, the preceding letters are destroyed. There remains no possibility of all the letters staying together at the same time making it impossible to perceive all the letters at the same time. Through the sequential perception of the letters, impressions of those letters get printed on the mind. The perception of the last letter along with the impression arising out of the perception of the previous letters, produces the knowledge of the word. Now each word has a specific relation with its meaning. This specific relation is known as the semantic power (*śakti*). A person who knows the specific relation of a word with its meaning comes to know the meaning of a word after the person grasps the word thus described. On this account, a person first grasps the word and then due to his knowledge of the relation of the word to its meaning he comes to remember the meaning.

Mīmāṁsakas, however, contend that even though letters are eternal, our knowledge of them is not. Even if there is a pot in the room, we might not have any knowledge of it, maybe because the room is dark. It is only when the pot gets in contact with light, that we come to perceive the pot. Light is that which manifests the pot. Similarly even if the letters are eternal, our auditory sense-organ remains covered with the external air and so we are not in a position to know them. But when a speaker utters a word, the air from within the speaker comes out touching all his vocal organs and removes the air cover from the hearer's auditory sense-organ. Thus the hearer comes to know the letters that constitute a word or a sentence. The perception or knowledge of the letter depends on whether the air cover of the auditory sense-organ of the hearer remains open or not. So the letters are always there, sometimes they are manifest and sometimes they are not. This manifestation amounts to knowledge. Since knowledge is born at one moment, stays on the second moment and gets destroyed in the third moment, knowledge of the letters is also temporary; it stays for two moments only, while the letters themselves are eternal. Like the Naiyāyikas, as mentioned above, Mīmāṁsakas also hold that the perception of the last letter along with the impression of the preceding letters produces the knowledge of the word.

The grammarians, of course, do not accept this account of

the Naiyāyikas and the Mīmāṁsakas. Grammarians argue that if perception of the last letter along with the impression of previous letters was able to produce the knowledge of the word, then had there been an interval in uttering the letters, even then knowledge of the word would have been produced. But this is not the case. So it is not enough to say that the knowledge of the word is produced from the collection of letters.

The uniqueness of the grammarian position lies in their proposing the theory of *sphoṭa*. It is the *sphoṭa* that produces the knowledge of the word. The etymological meaning of the word *sphoṭa* is that which manifests or uncovers. Once we analyse the word *sphoṭa,* we see that this is not a *yaugika* word rather a *yogārūḍha* word. A *yaugika* word is that where the meaning of the word is explained in terms of the stem and the suffix. The meaning of the word *pācaka* can be explained in terms of the meaning of the stem *pac* (to cook) and the meaning of the suffix *ghan* (performer of the action). In the case of a *yogārūḍha* word, the meaning of the word is something more than the meanings of the elements that constitute the word. *Paṅkaja* simply does not mean that which is born in mud (*paṅka*). But the word stands only for lotus and not anything and everything that is born in mud. Similarly the word *sphoṭa* does not mean anything and everything that manifests. It only stands for that which manifests meaning.

In the grammarian literature we find eight kinds of *sphoṭa* being mentioned, which are:

1. *Varṇasphoṭa,*
2. *Padasphoṭa,*
3. *Vākyasphoṭa,*
4. *Akhaṇḍapadasphoṭa,*

5. *Akhaṇḍavākyasphoṭa,*
6. *Varṇajātisphoṭa,*
7. *Padajātisphoṭa,* and
8. *Vākyajātisphoṭa.*

The analysis of a word into stem and suffix is called *vikaraṇa* in the grammarians' jargon. Grammarians hold that *vikaraṇa* by itself does not stand for anything, it has got no meaning. *Vikaraṇa* only helps manifesting the meaning of the word when the stem and the suffix get conjoined. *Sphoṭa* works behind only that which has the ability to express meaning. The sequence of letters expresses a meaning and so *sphoṭa* is said to be present here (*varṇasphoṭa*). Of course, as we have seen, how this sequence of letter gives rise to knowledge of meaning is a matter of debate.

While the letters constitute a word, it is impossible to say which letter manifests how much of the meaning. In linguistic use, we use stem and suffix. Analysing a word into stem and suffix is a product of intellectual imagination. The stem and the suffix do not convey any meaning by themselves. Whatever meaning we come to know is through the whole word. In linguistic communication of meaning, using a word is the way to grasp the meaning. So it is the word that has the ability to express a meaning. Thus a word, which is a collection of letters, possesses *sphoṭa* that expresses meaning (*padasphoṭa*).

If people use words separately, this does not produce any knowledge that people can use or communicate. In communication we not only use words, we use sentences. It is through sentences that we come to know the meaning. It is a sentence that has the ability to produce knowledge of meaning. Thus *sphoṭa* resides in a sentence (*vākyasphoṭa*).

All the above three views accept the ontology of the letter.

Since a sentence and a word can be analysed into smaller parts, the letters are parts of a larger whole. There are people, however, who think that a word is an indivisible whole. This indivisible word gives rise to the knowledge of meaning. The ability to express meaning can only be ascribed to a word. On this view, this indivisible word is the bearer of *sphoṭa* (*akhaṇḍapadasphoṭa*).

Following the above line of argument some people argue that a sentence is an indivisible unit. It is a whole sentence that expresses meaning. We imagine the words as parts of a sentence, but they do not have any ultimate reality. The whole sentence is the bearer of *sphoṭa* (*akhaṇḍavākyasphoṭa*).

The five kinds of *sphoṭa*s that have been discussed so far are concerned with an individual letter or word or sentence. All these views come under what is known as individual *sphoṭa* theory (*vyaktisphoṭavāda*). Some philosophers, for example Mīmāṁsakas, hold that the reference to the word 'pot' does not denote an individual pot but the universal potness. Words stand for the universal that resides in the corresponding objects. Echoing this view, some people think that the letters stand for the universal that reside in all the instances of that letter. By 'letter' here is meant the stem and the suffix. The universal residing in the stem or the suffix is the reference of the *sphoṭa* (*varṇajātisphoṭa*).

Another universalist view holds that the universal in the stem and the suffix do not have any referring power. They do not have the power to produce meaning. The stem and the suffix constitute a word and there is a universal that resides in the word and this universal is that which is manifest by *sphoṭa*. So the universal is manifested by *sphoṭa*, but this universal resides in the word (*padajātisphoṭa*).

Another universalist view holds that in communication we not only use words, but also sentences. Linguistic communication takes place through sentences. If a word was enough for communication, then we would not use sentences at all. Knowledge of meaning takes place only after using sentences and not words. The sentence has the capacity to express meaning. Different sentences having the same type (*ākṛti*) are permeated by the same universal. This universal is that which is manifest by *sphoṭa*.

One point to be noted here is that universal *sphoṭa* theorists hold that letters, words and sentences are multiple. Otherwise there would be no point in asserting the existence of universal. Universal is that common feature which is present in all the similar things. Commonality in different individuals is the mark of the universal. Unless there are multiple individuals, there is no point in accepting the universal. If an entity is unique and one of its kind, then universal cannot be said to be present there. So the universal *sphoṭa* theorists must hold that letters, words and sentences are multiple in nature. As the universal cowness is manifest in different individual cows, similarly, the universalist holds that *sphoṭa* is to be explained in terms of the universal that resides in the letters, words and sentences.

Bhartṛhari accepts the sentence *sphoṭa* theory (*akhaṇḍavākyasphoṭa*). Bhartṛhari takes sentence to be the unit of meaning, for it is through sentence that communication takes place. The words do not exist independent of the sentential context in the sense that words do not convey anything outside the sentence. It is only for the sake of understanding or grammatical analysis that we analyse a sentence into words. It is a sentence that is indivisible and devoid of any part. Words are analysed into stem and suffix only to explain to the ignorant person. The stem and suffix do not have any existence independent of the word. Similarly, Bhartṛhari holds, a sentence is analysed into words only to explain things to a person. Talk of words is the product of our intellectual imagination (*apoddhāra*).[2]

One point worth exploring here is that if we accept Bhartṛhari's position, then is there any justification of accepting other kinds of *sphoṭa*s? If Bhartṛhari's arguments are taken seriously, then the only kind of *sphoṭa* that one could find philosophically defensible is the sentence *sphoṭa*. Bhartṛhari's main thesis seems to be that meaning plays an important role in communication and so an account of meaning must take communication into account. And in an account of communication, the sentence is of crucial importance, not the letter nor the word. Thus it might be philosophically lavish to entertain all the different kinds of *sphoṭa*s other than sentence *sphoṭa* and that too without any significant gain.

One important consequence of Bhartṛhari's attaching importance to communication in an account of meaning is that knowledge and language are said to be inextricably related. Knowledge that is not interwoven with language is not knowledge worth the name. Knowledge by its very nature manifests its object and knowledge could not do so if it is not followed by language.[3]

As the air inside the speaker's body rises above from *nābhimūla* via the different vocal organs, *sphoṭa* gets manifest. But it is not that *sphoṭa* is created. That which manifests *sphoṭa* is called *dhvani*. Sometimes letters are also said to manifest

2. I have analysed Bhartṛhari's arguments for sentence holism in my paper "An imaginary Dialogue of Bhartṛhari and Quine", in *JICPR*.

3. For details see my "Knowledge and Language in Classical Indian Philosophy", Raghunath Ghosh (ed.), *Language and Meaning*, Kolkata: Allied Publishers, 2003, pp. 49-125.

sphoṭa. But the grammarians seem to hold that *sphoṭa* appears to us in the form of letter. Grammarians of post-Patañjali period can be divided into the old and new schools. The old grammarians hold that as the internal air gets in contact with the vocal organs, *dhvani* is produced. This *dhvani* manifests *sphoṭa*. The argument behind this thesis is that if by mistake the air does not get in contact with the required vocal organs, then no letter is pronounced even though *dhvani* is produced. Thus both where *sphoṭa* is manifest and where *sphoṭa* is not manifest *dhvani* is produced. If we deny this, then the cause of manifestation of *sphoṭa* would be regarded as an impediment to the production of *dhvani*. But this leads to postulating more things than required.

However, this raises another problem. When the air gets in contact with the vocal organs, we get the knowledge of 'pot,' for example. This 'pot' is nothing but a manifestation of the *sphoṭa*. Here, all the knowledge that we have is that of the pot and we do not have any knowledge of *dhvani*. If *dhvani* is the cause of the manifestation of *sphoṭa*, then in all the cases of the manifestation of *sphoṭa*, *dhvani* also must be an object of knowledge. But we do not come to know *dhvani* in all those cases.

There are different possible accounts of this situation.[4] According to some grammarians, *dhvani* is known as and when *sphoṭa* is known. They come together to us. *Dhvani* is not known separately. But other grammarians hold that *dhvani* is not a proper object of knowledge. *Dhvani* is compared with a sense-organ. Eyes, for example, are the cause of the knowledge of colour. But eyes themselves are not subject to our knowledge. Each sense-organ has its own specific quality and this is why each sense-organ is capable of perceiving that specific quality

4. See Bhartṛhari's *Vākyapadiya*, I.81-84.

and not others. Thus while each sense-organ and its quality is the cause of perception of its specific object, the sense-organ and its quality are not subject to knowledge. Similarly *dhvani* itself is not subject to knowledge, while it is the cause of the manifestation of *sphoṭa*.

According to the other view, *sphoṭa* is completely distinct from *dhvani*. When the words are uttered from a distance, we do not have knowledge of the corresponding *sphoṭa* though we do have knowledge of *dhvani*. When the *sphoṭa* is manifest, normally *sphoṭa* and *dhvani* become objects of knowledge intermingled with each other and so we fail to apprehend *dhvani* separately. But *dhvani* is very much there. When milk and water are mixed together, we cannot have the knowledge of water separately. Similarly when *sphoṭa* and *dhvani* are mixed together we fail to know *dhvani* separately.

Arguments have been given against the grammarian view that *dhvani* is the cause of the manifestation of *sphoṭa*. People argue that *dhvanis* stay for one moment only, and so we can never have a collection of *dhvani*. Thus in the absence of a collection of *dhvani, sphoṭa* can never be manifested. If, on the other hand, we accept that each and every *dhvani* individually manifests *sphoṭa*, then after one *dhvani* manifests *sphoṭa* other *dhvanis* would be redundant. Remember the same kind of argument was given by the grammarians while arguing against the view that the collection of letters produce the knowledge of meaning.

The grammarians contend that each and every *dhvani* manifests *sphoṭa*. But the first *dhvani* manifests *sphoṭa* in an undifferentiated manner. The manifestation of *sphoṭa* gets more articulate and clear and specific as all the other *dhvanis* are made successively. With the pronunciation of the last *dhvani* manifestation of *sphoṭa* becomes complete. It is only after the manifestation of *sphoṭa* is complete, that the knowledge of meaning dawns. Preceding *dhvani*s manifest *sphoṭa* only partially and so meaning is not known at that stage. *Sphoṭa* is manifest through *dhvani* and becomes the cause of the knowledge of meaning. This *sphoṭa* by manifesting meaning makes it possible for humans to behave with the world in an appropriate manner.

Bhartṛhari develops a whole metaphysical system banking on the idea of *sphoṭa*. Bhartṛhari identifies this *sphoṭa* with the ultimate reality. *Sphoṭa*, according to Bhartṛhari, consists of three stages. The *sphoṭa* that is audible to our auditory sense-organ is called *vaikharī*. Before the manifestation of *vaikharī* laid open by a speaker's utterance there remains a *sphoṭa* in the mind of the speaker and after listening to *vaikharī* there arises a *sphoṭa* in the mind of the listener. These are called *madhyamā*. Truly speaking, this *madhyamā* gives rise to the knowledge of meaning. The last stage of *sphoṭa* is called *paśyantī* and this is beyond the comprehension of the ordinary auditory sense-organ. This *paśyantī* is regarded as identical with the unchanging reality known as *Brahman*. Even if Patañjali talks about *sphoṭa* and explains the nature of word in terms of *sphoṭa*, it is Bhartṛhari who develops the theory of *sphoṭa* in its full detail which is followed by a series of important works, some defending *sphoṭa* and some others refuting it.

Patañjali, of course, mentions the view where a word is explained in terms of *dhvani*. But as we have seen earlier, this is not a view that is endorsed by Patañjali. Patañjali is keen to prove that the attempts to explain the nature of a word in terms of substance, quality, action and universal are headed in the wrong direction. To set aside these wrong views Patañjali talks about the attempt to explain the nature of a word in terms of *dhvani*. It is true that we request somebody who is about to stop singing to 'go on singing' (manifesting sound) or we request somebody who is manifesting a horrible sound to 'stop making that sound.' This might lead one to understand the essence of a word in terms of *dhvani*. But this is not the official view of Patañjali.

References

A Pāṇinian Approach to Philosophy of Language, Kolkata: Sanskrit Pustak Bhandar, 1990.

Gaurinatha Sastri, *A Study in the Dialectics of Sphoṭa*, New Delhi: Motilal, Banarsidass, 1980.

K.A.S. Iyer, *Bhartṛhari*, Poona: Deccan College, 1969.

Gangadhara Kar Nyayacharya, *Mahābhāṣyam*, Kolkata: Sanskrit Book Depot, 2002.

Karuna Sindhu Das, *Prācīn Bhārater Bhāṣā Darśana*, Kolkata: Progressive Publishers, 2002.

Gaurinath Sastri, *The Philosophy of Word and Meaning*, Kolkata: Sanskrit College, 1959

Rudranath Jha (ed.), *Vyākaraṇamahābhāṣyam*, Varanasi: Chaukhamba, 1996.

Gurupada Halder, *Vyākaraṇa Darśaner Itihāsa*, Kolkata: 1943.

Vyākaraṇa-Mahābhāṣya, Kolkata: Dandiswami Damodar Ashram, 1904 Saka.

Raghunatha Sharma (ed.), *Vākyapadīya* of Bhartṛhari, Varanasi: Sampurnananda University, 1980.

Bishnupada Bhaṭṭacharya (ed.), *Vākyapadiya* of Bhartṛhari, Kolkata: Pascimbanga Rajya Pustak Parsad, 1985.

11

The Centrality of Mind in the Cognitive Process
The Nyāya Perspective

*K.S. Prasad**

Mapping the Domain

THE issue of cognition offers a most welcoming invitation to rethink the whole field in depth and in perspective. All of us engage in various cognitive episodes throughout our life. Whether it is reading a book, talking to a friend, watching a movie or simply listening to music, we are attempting to, make sense of and sometimes remember what we saw or heard. While all these cognitive episodes are routine, seemingly simple and often effortless, the mechanism involved in them is more sophisticated than is apparent. Philosophers of all ages have been troubled with this apparently simple question of what cognition is. A complete account of the cognitive system must explain how it takes information in and retains it as well as how it transmits the same. Indian philosophers in general and the Naiyāyikas in particular have addressed this issue within the framework of their discussion on *pramāṇas* (methods of valid cognition). *Śabda* or verbal testimony is regarded as an important epistemic tool in knowledge acquisition in Nyāya

* Reader, Department of Philosophy, University of Hyderabad, Hyderabad, India.

philosophy, for a major portion of our knowledge comes from the testimony of our fellow beings. Naiyāyikas firmly believe that language is competent to describe everything that is there. Whatever exists, according to Nyāya, is potentially capable of being known and whatever is known is capable of being expressed. The basic thrust of this paper is to pinpoint the role of the mind in the Nyāya theory of cognition, more specifically cognition generated from *śabda pramāṇa*. Broadly, attempts to understand cognition may be approached from three perspectives: nature, structure and process. Accordingly an effort is made in this paper to present the Nyāya theory of cognition from these three perspectives. I begin with a note on translation of the term *buddhi* which is an approximate equivalent of the term cognition followed by a detailed account of the nature of *buddhi,* so to say, cognition as understood in the Nyāya system. Next, I consider the structure of cognition which includes various components involved in cognition and the centrality of mind in the cognitive process. Finally, I present the Nyāya account of the step by step process of cognition and indicate briefly the role of the mind in the cognition generated from linguistic utterances.

A Note About Translation

The term *buddhi* is regarded as an approximate equivalent of the term 'cognition.' However, according to Naiyāyikas, *buddhi* is taken to mean the same as *jñāna* (cognition), *darśana* (perception), *upalabdhi* (apprehension), *bodha* (understanding), *pratyāya* (cognizance), and *adyavasāya* (ascertainment). In other words, they treat these three words — *jñāna* (cognition), *upalabdhi* (apprehension) and *bodha* (understanding) — almost as synonyms.[1] In fact, our regular use of these words confirms

1. *Nyāya-Bhāṣya,* 3.2.3 tr. Ganganath Jha, *The Nyāyasūtras of Gautama with the Bhāṣya of Vātsyāyana and the Vārttika of Uddyotakara,* vol. III, Delhi: Motilal Banarsidass, 1984, p. 1269.

this view. When we say of an object that it has been known, we may also say of it that it has been cognized or that it has been apprehended or that it has been understood. Similarly when an object is not known we may also say of it that it has not been cognized or it has not been apprehended or it has not been understood.

Nature of Cognition

In his celebrated work *Nyāya-Sūtras,* Gautama has devoted fifty-six *sūtras* on cognition (*buddhi*).[2] Two important issues were raised and discussed in this connection. They are: 1. What is cognition as a fact of reality? and 2. Is cognition eternal or non-eternal? Cognition, according to Nyāya, consists in the manifestation of objects (*arthaprakāśo buddhiḥ*). Things are made manifest or revealed to us only when they become objects of cognition. The object of cognition may be a substance or a quality, an act or an emotion. But in each of these cases whenever there is cognition, there must be something that stands out as the object of cognition. It can either be the cognition of what is already known, or the cognition of what was previously unknown. Nyaya believes in the causal theory of cognition. That an object produces cognition is proved by the method of agreement and the method of difference. For instance, when *A* goes to the house of *B* in search of him, he does not see him if *B* is absent. But at a later moment when *B* comes home he sees him. Thus when *B* is present, cognition of him is present, and whenever *B* is absent cognition of him is absent. So we must conclude that *B* is the cause for the cognition of *B*.

Further it is on the basis of cognition of some kind that all

2. *Nyāyasūtras* 1.1.15 & 3.2.1-55, tr. M.M. Satish Chandra Vidyabhusana, Delhi: Motilal Banarsidass, 1981, p. 7. & pp.105-127.

our actions are governed. Hence cognition is regarded as the ground of what may be called the human behaviour. We behave differently in relation to different objects because we know them to be different. That is, our action or behaviour towards an object is governed by our desires and our desires again have cognitions as their causes. Some of our actions are successful and some are not. For instance, when a greedy man notices a shiny object, he considers it to be a rupee coin, since a rupee coin is manifested to him. He desires to have it and acts accordingly. If the object that he takes in possession is really a rupee coin, his action is successful. On the other hand, if it is not a rupee coin, he fails to get what he desired to get and his action is termed unsuccessful. We come across a stream of such successful and unsuccessful actions in our life, and accordingly we may hold that of the manifestations at the back of them, some tally with their objects and some do not. Nevertheless, they are all cognitions. Thus within the ambit of cognition, Nyāya brings in all cognitive episodes such as feelings, sensation, memory, doubt, illusion and the like. This being the general framework of cognition, it remains to be seen what it is as a fact of reality.

Being uncompromising realists, the Naiyāyikas strongly believe in the objective order of reality external to and independent of the cognizer. The realm of experience with which an individual starts is the basis for such a position. The reality consists of objective facts, cognizable no doubt, but existing prior to, and making possible the cognition of them. Gautama in his *Nyāyasūtras* enumerates only twelve cognizables as objects of cognition.[3] Vātsyāyana points out that the list neither is, nor intended to be, a comprehensive enumeration

3. *ātmaśarīrendriyārthabuddhimanaḥpravṛttidośapretyabhāvaphala-duḥkhapavargastu "prameyam"* — *Nyāyasūtras* 1.1.9. op. cit., p. 5.

of all possible objects. Besides these twelve objects of cognition there are countless other cognizables that can be subsumed under the list of seven categories namely, *dravya* (substance), *guṇa* (quality), *karma* (action), *sāmānya* (universal), *viśeṣa* (particularity), *samavāya* (inherence) and *abhāva* (non-being) admitted by the Vaiśeṣikas.[4] The fact that when an object is cognized through perception, not only is the object perceived, but the cognition of it that had been known before is also perceived. For instance when a book is perceived as a book, only the book is perceived. But when the book is perceived as a known book not only the book but also the fact that it had been cognized before is also perceived. Just as the book this 'cognition' of the known book is also an objective fact.

Cognition being an objective fact must be subsumed under one of the categories mentioned above. Cognition cannot be subsumed under *abhāva* for it is an existent fact which is quite obvious. In fact, *abhāva* is itself an object of cognition. A cognition that cognizes no object is impossible to conceive. Even when there is a cognition of nothing, it is not a cognition that is cognizing nothing, for it is a cognition that cognizes something and that something is nothing. It is the very nature of cognition to be the cognition of an object. Cognition cannot be subsumed under *sāmānya* and *viśeṣa* for it is admitted by Kaṇāda himself that *sāmānya* and *viśeṣa* are dependent on cognition (*buddhi*).[5] Cognition cannot be subsumed under *samavāya* for *samavāya* is a relation between two inseparables. Although the relation between subject and object takes the form of cognition, cognition itself is not a relation. It is something different from relation. We can at best say that cognition appears when the subject becomes related to the

---

4. *Nyāya-Bhāṣya*, 1.1.9. op. cit., vol. I, p. 212.
5. *sāmānyaviśeṣa iti buddhiāpekṣam* । — *Vaiśeṣika-Sūtras of Kaṇāda*, 1.2.3.

object, but it is a new phenomenon other than the subject-object relation. Just as the contact of the visual sense with the object serves to manifest its colour but does not produce it, similarly the relation of the subject with the object does not produce cognition but manifests it and the cognition is something different from relation. Hence cognition cannot be a relation. Cognition is not a *dravya*, for it cannot be the constitutive cause of anything, nor is it the substratum of certain qualities.[6]

According to some, cognition can be subsumed under *karma*.[7] In fact, the transitive nature of cognition suggests that cognition is an activity. This activity is always directed towards the object. There cannot be any cognition unless the mind is directed towards the objects. At any moment of inattention we will not cognize the objects although they are in contact with their respective senses. Cognition is a process wherein the mind actively reaches out to objects and illuminates them. Cognition, at best, may be construed as an illuminating activity. This view is not acceptable to the Naiyāyikas. According to them, in cognition itself as awareness we find an object that is cognized and a subject that cognizes it, but not any activity. An act is as much an object of cognition as any other. It is simply manifested in cognition and not identical with it. Hence cognition cannot be subsumed under *karma* (action).

---

6. Sāṁkhya notion of *buddhi* differs from Nyāya. For Sāṁkhya, *buddhi* is the first evolute of *prakṛti* and thereby regarded as the constitutive cause of the rest of the objects of the world. *Sāṁkhya Kārikā of Īśvarakriṣṇa*, 22-23. Ed. and tr. S.S. Suryanarayana Sastri, Madras University Philosophical Series no. 3, Madras, 1973, pp. 55-57.

7. In classical Indian thought, the Buddhists and the Mīmāṁsakas support this view.

The Naiyāyikas consider cognition as a *guṇa* (quality). As a quality it must subsist in a substratum. Substance is the substratum of qualities and actions. Then what exactly should be the repository of this quality namely cognition? According to Nyāya, cognition is a quality neither of the body, nor of the senses, nor of the mind. The body cannot be the abode of cognition, because it is a material substance like a pot. That which is material is not active, but once it is endowed with a conscious agent it becomes active. Cognition, desire, aversion are all associated directly with the soul and only indirectly with the body. Further a physical substance has two kinds of qualities, firstly those which can be known by the external senses like shape, colour and so on, and secondly those which cannot be known by external senses like weight, etc. Cognition belongs to neither category; because the external senses do not know it and yet, unlike weight, we are aware of it. So cognition cannot be the quality of a material substance like body.[8]

Cognition cannot be a quality of any of the five external sense-organs, for these sense-organs are only instruments of cognition. In fact, we have two kinds of cognition: (i) ordinary perceptual cognition which proceeds from the contact of the sense-organ with the object and ceases upon the destruction of sense object contact, and (ii) recollections which proceed from the contact of the mind with the *ātman* which continue even after the destruction of the contact between the sense and the object. If it is the quality of the sense-organ, recollection of things which a sense-organ cognized before could not be possible after that sense is destroyed.[9] Cognition continues

8. *Nyāya-Vārttika,* 3.2.53. op. cit., pp. 1392-93.

9. *naindriyārthayostatvināśepi jñānavasthānat.* — *Nyāyasūtras,* 3.2.18. op. cit., p. 111.

to exist even after the destruction of a particular sense-organ. For instance a person born blind can never have an idea of red colour, whereas a normal person can have the idea of red colour even after the destruction of his visual sense. This clearly suggests that cognition is not a quality of the senses.

Cognition cannot be the quality of the mind for the existence of mind is inferred from the non-simultaneous character of cognitions of objects and also because the mind is an internal sense governed by the cognizer.[10] If cognition be the property of the mind, the mind would cease to be an instrument. Just as the objects of the surrounding world are known through sense-organs, the internal states of experience such as pleasure, aversion, etc. are known, according to Nyāya, through an internal sense namely the mind, and hence cognition cannot be a quality of mind.

According to Nyāya, cognition is a quality of the self. Vātsyāyana states: "of what then is the quality? It is the quality of the Cognitive Agent, as it is he who is the controller. As a matter of fact, the controller is the cognizer and that which is controlled is the instrument."[11] As stated earlier it cannot be the quality of any material substance, for, unlike that, it does not admit of external perception. Physical qualities are perceived by the external senses, but cognition is not so perceived. Being thus fundamentally different from all physical qualities, cognition is to be regarded as the quality of the immaterial substance called soul. To quote:

> By reason of Elimination — The quality of cognition being denied in reference to the Body, the sense-organs and the Mind, there being no other Substance left to which the said

10. *yugapatjñeyānupalabdheḥca na mānasaḥ* । —'Ibid., 3.2.19.

11. *Nyāya-Bhāṣya*, 3.2.19 op. cit., p. 1332.

> quality could belong, and the Soul being the only likely Substance left, — Cognition is regarded as being the quality of the Soul.[12]

Further, cognition is not an essential quality of the soul. The soul has acquired this property in its bodily setting. When an individual cognizes that a certain thing is a source of pleasure or pain, he/she desires to acquire or to avoid it and accordingly his/her efforts are directed towards these ends. Thus cognition, pleasure, pain, effort and aversion are all connected with a single agent. They all subsist in a common substratum and are therefore properties of such an agent. These properties cannot be attributed to something that is unconscious. Our ordinary experience also confirms this. For instance when I judge that there is a book on the table then 'that there is a book on the table' is a particular kind of cognition that belongs to me. It may be restated as 'I am the one who is predicated of having the cognition of the fact that there is a book on the table.' Thus cognition is a quality that pertains to the cognizer. To the question of how cognition is related to the cognizer, the Naiyāyikas bring in *samavāya* as a special kind of relation that subsists between two inseparables such as a quality and a substance. Granting that cognition is a quality of the soul, so to say, the cognizer, it remains to be seen whether cognition is eternal or non-eternal.

According to Nyāya, cognition is non-eternal. The principle argument to substantiate the non-eternal nature of cognition, for Naiyāyikas, is based on the transitory nature of cognitions which suggests that a cognition arises and then another one destroys it and takes its place; then that one is destroyed and another takes its place and so on. Each cognition illuminates a distinct object from among several objects that are coming

12. *Nyāya-Vārttika,* 3.2.39 op. cit., p. 1370.

into existence at one moment and disappearing at another. Hence cognitions must be fleeting in character. Vātsyāyana explains:

> In the case of an arrow shot form the bow we perceive a series of motions till the arrow drops down; and since every cognition is restricted to a single object, it follows that, just as there is a series of (fleeting) motions (in the arrow), so must there be also a series of corresponding cognitions.[13]

Even in the case of a static object such as a pot there is a series of cognitions, which function till we have ceased to apprehend the pot as soon as something comes in the way of our vision. If cognition is not fleeting in character, then the perceptual cognition of the pot would have continued to exist even after the pot is taken away from our view.

Another argument to support the non-eternal nature of cognition is based on recollections. Recollection, according to Naiyāyikas, is the name of that recognition of things which is preceded by the cognition thereof, and which appears on the disappearance of that cognition. For instance, in the case of a recollection in the form 'I saw him before,' it would be possible only when the original perception of him itself has become a matter of the past. As a matter of fact, recollection is possible due to the impressions generated by cognition, and these impressions are recollected at an appropriate time. What continues to exist, is the impression of cognition and not the cognition itself. As stated earlier, if cognition is not transitory then cognition continues to exist even after the object of cognition has ceased to exist, and in such case the term 'recollection' loses its significance.[14] Further, the fact that we

13. *Nyāya-Bhāṣya,* 3.2.42 op. cit., p. 1374.

14. *Nyāya-Vārttika,* 3.2.42 op. cit., pp. 1377-78.

often fail to recollect certain data of our earlier experience suggests that cognition is non-eternal. The notion of forgetting makes no sense if cognition is eternal.

Thus, from what has been said above it appears that cognition according to Nyāya is used in a wide sense to include all cognitive episodes such as feelings, sensations, illusions, etc. and it is a non-eternal quality that belongs to the cognizer (soul). This takes us to a discussion on the cognitive apparatus.

Cognitive Apparatus

In a simple cognitive process like perception[15] we have four entities and three contacts. The four entities are: self, object, sense-organ and mind. The three contacts are: sense-object, sense-mind and mind-self.

The presence of cognizer (*ātman*) is an indubitable fact in the process of cognition. Even those schools of Indian philosophy which are skeptical about the existence of *ātman* also recognize the importance of a cognizer in a cognition though there are differences among them with regard to the essential nature of the cognizer. *Ātman* is the first in Gautama's list of objects of cognition. According to Gautama the marks of the self are: desire, aversion, effort, pleasure, pain and cognition.[16] It is on the basis of these marks that we can infer the existence of *ātman*. Uddyotakara, while commenting on this, explicitly states: ". . . because Desire and the rest have the same object as Recognition, they prove that all cognitions appearing in the Recognition must have a common agent; it is

---

15. Perception being the most primary and fundamental of all sources of cognition in any system of philosophy, it is appropriate to consider this as an illustration.

16. *icchā dveṣa prayatna sukha duḥkha jñāni "ātmanoliṅgam" iti* । — *Nyāyasūtras* 1.1.10. op. cit. p. 6.

a well-known fact that no 'recognition' of cognitions is possible, (a) when these cognitions have different agents, or (b) when their objects are not the same, or (c) when they are brought about by different instruments."[17] We find, for instance, a cognizer can remember and recognize what (s)he has perceived and not what remained unperceived for him/her or what others might have perceived. Desire to acquire a thing or aversion towards a thing originates only from the remembrance of previous cognitions. This is possible only when all the cognitive events are registered as attributes of the cognizer. Thus cognizer (*ātman*) is the substratum of cognitions. The main objective of Nyāya philosophy is the logical substantiation of proper cognition with respect to the acquisition of the highest end of the cognizer.

Proper cognition necessarily presupposes an inventory of objects of cognition which are discussed under the caption of *prameyas* in Nyāya philosophy.[18] These *prameyas* constitute the basic types of cognitive reality which exist independent of cognitions. We can as well bring those under two varieties: (i) Entities which are directly related to the senses, such as table, etc. and (ii) Entities which are indirectly related to the sense-organs, such as colour of the table, etc. We cannot withhold the acceptance of the evidential value of our experience which guarantees the reality of these objects of the world. A detailed Nyāya discussion on the cognition of different kinds of objects is beyond the scope of this paper. I rather confine myself to the point that the Naiyāyikas being committed to realism believe in the reality of the external world consisting of objects, and a proper understanding of these objects alone will show

---

17. *Nyāya-Vārttika*, 1.1.10. op. cit., p. 220.
18. *ātmaśarīrendriyārthabuddhimanaḥ pravṛttidiśāpretyabhāvaphala duḥkhapavargastu "prameyam"* — *Nyāyasūtras*, 1.1.9. op. cit., p. 5.

the way to the attainment of the highest good.

The next entity in the cognitive process is the sense-organ. According to Gautama the sense-organs are third in the list of objects of cognition (*prameyas*). There are six sense-organs. Of these five are external senses and one is the internal sense.[19] The internal sense is known as the mind which will be considered later. Gautama establishes the reality of the five external sense-organs in two stages. To begin with, he rejects the view that there is only one external — the cutaneous — sense-organ and the other sense-organs are simply the special parts of it. He then proceeds to explain the reality of all the five external sense-organs.

The thesis that there is only one sense-organ and the other sense-organs are the modifications of it is supported by the fact that the cutaneous organ is the only organ by which all sense-substrata are pervaded and in whose absence no cognition is possible.[20] This argument is counter-intuitive for, if the cutaneous organ is the only sense-organ to apprehend all sensible objects, then even a blind person could appreciate a painting and a deaf person could enjoy music, which is not the case. Further the argument that various sense-organs are nothing but special parts of the cutaneous organ and the different kinds of sensible objects are perceived through these parts, so that when these parts are destroyed the

19. It is interesting to note that in *Nyāyasūtras* 3.1.54-55, we find only five sense-organs listed on the basis of their corresponding objects. Mind which is considered as an organ of internal perception in *sūtra* 3.1.16 is not mentioned along with these sense-organs. However, Gaṅgeśopādhyāya in his *Tattvacintāmaṇi* enumerates six senses, the five external and the one internal. (S.C. Vidyabhusana, *History of Indian Logic,* Delhi: Motilal Banarsidass, p. 411.

20. *Nyāya-Bhāṣya,* 3.1.51, op. cit., pp. 1222-23.

corresponding sensible objects are not perceived, is not reasonable, for this argument is self-contradictory. If the cognition of colour, sound, smell, etc. is held to be brought about by different parts of the cutaneous sense-organ, then it goes against the theory of a unitary sense-organ. If those special parts of the cutaneous sense-organ are of the nature of a sense-organ, then all those being many, the sense-organs are also many. On the other hand, if those special parts of the cutaneous sense-organ are not of the nature of a sense-organ, then colour, sound, smell, etc. cannot be regarded as perceptible by the senses. Another problem associated with the theory of a unitary sense-organ is that it results in simultaneous cognitions of a colour, sound, smell, etc. The cognizer would come in contact with the mind, the mind with the unitary sense-organ (cutaneous sense-organ) and this sense-organ in contact with various objects which would result in the cognition of many objects at a time, which is impossible.[21]

Having argued a case for the plurality of sense-organs by rejecting the theory of a unitary sense-organ as self-contradictory and contrary to facts, Gautama proceeds to establish his theory that there are five external senses. Vātsyāyana while commenting on *Nyāyasūtra* (3.1.54) explains that the existence of five sense-organs is inferred from five distinct varieties of sense experience namely, touch, colour, smell, taste and sound. These five distinct types of sense experience require five distinct sense-organs for their cognition. For instance colour is cognized by the visual sense-organ (eye) but eye does not apprehend smell. Similarly, we infer the existence of the olfactory sense which serves the purpose of apprehending smell. Likewise, the existence of the

21. Ibid., 3.1.52, p. 1226.

other sense-organs also can be inferred.[22] Thus, from the five kinds of apprehension, visual, auditory, olfactory, gustatory and tactile, we can validly infer the existence of the five different sense-organs. Further, the multiplicity of the sense-organs is also inferred from the diversity of their locations. Thus the author of *Nyāyasūtras* established the reality of the five external senses. These sense-organs are responsible for receiving sensations. Sensations are those which make the object intelligible to the cognizer through the mind. It is imperative that the sense-organs should function and be in contact with the mind before sensations of objects can have some meaning to the cognizer. This takes us to the concept of mind in the cognitive process.

The concept of mind has a long history in the Indian philosophical scenario. However, my task here is not to present an elaborate analysis of the development of this concept, rather to situate its role in the cognitive process. Mind is considered both as an object of cognition and also a material means for cognition in Nyāya literature. It is sixth in the list of objects of cognition enumerated in the *Nyāyasūtras*.[23] Gautama establishes the existence of the mind on the basis of the non-appearance of simultaneous cognitions. There are two kinds of non-simultaneity of cognition: (i) Non-simultaneity of several cognitions produced by the same sense-organ, and (ii) The non-simultaneity of several cognitions produced by different sense-organs. The first kind of simultaneity is impossible to conceive, for one and the same sense-organ cannot come into contact with different objects at one and the same time. For instance, when our visual sense is connected with an object on the table, at the same time it cannot come into contact with another object hung on the wall. It is the second kind of non-

22. Ibid.. 3.1.54, p. 1232.

23. Supra, 18.

simultaneity that Gautama is talking about to prove the existence of the mind.[24] It is a matter of common observation that even though several sensible objects are in contact with their respective sense-organs at one and the same time, there is no simultaneous cognition of these objects. From this we conclude that there is some instrumental cause other than the five sense-organs that is responsible for all our cognitions and that instrumental cause is none other than the mind. If merely the sense object contact were able to bring the cognitions, independently of mind-sense contact, then we should have simultaneous cognitions, which is not the case. Hence we have to admit the existence of the mind as an instrument that connects the sensations with the cognizer. An informal example of our everyday behaviour may serve to contradict this view. Imagine that we are watching a programme on television. Apart from cognizing the visual images we are also cognizing auditory sensations simultaneously. This apprehension of simultaneity among cognitions, according to Nyāya, is due to the fact that the mind comes in contact with different senses in such a rapid succession, that it looks like the apprehension of a circle of fire-band.[25] When a fire-band moves rapidly in a circle, there is a succession among several cognitions of the fire; but because it moves with extreme rapidity, we perceive continuity in the circle of fire as if it is a single continuous circle of fire. The fact of non-simultaneity of cognitions also suggests that there is only one mind in a body. To quote Vātsyāyana:

> If there were several minds, it would be possible for several sense-organs to be in contact with several minds

---

24. *jñānayaugapadyatekam manaḥ* । — *Nyāyasūtras*, 3.2.56 op. cit., p. 127.

25. *alātcakradarśanāvat tatupalabhiasusañcārat* । — *Nyāyasūtras*, 3.2.58. op. cit. p. 128.

> simultaneously; whereby there should be several cognitions appearing (through these contacts) at one and the same time — but this never happens; — hence the conclusion is that, inasmuch as cognitions of things appear only one after another — and never simultaneously — there is a single mind (in one body).[26]

Another argument to demonstrate the existence of the mind is based on conations. It is a fact that cognitions of pleasure, pain, aversion and the like are different from the objects of the external senses; still they are objects of cognition no doubt and hence they need an instrument for the manifestations of such cognitions. Such an instrument is none other than the mind.[27] The fact that our feelings are also successive and not simultaneous supports the idea that there is only one mind in one body. Even our efforts that are based on our feelings appear only one after the other. When there is an effort in one direction, we do not put our effort in any other direction. These activities also indicate that there is only one mind.

Having established the existence of mind, we need to look at the nature of mind. According to Nyāya, mind is a non-physical substance. It is a substance because it has qualities such as conjunction and it is non-physical because it is not constituted by any of the physical elements of earth, water, etc. Further it is atomic in magnitude. If the mind is something

---

26. *Nyāya-Bhāṣya*, 3.2.56, op. cit., p. 1396.

27. . . . *manograham sukha duḥkhamicchā dveṣā matiḥ kṛtiḥ*, — *Bhāṣāpariccheda* 57, and *sākṣātkāre sukhādinām kāraṇam manocchate*, — Ibid., 85, tr. Swami Madhavananda, Kolkata: Advaita Ashrama, 1977, pp. 85, 175.

    sukhadupalabdhisādhanamindriyam manaḥ tacca pratyātmāniyatatvatanantam paramāṇurūpam nityam ca I Annambhaṭṭa, *Tarkasaṁgraha*, Section II.9, tr. Swami Virūpākṣānanada, Chennai: Sri Ramakrishna Math, 1994, p. 79.

non-atomic in magnitude, then it is quite possible for the mind to come in contact with several sense-organs at one and the same time through its different parts, giving rise to simultaneous cognitions. The fact that our cognitions are always successive and not simultaneous establishes the fact that the mind is atomic in magnitude.[28]

With regard to the location of the mind, Upaniṣads consider the heart as the seat of the mind,[29] whereas the Naiyāyikas are more general in stating that the mind lies within the body.[30] Here the term 'lies' should not be taken literally in the sense of a container and contained. Uddyotakara while commenting on this explicitly states that "all that is meant by the mind lying within the body is that the mind never functions except through the body."[31] Of course, the functioning of the mind has meaning only when it is connected with the *ātman*.

Thus according to Nyāya, mind is an instrumental cause of cognition through which all cognitions both external and internal objects get actualized. If we take *ātman* to be the cognizer of cognitions, then the mind is the material means of communicating to the *ātman* the impressions as well as sensations brought through sense object contact.

Centrality of Mind in the Cognitive Process

Indian thinkers in general have recognized the centrality of mind in the cognitive process since time immemorial. In

28. *Nyāya-Bhāṣya*, 3.2.59. op. cit., p. 1399.

29. *Aitareya Upaniṣad*, III.i.2, tr. Swami Gambhirananda, *Eight Upaniṣads*, vol. II, Kolkata: Advaita Ashrama, 1992, p. 63.

30. *nantaḥ śarīravṛttitvanmanasaḥ* । — *Nyāyasūtras*, 3.2.26. op. cit., p. 114.

31. *Nyāya-Vārttika*, 3.2.26. op. cit., p. 1344.

Bṛhadāraṇyaka Upaniṣad, we have the following verse: (we say) "My mind was elsewhere; I did not see it. My mind was elsewhere, I did not hear it. It is through the mind that one sees and hears."[32] Commenting on this, Śaṅkarācārya says,

> There is a mind apart from the external organs such as the ear. For it is well-known fact that even when there is a connection between the external organ, the object and the self, a man does not perceive that object, which may be just in front, and when asked, "Have you seen this form?" he says, "My mind was elsewhere — I was absent-minded, I did not see it." Similarly when asked, "have you heard what I have said" he says, "I was absent-minded, I did not hear it." Therefore it is understood that something else, viz. the internal organ called mind, which joins itself to the objects of all the organs, exists, in the absence of which the eye and other organs fail to perceive their respective objects. ...[33]

This clearly indicates the centrality of mind in the cognitive process. There can be no cognition unless the mind responds to the influences of the surrounding world. At any moment of inattention or absent-mindedness we do not perceive sounds or things other than those in which we are engrossed, although the sounds or things may be acting on our sense. Thus in a cognitive process such as perception, mind must be in contact with the object through the medium of the sense-organs on the one hand, and with the self one the other, and in this sense the mind seems to be a liaison between the objects and sense-organs on one hand and with the self (*ātman*) on the other. However, cognitions such as pleasure and the like are directly apprehended by the self through the

32. *Bṛhadāraṇyaka Upaniṣad*, I.v.3, tr. Swami Madhavananda, Kolkata: Advaita Ashrama, 1988, p. 147.

33. Ibid., p. 148.

instrumentality of the mind. In either case the role of the mind is indispensable.

Algorithms of Cognition

A simple cognitive process such as perception leading to a definite cognition, as mentioned earlier, involves at least three contacts. They are, the contact of the sense-organ with its object, the sense with the mind, and the mind with the self. According to Nyāya, cognition being an attribute of the self depends on mind-self contact. Secondly, sense-object contact cannot generate cognition independent of mind-sense contact which is established by the fact of non-simultaneous apprehension of cognitions. Thirdly, sense-object contact is an essential prerequisite for perceptual cognition in the absence of which cognition is impossible. This, in fact, is the reason for Gautama to define perception in terms of *indriyārthasannikarṣa* (sense-object contact).[34] The sense-object contact may be intentional or accidental. For instance, if we have a desire to perceive a particular thing, we direct our mind to perceive that thing. Here the sense-object contact is intentional. But sometimes we are forced to perceive an object without any desire or effort on our part as in the case of thunder. This is an instance of a sense-object contact which is accidental. Nevertheless, sense-object contact is mandatory for all our perceptual cognitions and these perceptual cognitions are the bases for other methods of cognition such as inference, comparison, testimony and the like. The various steps involved in the case of perceptual cognition are as follows:

Step I: Sense-object contact: Of the five external senses, the sense of sight and sense of touch can give us perception of

34. *indriyārthasannikarṣotpannamjñānam* — *Nyāyasūtras*, 1.1.4. op. cit., p. 3.

substances while the sense of smell, sense of sound and sense of taste can give us a perception of qualities. These sense-organs are capable of receiving sensations of their respective objects only when they are in contact with their respective objects. This contact between a sense-organ and its object is technically termed as *saṁyoga* which is a separable relation. When a sense-organ, say visual sense, is in contact with its object, say a mango, it (visual sense) receives sensation of that object (mango).

Step II: Mind-sense contact: Among the different sensory inputs received, the mind comes into contact with only one sensory input at a time depending **on the preference of the cognizer** so that only one sensation reaches the cognizer at one time.

Step III: Soul-mind contact: The sensation so received from the mind is an apprehension of the object as something indefinite and uncharacterized. It is a simple apprehension of the existence and attributes of an object without any corresponding judgement of it. According to Nyāya this cognition is termed as *nirvikalpaka*. It is a **conscious state but not a self-conscious state.**

Step IV: Transition from nirvikalpaka to savikalpaka[35]: The

35. We do not find an explicit reference to the distinction of *nirvikalpaka* and *savikalpaka* states of perception in *Nyāyasūtras, Nyāya-Bhāṣya* and *Nyāya-Vārttika.* Vācaspatimiśrā in his *Nyāyavārttika Tātparyaṭīkā* interprets the words *avyapadaśya* and *vyavasāyātmakam* present in the *Nyāyasūtras* definition of perception to mean *nirvikalpaka* and *savikalpaka* respectively. Later Naiyāyikas, following Vācaspati, distinguish between *nirvikalpaka* and *savikalpaka* as two stages of the same perceptual process.

    indriyārthasannikarṣajanyam jñānam pratyakṣam I *taddvividham nirvikalpam savikalpam ceti* I *tatra niṣprākārakam jñānam nirvikalpakam yathedamkiñcit saprākārakam jñānam savikalpakam yathā ditthahayam* →

apprehension of an indefinite object of *nirvikalpaka* perception being associated with a certain class name in our past experience revives the word-image answering to that name. With this we remember the class-name of the perceived object and call it by that name. It is here that we have **determinate perceptual cognition** of the object expressed in language in the form of "this is a mango." In Nyāya terminology this is known as *savikalpaka* cognition. This does not add anything that is not contained in the object, rather it brings a change in the perceptive consciousness of the object. There is a development from the feeling of something there to an articulated expression of the feeling of a definite cognition of an object. In fact, this is a kind of recognition in a broader sense brought about by the recollections of the impressions of previous cognitions. To the question how recollections are possible, it is answered by the Naiyāyikas that when the mind comes into contact with such parts of the soul that are impressed by the previous cognitions there is a recollection of the corresponding original experience by the cognizer.[36] But what exactly is the cause of recollection is a significant question. In *Nyāyasūtras* there is a list of twenty-five causes for recollections.[37] Thus all determinate cognitions are verbal expressions. Language plays a crucial role in our cognitions. It acts as an intermediary between the cognizer and cognition. In fact, our cognitions cannot go beyond words. Words are always present wherever cognition is present. No cognition is possible without words.

→ *brahmaṇahyam syamahayam pacakahayamiti* ॥ — Annambhaṭṭa, *Tarkasaṁgraha*, Section IV.32, tr. Swami Virūpākṣānanda, Chennai: Sri Ramakrishna Math, 1994, p. 79.

36. *jñānasamavetatmapradessannikarṣanmānasaḥ smṛtyutpattina-yugapatutpattiḥ* । — *Nyāyasūtras*, 3.2.25, op. cit., p. 114.

37. *pranidhānanibandhabhyāsaliṅgalakṣaṇasādṛśyaparigrahaāśryaśrita-sambhandhantarāyaviyogekakar*

From Words to Words

Naiyāyikas recognized the irreducible character of linguistic utterances as a separate source of valid knowledge, because the cognition generated from linguistic utterances can neither be understood in terms of perception nor inference. Naiyāyikas use the expression *śābdabodha* to mean the cognitions generated from linguistic utterances. The purpose of *śābdabodha* thesis of Nyāya is to show how there is a close connection between linguistically generated knowledge and the mind. Something is known to us whenever a word is uttered. This awareness necessarily involves some relation between the word and the thing for which it stands. The verbal cognition arises from words, goes through words and ends in words. This transition is quite significant. In a communicative episode the words of a speaker (determinate cognition) reach the hearer through words and these words having been understood by the hearer end in determinate cognition which again is in the form of words. The cognition so generated is quite distinct from other methods of knowledge such as perception, inference and comparison. However the role of perception in *śābdabodha* is not denied for it is through the perception of words that the hearer is able to understand the meaning connected with it. We perceive words either through ears if they are spoken or through eyes if they are in a written form. The moment the words are perceived there is a mental process in the hearer. The mind of the hearer relates the words with such parts of the soul that are impressed by the previous cognitions of those words and their corresponding objects. Once the relation between the words and the objects is established, there is the cognition of the utterance namely *śābdabodha*.

Conclusion

The term cognition, for Nyāya, is a mode of apprehending the objects. In this sense it includes all cognitions irrespective of their epistemic validity. Being realistic in its approach, Nyāya believes in the reality of the objects of cognition independent of the cognizer, and maintains that there is an essential difference between a cognition and an object. Cognition is always referred to as an attribute of the cognizer. It is a private property of an individual. On the other hand, an object is open to public. The cognitive process is a complex one wherein the role of the mind is quite significant for it is through the mind that one acquires knowledge. The mind is instrumental in bringing about a direct experience of pain, pleasure and the like and acts as a mediating principle in perceptual cognition and the like. The Naiyāyikas rely on attention as an important factor in their proof for the centrality of mind in the cognitive process.

Index